PASSION AND PURPOSE

How to identify and leverage the powerful patterns
that shape your work/life

By
Marlys Hanson, M.S. with Merle Hanson, Ph.D.

In collaboration with
Arthur F. Miller, Jr., Founder, People Management International LLC

Hanson, Marlys.
    Passion and purpose : how to identify and leverage
the powerful patterns that shape your work/life / by
Marlys Hanson with Merle Hanson ; in collaboration with
Arthur F. Miller, Jr. -- 1st ed.
    p. cm.
    Includes bibliographical references and index.
    LCCN 2001092260
    ISBN 0-9717215-4-8

    1. Success in business. 2. Success. 3. Motivation
(Psychology)   I. Hanson, Merle. II. Miller, Arthur F.
III. Title.

HF5386.H36 2002   650.1
                QBI02-200178

Printed in the United States of America

Cover Illustration: Ken McGhee and Lori Hanson, Artists/Illustrators, Alameda, CA (209) 785-8720

Layout: Deena Quilty, Quilty Communications, Farmington, CT (860) 678-8622

PASSION AND PURPOSE

How to identify and leverage the powerful patterns that shape your work/life

"Successful" people* in every walk of life have one thing in common: they follow their passion. Like most successful people, the individuals on the cover of this book were not born successful, but they each leveraged their unique passion to achieve their purpose—and found success in their efforts.

Passion frequently appears in early childhood. World famous cellist *Yo-Yo Ma*[1] learned to play an improvised viola while seated on stacks of phone books—he was 4 years old when he decided he wanted to play the cello. But music critics agree that his unique power is knowing how to communicate with his audience.

Some passion emerges more clearly in the teens. *Bill Gates,*[2] computer scientist-entrepreneur, formed his first start-up at age 13, when he teamed up with two friends to create a programming company. One of their products was a game called Risk; the object of the game was world domination. At age 16, *Albert Einstein*[3] wrote in a school essay: *One always likes to do those things for which one has talent. I imagine myself becoming a professor of the natural sciences.... choosing the theoretical parts of them...because of my individual disposition for abstract and mathematical thought...and my lack of fantasy and of practical talent.*

For most of us, our actual calling or career requires more time in order to manifest itself. The potential may be present but it is not always clear just how that potential should be nurtured. *Oprah Winfrey,*[4] all-time favorite talk show host, was reciting Bible verses in church at age 4. But her real gift is a masterful understanding of human emotion, which blossomed when she began her career in radio.

Cesar Chavez's[5] sense of injustice surfaced early in his life, when his father was bilked out of his farm by an unscrupulous lawyer. While others suffered in silence, Cesar's amazing inner strength and commitment to helping others found expression. His lifetime achievements in leading non-violent labor organizations are monuments to his passion for justice, and he lives yet in the hearts of farm workers everywhere.

Julia Child,[6] world famous chef and author, literally "did not know how to boil an egg until she was 35." But she did have an appetite for learning everything there was to know about whatever she did—whether in her work with the predecessor of the CIA during WWII or cooking a French soufflé. Her life stories reveal pioneering and experimental activities of all kinds—and an extraordinary appetite for life itself!

---

* These individuals were selected because most readers will know something about their work and even their personalities.

Thurgood Marshall's[7] home as a young man was known as "The Friendly Inn" because he regularly entertained friends of all ethnicities and economic status. Who would have guessed that his passion for getting multiple perspectives on issues would lead to a seat on the Supreme Court and involvement in the nation's early integration legislation? *Christiane Amanpour,*[8] broadcast journalist, was a youngster with incredible determination to get what she wanted. She recalled clambering onto a table to retrieve a balloon which had become stuck on the ceiling—and pulling down the entire chandelier! She was only 5 years old but years later, she recalled the joy in getting that balloon. Her gutsy, unflappable passion for adventure eventually led to her reputation for being where the action is. As they say, "Where there's war, there's Amanpour!"

Everyone, not just "successful" people, has a story to be told. By reflecting on your story, you will begin to understand why you remember (in great detail) certain events in your life—yet can hardly recall others. You will begin to recognize the unique and powerful themes in your life/work activities. You will identify—and thus be more prepared to successfully leverage—your passion and your purpose.

REFERENCES

1. ICM Artists, Ltd., YO-YO MA, New York City, 1997.

2. Gatten, Jonathan, BILL GATES, THE PATH OF THE FUTURE, Avon Books, 1999.

3. Dukas, Helen and Banesh Hoffman, ALBERT EINSTEIN, THE HUMAN SIDE, Princeton University Press, 1989.

4. Triumph Entertainment, THE SOUL AND SPIRIT OF A SUPERSTAR, 1998.

5. United Farm Workers Website, THE STORY OF CESAR CHAVEZ, www.ufw.org, 2001.

6. A & E Biography Series, JULIA CHILD: AN APPETITE FOR LIFE, 1996.

7. Williams, Juan, THURGOOD MARSHALL, AMERICAN REVOLUTIONARY, Times Books, 1998.

8. Newsmaker, CHRISTIANE AMANPOUR, Cumulative Issue #4, 1997.

ENDORSEMENTS

from individuals, managers and management/career consultants

From Individuals...

I am certain that I am one of millions who has suffered intensely from poor job-fit, unrealized potential, and years lost in frustration because of inability (read fear) to admit my unhappiness, and to change course. Wide use of the concepts presented in this book could prevent much of this unhappiness and suffering, and give us a world where people have a sense of joy on Monday morning, instead of dread. We would be more fulfilled, productive, attentive and look back on our careers with pride instead of regrets. I highly recommend that every career counselor, admissions committee member, business owner, and anyone else who knows deep in their heart that they are not doing their 'true work' read this book.

Karen Roberts, M.D, M.P.H., Atascadero, CA

In my 35 years as an engineer and manager with aerospace and high technology organizations, I have had many job assignments offered to me. Some have worked very well while others have been disasters. Until I was introduced by Marlys and Merle Hanson to the SIMA® instrument, I did not have the insight I need to help me evaluate my career choices. Their analysis pointed out specifically what I need to be "motivated" in my work and how I can leverage my "passions" into a fulfilling work life. I now have a clearer understanding of myself so I can make accurate and informed decisions about my job/career directions. I truly had not recognized the power that lies in having a passion for one's work until I completed the SIMA® process. I recommend this book and SIMA® to all who are just entering the workforce as well as those who are evaluating their careers.

William M. Robson, P.E., Program Manager, Lawrence Livermore National Laboratory, Los Alamos National Laboratory

For the first time in my life, I am gaining genuine clarity on the aspects of work that I find fulfilling, as well as those that can cause significant personal frustration and stress. Having taken a large number of assessments in my life, I can say that I have greater confidence in SIMA® than anything else I have seen of this nature, because the information you get from it is not a generic description—it's you! As I continue to understand the information I have received (and its implications), I expect to see both professional and personal benefits from SIMA® for the rest of my life.

Jim Wheeler, Learning Analyst, The Williams Companies, Tulsa, OK

The SIMA® process was very helpful, focusing my attention on those areas of work that are most enjoyable. In life, many things come easy; but investing more time on the fun things brings a great deal more satisfaction.

Art Rebrovick, President, Warner Street Company, Inc., Nashville, TN

I don't know if you remember me. We met in London in September, when you held a career-planning seminar for my organization. I was at the time 25 years old. I had been working for that company for about three years. I was also very unhappy in my job and was contemplating graduate work as an honorable way out. I have kept your address and, at this point, I believe that I do have some good news to share. I want to write both to thank you for your insight and understanding and the catalytic role you played in helping me to begin to develop a career path that really is a "fit" for me. No more pretending to be something I am not! Best regards,

William Strand, Engineer, Fortune 10 Company, London

The SIMA® process was the perfect solution to my job dissatisfaction. Through the process I discovered my natural motivations, why certain jobs were naturally poor fits, and how to find a position that maximizes my natural abilities. The result of the process—a best fit job description—has proven valuable in all phases of my career: job searching, interviewing, and career development.

Roy Chancellor, Process Development Engineer, Durel Corporation, Chandler, AZ

I have worked with Marlys Hanson on her method of interview and assessment of motivated abilities and found her feedback insightful and thought-provoking. Her counsel on what to pursue and what to avoid has remained with me since, proving useful over and over again. Her method and style fit particularly well into conservative business cultures seeking to evolve their practices but not wanting to take too radical a step at a time. You might call this method "slow and steady wins the race" which, despite the media attention on fast change, is still a dominant preferred style in large American business.

James Neville, Internet Consultant, Petroleum Chemical Company, Houston, Texas

Never again will I trade job security for the opportunity to reach my potential. This book is a treasure map to ultimate career satisfaction.

Paul Hugo, Trial Consultant, Litigation Communications, Inc., Washington, D. C.

What helped me the most about my SIMA® assessment is the ability to put my finger on something that had been elusive to me for a lot of my life—where I fit in the working world. It has greatly helped me understand why I naturally gravitate toward certain skills and shy away from others. It has helped me broaden my scope and to consider jobs that I didn't even know were jobs!

Susan Sutherland, Salesperson, Export Sales, Naperville, IL

PASSION and PURPOSE is an extraordinary achievement that inspires, motivates and profoundly impacts one's life—professional and personal. This book has been such an inspiration to me and has provided me with valuable guidance to making changes towards a higher quality of life and fulfillment at work and at home. Marlys hits the mark again and again with her insights. I am amazed at how she can succinctly articulate what one suspects and feels but cannot exactly pinpoint.

Going through the SIMA® assessment and counseling process was a journey of self-realization and greater understanding of why people behave as they do. It concretized and put to practice the observations and insights shared in the book. Above all, it provided the means to indeed enable me to "Know myself...and become who I am"...in the best way that I can. The value of this book cannot be expressed enough.

Wilma Gamboa-Guez, Director of Strategic Partnerships, Edutorium A/S Copenhagen, Denmark

In the competitive corporate world, it is essential in managing your career to have a correct and accurate understanding of your individual 'giftedness' and how best to leverage your abilities to maximize personal performance. I believe the concepts discussed in this book assist an individual in accomplishing this objective.

Jim Morgan, Accountant, Houston, TX

From Managers…

An enormously powerful tool that has become a cornerstone of our personnel development process. Through the use of SIMA®, we not only fill positions based on "skill match," but perhaps more importantly, on "motivation match." It's a win/win for both employees and the company: Employees gain insight into where their passions lie and are assigned to areas where their energies can be tapped, and the company gets big productivity gains from their truly motivated employees.

Manager, Fortune 10 Petrochemical Company

This book is definitely one that I will have as a reference for myself and all my clients. I have used the SIMA® for the last six years within my agency. It has helped all levels of employees to find how they "fit" into the organization and what career paths to take to further develop their individual strengths. SIMA® is a great tool for retaining new hires, retraining people, and keeping retirees as part-time consultants.

Ornella L. Pensyl, Career Development Officer, Defense Intelligence Agency

As adults, most of us spend the vast majority of our lives doing work that is not personally rewarding and-or fulfilling. Marlys' approach details a cogent way to change this. Read her book and you'll have a clear set of choices that will get you what you want. I've seen it work, and I highly recommend it to you.

Mat Juechter, Past Chair, Board of Governors, ASTD; former CEO at ARC International, Wilson Learning and Xerox Learning

In a Department of Energy national workshop I directed, and which won White House recognition, several instruments were used to help senior engineers/scientists assess their "fit" for transferring their technologies from DOE to the private sector to begin businesses and entrepreneurial careers. Participants gave Marlys Hanson and the SIMA® session the highest evaluation of the six-day workshop. Many called in subsequent months to discuss how they were able to apply SIMA® insights not only to this important life changing career decision, but also to even broader issues of work/life planning. SIMA® is uniquely powerful and comprehensive; people do not forget what they learn from this assessment.

Ladonna Robson, Managing Partner, The Robson Group; Past Organizational Change Consultant and Manager at Lawrence Livermore National Laboratory and Los Alamos National Laboratory

After going through the SIMA® process, I began to actively select roles that complimented my natural motivated abilities and to better understand why I struggled with activities that did not engage my motivated abilities. This knowledge gave me a whole new outlook and influenced all future dealings with others. I insisted that my whole team take the class. We worked together to restructure the team participation responsibilities based on their motivated abilities and immediately became a more effective team.

Even when life calls on us to perform responsibilities that do not match our motivated abilities, this knowledge of our inherent success skills drives us to get the job done in a manner which meets the expectations and feels good.

Janet S. Brooks, Project Manager, Houston, TX

From Management Consultants and Career Counselors:

I believe that SIMA® represents a breakthrough in our understanding of intrinsic motivation. This methodology has proven to be a reliable, valid and powerful tool to help individuals manage their careers in specific work settings and to enable managers to harness the talents of their staff members with more precision. Nothing else comes close to SIMA®'s ability to define person-job-fit in behavioral terms.

Among those using the SIMA® technology today, Marlys Hanson stands out as one of the foremost practitioners in the world. Her work with SIMA® is grounded in more than twenty-five years of experience with top scientists, engineers and executives. Marlys Hanson has created innovative SIMA® workshops and instructional guides to bring this technology to thousands of individuals and hundreds of organizations. I highly recommend Marlys Hanson's book to those individuals interested in understanding their core competencies, in demystifying their intrinsic motivation and in improving their work satisfaction.

William J. Banis, Ph.D., National Certified Career Counselor, Interim Vice President for Student Affairs and Director of University Career Services, Northwestern University

I first encountered SIMA® shortly after making a significant career change, from engineering to organizational development consultant. The SIMA® process confirmed my choice, and has guided my own career decisions ever since. No other assessment instrument helps people do career planning better than SIMA®. It really gets at what makes the person thrive— uncovering that has changed the lives of countless clients with whom I have worked over the past ten years.

Debra Franke, Career Counselor, Philadelphia, PA

The SIMA® assessment process really made sense to me. I've taken a lot of assessments over the years. SIMA® gave me extra insight others had not. Complexity and change are motivators to me. I wondered why I was drawn to challenges that always seemed hard—the more complex they were, the more I liked it. SIMA® finally put a name on what was going on for me and helped me understand it. After that I was firmly convinced that I needed the complex challenges to keep me engaged. Otherwise I got bored. I've since walked away from assignments that are straightforward knowing that I may not stick with them through completion.

Julie O'Mara, President, O'Mara and Associates, Past National President American Society for Training and Development, Co-Author, Managing Workforce 2000

I have used SIMA® extensively in consulting with leadership in local churches and parachurch organizations. I find that SIMA® provides the most accurate, comprehensive determination of inborn abilities and motivations for ministry.

Dr. H. Thomas Walker, President, Ministry by Design, Minneapolis, MN, (United Methodist Minister, Ret.)

For those serious about understanding the motivational dynamics of each individual, SIMA® will prove to be an invaluable tool. In my consulting practice, after more than 10 years of searching for definitive answers on how people are wired, SIMA® has been, to me, an answer to an heart-cry!

John B. Samuel, Director, SIMA®Asia Pte Ltd, Singapore.

My clients—senior executives who find themselves in changing and challenging times—frequently need solid data to help them understand their team, how they might succeed in a new position, or the dynamics of a merging two seasoned and senior teams. The SIMA® assessment consistently provides personal insight and the material on which they can make informed decisions.

Ron Galbraith, CEO, Management 21, Nashville, TN

In over twelve years of working as a career counselor and outplacement consultant I have found SIMA® the most effective instrument in helping people find work they are successful at and enjoy doing.

Anton Philips, President, Emergo Consulting, Amsterdam, Netherlands

Contents

ABOUT THIS BOOK

This book is about innate motivation—the naturally endowed needs, drives or desires that motivate a person to some particular action or behavior. Many terms are used to describe this phenomenon. Giftedness, talents, motivated abilities, natural strengths, motivational patterns, or passion and purpose are some of the most common. Regardless of the specific term used, all are intended to convey the fact that every time a person accomplishes something personally significant and enjoyable, he or she will inevitably repeat some or all of the aspects of his or her innate motivation. Over time, a consistent pattern emerges that, if recognized and understood, reveals the basis for fulfillment and productivity for that individual. **This book presents the System of Identifying Motivated Abilities (SIMA)®, a behavior-based* assessment process designed to identify this unique but consistent pattern of your natural strengths.**

The outcome of this SIMA® Assessment is a description of your vocationally significant motivations—what you enjoy doing and feel you do well. It describes:

✧ The "motivated" abilities that recur in your work/life achievements.

✧ The subject matter or content with which you are motivated to work.

✧ The circumstances that trigger and sustain your efforts.

✧ The way in which you prefer to relate to others when you are working.

✧ The overall outcome or payoff that you seek to achieve from your efforts.

This set of information, which is your Motivational Pattern, should be the foundation of every decision you make about your job, your career and even your life.

You may elect to complete this behavior-based SIMA® Assessment as a self-directed process by completing the step-by-step guidance presented in this book, or you may choose to seek expert assistance via our website www.motivationalpattern.com. After you have identified your Motivational Pattern, you may elect to have your pattern compared to profiles of more than 400 professions and occupations to determine the

---

*Many popular personality or vocational assessments (e.g. Myers-Briggs Personality Profile or Strong Campbell Interest Inventory) are preference-based assessments; the results are determined by the participants' choices as they respond to the options presented for each question. Obviously, such choices can be heavily biased by our social and cultural values. For example, in most organizations, "managing others" has more status than "working independently." "Doing original work" sounds more professional than "performing repetitive tasks." In contrast, a behavior-based assessment is based on the actual behavior as performed and reported in detail by the participant, without benefit of options from which to select a response. Behavior-based assessments are much more reliable and valid as predictive data.

"best fit" roles for you.

Everyone has motivational issues and career concerns. While we recommend the entire book to everyone, to meet your unique situation you may wish to select the sections of the book that are most relevant for where you find yourself today. The following is designed to help you make the most of this book:

Part I: Defining Passion and Purpose

Section A.
What Are Motivational Patterns?   page 3

This section explains the phenomenon and the power of innate motivation. It describes how "evidence" is gathered to develop recurring themes or patterns, regarding the work you enjoy and do well. Advantages of "matching" motivations to one's work and disadvantages of mismatches are discussed. Personal stories covering a variety of life/work achievements of "ordinary" people will start you thinking about your life/work achievements—and prepare you to recognize and differentiate your own motivations.

Recommended for all readers—the Foundation for the book.

Section B.
What Are You "Motivated" to Do?   page 40

This is the heart of the book and provides the process for you to discover and define your innate motivation—your Motivational Pattern. Everything you need to "do it yourself" is provided in this section, but you can also contact us for assistance, if desired.

Recommended for all readers—the SIMA® assessment process.

Section C.
Understanding Innate Motivation   page 92

This section is designed for the reader who wants more background or "proof" regarding the concept of innate motivation. It addresses issues like "nature" vs. "nurture," the relationship of motivation to competencies, and money as a motivator. If you are already convinced of the power in your innate motivation, you can skip this section and go right to work on Part II: Leveraging Your Passion and Purpose.

Recommended for skeptics and readers who want to investigate this subject in greater depth and detail. (For others, it will strengthen your appreciation of the profound nature of your pattern.)

PART II: Leveraging Your Passion and Purpose

Section A.
Finding (or Creating) Work That "Fits"   page 105

This section gives you an opportunity to apply what you have learned about your innate motivation. What is the nature of your potential? Are you a manager or a leader? Can you recognize and resolve mismatches? What criteria do you use in making job/career decisions? Does your current job "fit" you? How do you negotiate for a better "fit"?

Recommended for readers who are concerned about their job "fit."

Section B.
Managing Your Career   page 161

This section is about selecting and maintaining a career direction that capitalizes on your innate or natural talents. Building on your strengths, developing critical skills that "fit," exploring entrepreneurial talents and avoiding mid-career plateaus are addressed. And if a new career direction is in order, this section provides assistance in defining your "best-fit" scenario!

Recommended for readers who are concerned about their career direction.

Section C.
Recognizing the Talents of Others   page 191

This section provides insight to help you recognize, nurture and utilize the innate motivation of others. And because so many participants have asked about how this concept of innate motivation applies to their children, there is a chapter especially for parents.

Recommended for team leaders, supervisors, managers and parents.

PART III: Getting What You Need

Section A.
ACT II: One Last Chance to Be Who You Are   page 207

This section is for the reader who is looking ahead to "retirement." As Peter Drucker says: *There is one prerequisite for managing the second half of your life. You must be doing so long before you enter it.* If you are in your 20's or 30's, you can skip this section (unless you are interested in this subject).

Recommended for readers over 40 years of age.

Section B.
Creating What Will Be   page 214

This last section brings closure to the book with a guide for how to keep your motivational insights alive and well. You will want to consider each step carefully—and to reflect seriously on the rewards for the "good-fit" life.

Recommended for all readers—a "must do."

FOREWORD

By Arthur F. Miller, Jr.
Founder, People Management International LLC.

For all those knowledge workers who are still relying on someone else to manage their careers . . . this is your wake-up call!

The purpose of this book is to provide a process for you to discover, once and for all, the parameters of the life you were meant to live—and then to use that knowledge in making more accurate and informed decisions about your work and your life.

For over 40 years, my organization has worked with both employers and employees on the issue of job "fit" and its relationship to performance and career satisfaction. After examining the "match" of the individual's talents to the requirements of the job for over 50,000 individuals, we have arrived at the following conclusions:

> *The ONLY way you can find a meaningful, fulfilling life is by performing work that engages your heart and mind. There is no Plan B. And, what is true for you is also true for your employer, who can attain and sustain a competitive advantage (which means "an economically fulfilling life") ONLY through employees who are both gifted at their tasks and passionate about securing the results desired.*

This may seem like a simple statement of the obvious, but, in many cases, the conundrum is that neither you nor your employer knows what kind of work will engage your heart and mind. As Peter Drucker says:

> *Most people think they know what they are good at. They are usually wrong. More often, people know what they are not good at—and even then more people are wrong than right. And yet, a person can perform only from strength.* [1]

It would be wonderful if everyone had recognized and were making fulfilling, productive use of their strengths. However, our work has shown that there are far too many examples of "mismatch" (situations in which the "motivated" abilities and interests of the person are significantly at odds with the demands of the job in which they are working) in the workplace today. The evidence for "mismatch" comes from a variety of perspectives:

❖ *In a survey of 1.7 million employees in 101 companies from 63 countries, only 20% said that their strengths are in play every day.* [2]

❖ *A recent Career Education Corporation survey reported that half of employed adults in the United States would consider changing their careers, and nearly 25% plan to do so in the next 12 months.* [3]

❖ *Termination rates of 50% (for professional employees) in the first five years of employment are typical, even during periods of high unemployment.* [4]

These "mismatch" scenarios are very common and very costly—and yet there is a remedy. You and your employer both need the same information to achieve your mutual objective: the productive use of your strengths. The secret to achieving this mutually beneficial match of "talents to tasks" is contained in how you and your organization perceive human nature.

THE "BECOMING CULTURE"

One way is to view an individual as a work-in-progress, on the road to becoming what others want or need him to become. In our experience of over 40 years of working with a wide variety of professionals, we have come to refer to this as the "becoming 0culture." This interpretation of human nature permeates our families, our schools and our organizations.*

Initially advocated by theorists like Ivan Pavlov and B. F. Skinner, this "becoming" approach to understanding human nature assumes individuals are malleable, like putty, and can be shaped and reshaped by others or themselves in response to values or needs.

Parents play a key part by encouraging their youngsters to become whatever the parents value, be it choice of profession or occupation, social skills or leadership, sports or music, fitting in or being unique. The emphasis is on some form of "getting ahead," which involves comparison and competition with peers, which necessarily creates the categories of winners and losers. Much of this lobbying is attempted in the context of the educational experience, where the faculty seeks to help the youngster become the best speaker, writer, researcher, historian, scientist, ad infinitum. With little regard to what, how and why the student is motivated to learn, teacher after teacher seeks to enable the student to become whatever the course and standards require. For 12 to 16 years this scenario continues, with the primary focus on "becoming" whatever is desired or required by the "system." Those who possess the innate abilities and motivation needed (reading, studying, writing, memorizing) to meet the demands of the educational system generally succeed; those who do not often struggle to keep up or merely tolerate

---

*A more complete discussion of "nature vs. nurture" appears in the section entitled "Understanding Innate Motivation."

the educational process.

Whether students are so endowed as to prosper a lot, a little, or hardly at all by means of their formal education, they nevertheless do not learn who they are, what their purpose is, what they have to give an employer, and what they want out of their career. In that state of mind and with limited self-knowledge, they enter the world of work, often confused and uncertain, but mostly hopeful. We meet many of these individuals during the first five years of their employment, when, on average, 50% of them elect to voluntarily terminate their employment. The problem is called turnover, and it is very costly to employers. [5] It is also very troubling to the employee, who discovers that she is not interested in performing the work of her chosen career—in which she has already invested a great deal of time, money and effort.

Rarely, if ever, do those who seek to so change an employee make the investment to discover the employee's interests and motivations.

Upon entering the world of work, employees tend to trust that someone knows better than they and will make good use of them. However, employers are primarily interested in getting the work done, regardless of how individual employees are "motivated." So, to close the gap between employee capability and work requirements, employers universally embrace the ubiquitous but baseless doctrine that, regardless of their unique make-up, employees can be trained, developed, motivated, changed, incentivized, rewarded—all to become what the employer needs them to become. It is a popular but mythical approach.

Rarely, if ever, do those who seek to so change an employee make the investment to discover the employee's interests and motivations. Pursuing the "becoming" agenda, they ignore the unique make-up, and especially the motivational engine, that drives the employee to superior performance.

It isn't as if managers who make hiring and promotion decisions are incompetent—far from it. *They simply do not have data about the candidates that reveal their "motivated" strengths.* The "becoming" culture, as it is practiced by most organizations, does not generate data about the kind of work that will engage the employee's heart and mind, or, what has been rightly called, the employee's *passion and purpose*. In fact, data gathered about employees are piece-meal and fragmentary and are not—and probably cannot be—integrated into a picture of the whole person in action. Why? Because it makes the terribly flawed assumption that employees are essentially malleable clay who can be shaped into anything they (or others) want them to be.

IMPACT OF THE "BECOMING" CULTURE

Believing in their powers to "mold and shape" employees, management makes critical decisions about hiring, promoting and transferring people, primarily on the basis of the individual's *past experiences*, as observed, evaluated and reported by others (e.g., college degrees, grade point average, references, 360 degree feedback, performance appraisals). The resulting decisions are effectively a toss-up. At least 50% of the time, people who are not good at making or motivated to make risky decisions, set new and different goals, or monitor activities which impact bottom-line issues are promoted into key positions that require these specific "motivated" abilities.

Brilliant, articulate, analytical, relational influencers who can't abide the idea of confronting others are put in command positions. Outstanding, knowledgeable specialists in areas critical to organizational success, who have built a reputation based on lengthy investigations and insightful recommendations, are promoted to operating jobs requiring quick, decisive response to a wide variety of unfamiliar issues and partial facts. Developers are promoted to managing positions where they struggle to find the motivation to maintain what they have developed. Scores of people are hired or promoted into functions for which they have no heart. Supervisors, effective when they can personally monitor and interact with subordinates engaged in a familiar activity, are promoted to manage multiple projects, specialties, functions or operations. Because they were so good at what they did, outstanding salespeople, scientists, engineers, accountants or buyers are frequently promoted. And these are often promotions into management jobs, which they, their subordinates and their management ultimately regret.

The greatest irony is that this "mismatch" is so common that it often isn't even recognized for what it is, even when we do see it.

The impact of this pervasive mismatch on productivity and growth, efficiency, costs, and workforce morale is practically beyond measure. Why? Because each mismatch not only affects the productivity of the incumbent, but also creates impediments in the performance of all those up, down and sideways who interact with and rely on the mismatched person. The greatest irony is that this "mismatch" is so common that it often isn't even recognized for what it is, even when we do see it.

As steep as the costs of mismatch are on the employer, there are usually other employees who can pick up at least some of the slack. *It is ultimately the mismatched employee who pays the real penalty.* The litanies of bad things that come upon the mismatched employee are even painful to recite. Frustration, anger, despair, self-doubt and depression are only the early signs. Sustained mismatch leads to continuing stress that takes serious—sometimes even deadly—toll on physical, economic and emotional health, and family relationships. (What mismatched work can do to the worker is discussed in more detail in the chapter entitled "Work Without Meaning is Deadly.")

The reason this plague of "becoming" takes so many down in every generation is due to the fact that people have not developed an accurate sense of identity; they don't know there is a better way to get more accurate information about themselves. At a practical level, they don't know who they are and what they would do and enjoy best in a job or career. Suffering from a crisis of identification, they are therefore most vulnerable to pressures or enticements for them to become what others want or need them to become. They enter into the "becoming culture," most frequently in their childhood or youth and may never escape its grasp. *They become quick to trade who and what they are for what beckons.*

THE CONCEPT OF "GIFTEDNESS"

There is another way to view human nature. We call it "giftedness." Evidence for this innate and unique make-up goes back as far as Socrates *(Know thyself and become who you are)* and is as current as the expressions of Jung, Adler, Fromm, May, Goldstein, Rogers, Allport, Maslow, Drucker, Gardner and Hillman. (James Hillman's *The Soul's Code*, is a "must read.") [6]

The Gallup Organization research (one million employees and 80,000 managers interviewed over 30 years) also offers strong support for the concept of giftedness:

> *A person's mental filter is as enduring and unique as her fingerprint. This is a radical belief that flies in the face of decades of self-help mythology.* [7]

Giftedness is an observable and provable fact of human nature; we have seen the phenomenon appear in the achievement data of 50,000 people. It emerges in people's lives as a consistent pattern of behavior, whenever they do something they feel they have done well AND they have enjoyed doing. This is the golden nugget of human nature:

> *Each person has innate abilities and motivation to achieve a certain unique purpose. Our equality does not lie in the nature of our talents but in the fact that we each are endowed with our own unique passion and purpose.*

People are born with a unique MO (modus operandi), a defined way of functioning, a pattern of certain competencies and motivations that governs how they attempt to perform any job or role. We refer to this pattern as a person's *giftedness* or *natural strengths*, because it is an endowment or inheritance, if you will, as contrasted to being the result of a developmental process. For ease of reference, we call this a Motivational Pattern. *

Although capable of prodigious development, the parameters of the Motivational Pattern define the potential of the person, not in organizational terms, but in what she would and would not bring to a job. Effectively, once you understand a person's Motivational Pattern, you understand the kind of work assignment that will engage his heart and mind. You will know what the person will be "motivated" to learn. You will

---

*Motivational Patterns are the product of an assessment process called the **System for Identifying Motivated Abilities (SIMA)**®, copyrighted in 1963. In 1989, Dr. John Crites, internationally recognized vocational psychologist, lead an extensive research program to evaluate the objectivity, validity and reliability of SIMA®. Dr. Crites reported that SIMA® met or exceeded the standards established by

know what type and level of performance will be stressful for the employee to sustain over time. You will know what he will avoid and where she will most likely encounter difficulties. Because the Motivational Pattern is irrepressible and constantly seeking expression, it is manifested and observable throughout people's lives, every time they do something that they find satisfying and believe they do well. In fact, its influence and power are so pervasive that people will—often without realizing they are doing it—subtly or even overtly transform elements of their jobs to fit with their pattern. The person who is motivated to organize will seek something to organize; the designer will look for something to design; and the influencer will find someone to influence.

The authority for these observations comes from the analysts at People Management International, who have spent 40 years studying the lived achievement experiences of over 50,000 people. Our conclusion: **To achieve a high level of performance AND personal fulfillment in any job, the person's competencies and motivations must "match" the critical requirements of the job.** The better this match, the greater the likelihood for success for the employee and the organization. Others concur in our conclusion. The Gallup Organization reports:

> *It cannot be overstated that being a great manager or a great salesperson or great analyst or great anything is much more about the natural abilities of a person and who they are vs. their skill and training.* [8]

THE IMPACT OF GIFTEDNESS

Human achievement is only possible through endowed giftedness. Pause and thoughtfully reflect on that comment for a moment. What it means is that **nothing of value has ever been achieved, except through the efforts of people "gifted" at the required tasks and passionate about attaining the desired result.** We see this when we look at the motivations of individuals who are considered "successful" (by themselves and others) in their fields. *Their successes are built on their strengths.*

You can find similar evidence in the biographies or autobiographies of "famous" people. The authors, knowing nothing about Motivational Patterns, inevitably tell a story of giftedness. We learn about World War II shipbuilder Henry Kaiser's childhood fascination with more efficient building processes; how Johnny Carson (all-time favorite talk show host) put together a magic show when he was six and started his career in the Lion's Club circuit in Nebraska; and how Pavarotti "entertained" his neighbors with his singing when he was five.

---

the American Psychological Association for determining the psychometric characteristics of assessment techniques. SIMA® scored exceptionally high (90%) on interscorer agreement, which means scores for it are almost as objective as standardized tests.
Dr. Crites' research is documented in detail in the SIMA® Theory and Research Handbook, PMI Shares, Inc., Avon, CT., 1992.

Robert Sapolsky, noted neurologist and author of the best-seller *Why Zebras Don't Get Ulcers,* [9] shares an example from his own childhood that gives us a glimpse into his early interest in science and his sense of humor, both of which have served him well throughout his life:

> *Some kids are born to biology. You can spot them instantly as kids—they're the ones comfortably lugging around the toy microscopes, stowing dead squirrels in the freezer, being ostracized at school for their obsession with geckos. Personally, I used to collect the leftover chicken bones from everyone at the Friday night dinner, clean them with my knife, and proudly display an articulated skeleton by the end of dessert. In retrospect, I think this was more to irritate my sister than to begin an anatomical quest.*

Generations of recorded history and experience, combined with evidence from modern scientific research, paint a compelling picture of the validity and power of the "giftedness" perspective. And yet, in the face of the fact that success by any name can only be achieved through the "match" of passion and suitable talents of employees, we know of only one industry that keeps "book" on the strengths of its employees and uses that information to run that business. Can you guess what it is?

IS THERE A LESSON HERE?

Teams in professional sports, like baseball, football, basketball and others, literally gather and maintain—for quick or studied access—data about the unique make-up of each player, as tested by a variety of circumstances or standards. Why this is true might seem obvious. The team's success or failure depends on 1) having the necessary "stuff" available and 2) making use of it in ways to defeat the competition and win the game.

Obscure philosophy? Complex metaphysics? See Jane run the 100 meters—fast, very fast. See Ishmael shoot the basket—with his left hand—from 20 feet out—off the backboard. See Raoul feint that guy out of his cleats. With such a payoff for winning, you would think every organization in the land would follow the lead of sports and make the gathering and productive use of strengths possessed by employees a Number One Priority! Are sports that much different from manufacturing and selling beepers, or cold cuts, or clothing? Or designing computer systems—or teaching and counseling students?

Acclaimed performance—whether in the production line, product or process design, in surgery, on stage, in the kitchen, in the studio, in the classroom, in the tool shop or in the laboratory—is only attainable when tasks match the endowed strengths of the performer. The sustained success or bottom-line effectiveness of a business (or function contained within it) is traceable to people *who possess the right stuff for the jobs required.*

And what is true of a business is true of a hospital, a labor union, a government agency, a church, a family and a scout troop.

"Success" in our personal lives involves accomplishing things meaningful to us and feeling good about ourselves and the lives that we lead. *A person can experience meaning in life only when gifts possessed by that person are used for purposes of personal significance.* Achievements driven by enabling our gifts and motivations are the ONLY means available to people for valid and continuing self-esteem.

WHY YOU CAN'T BE ANYTHING YOU WANT TO BE, YOU WILL LOVE BEING WHO YOU WERE DESIGNED TO BE [10]

Yes, we can change our bad habits, our values, our beliefs, our perceptions, our attitudes, our sensibilities, and our biases. But we have never seen any compelling evidence that proves that people can be changed at the level of innate motivation. Have you? Do you know of anyone who clearly was not and yet became a gifted, motivated decision-maker? An effective planner? Creatively innovative? A risk taker or a political animal? A team player? A big-picture person or detail minded? Highly observant, good with numbers or highly conceptual? When we ask this question of knowledge workers, only those whose ambitions require the addition of new talents respond in the affirmative.

Experienced and effective managers respond differently. In the language of the Gallup Organization research:

> The world's great managers realize that each person is motivated differently. They know there is a limit to how much remolding they can do. But they don't bemoan these differences and grind them down. Instead they capitalize on them. They try to help each person become more and more of who he is. [11]

As Peter Drucker cautions: *Do not try to change yourself—you are unlikely to succeed.* [12]

All of which brings us back to the purpose of this book. **The challenge to you is to discover, once and for all, the parameters of the life you were meant to live.** You will be able to use the knowledge you gain for the rest of your life, every time you have a decision to make, a personal performance puzzle to unravel, a possible new direction to pursue, or a criticism to ponder. It will be an investment of more than a few hours, but you will find the journey exhilarating and richly rewarding . . . I promise you.

PART I
DEFINING PASSION
AND PURPOSE

Section A.
What Are Motivational Patterns?

Section B.
What Are You "Motivated" to Do?

Section C.
Understanding Innate Motivation

SECTION A.
WHAT ARE MOTIVATIONAL PATTERNS?

Chapter 1. The Power Is in the "Fit"

Success in the knowledge economy comes to those who know themselves, their strengths, their values and how they best perform.

Peter Drucker

LEVERAGE YOUR NATURAL TALENTS

The essential ingredient for a successful life is the opportunity to engage our passions in the pursuit of a purpose that is personally meaningful. There is nothing neutral about our passions and our purpose. Either we respond to what these powerful forces present to us in our daily lives and in our fantasies, or we suffer from the neglect of ourselves.

What this means is that the scientist does not practice her calling but IS her calling. Just as the scientist needs her calling for a fulfilling and meaningful existence, each of us needs our calling. We need work that is more than a livelihood. We need work that is life itself. We need to listen to our passions and let them help us define our purpose and shape our work/life. It is only through this process that we find significant value in ourselves and thus build our feelings of self-worth.

For many of us, our passions and purpose became "fuzzy" early in our lives, when we decided that it was easier to do what was expected of us than it was to pursue what was meaningful to us. We may have lost sight of who we really are, by being focused on what we (or others) thought we should become. Sometimes we became so dependent on those external standards (and the related rewards) that we compromised our real passion and purpose. For many individuals, their successful performance in one position resulted in a promotion to another position that was not a good match. But regardless of the cause of our derailment, the good news is that we can uncover and retrieve the meaning in our work/life. By examining carefully what it is that we have enjoyed doing and found satisfying, we can refresh our understanding of our passion and our purpose.

We like to think that we have chosen our work, but it is probably more accurate to say that our work has found us. (The original meaning of the word *occupation* was "to be taken and seized.") [13] Our passion and our purpose are already within us, waiting to be discovered, if we will just take the time to examine our lives and our work. Once we have these insights about ourselves, we must acknowledge their enduring nature. We are not made of putty, waiting to be shaped into whatever the world wants or needs. Each of us possesses a *pattern* that orients and directs our behavior; it also defines what will be meaningful and fulfilling in our lives. The evidence of this pattern has shown through our entire lives. We just need to take the time to identify, understand and act on it.

Without the benefit of these insights that give direction to our lives, we are destined to wait until something comes along. We find ourselves waiting *to be discovered.* We keep

> *Our passion and our purpose are already within us, waiting to be discovered . . .*

waiting for the next promotion, for the company to reorganize, or for the new assignment. We may search the want ads or, these days, the Internet. But we are doomed to a reactive strategy if we have not set a course based on our own passions and purpose. In a time of perpetual change, we are also facing an existence paralleling that of a *cork on the waves of the permanent whitewater of the 21st Century.* [14]

This innate guidance is not just for the geniuses among us. It is waiting for all of us, no matter who we are or where we live. It is independent of our education, economic status, our gender and our ethnicity. And one purpose in life is not more important than another. *What is really important is NOT whether my gifts are more desirable than your gifts, but that we each have important gifts to share with the world.* We can learn from the gifts of others, but we cannot "adopt" the passion and purpose of another. We must discover our own. Recognizing and then achieving our own destiny is what life is all about.

GET THE RIGHT PERSON IN THE RIGHT JOB

I think I started to understand the "fit" concept about the time I started school. I grew up on a farm in North Dakota. Dad was a "dry land" farmer (no irrigation thus totally dependent on when and how much it rained). He also raised several hundred head of cattle and sheep. Mom raised five children...along with chickens, turkeys and a garden. I was in high school before we had electricity, so all the cooking, baking and laundry required considerably more time and effort than it does today.

I'm sure you get the picture. There was a lot of work to do. In fact, there was so much work to do that the best strategy for getting it all done was pretty obvious: Use the person who could do the job most efficiently. That meant the person who could do the job the most correctly, quickly and without requiring any help or guidance from anyone else was very likely to get the "opportunity."

Mom and Dad seemed to work all the time, doing whatever needed to be done. But as the five children respectively were able to participate, the opportunity for more selective "recruitment" became apparent.

My oldest brother Glenn was probably about nine or ten when he started driving the tractor and working in the field by himself. He loved the outdoor, physical labor, was mechanically talented and would do anything that looked like a challenge. He didn't really care much about schoolwork, and he didn't complain when he had to miss school to help in the field. He very quickly became a highly valued asset in the family's farming operation.

My sister Margie was the oldest. She is sufficiently older than me so that I don't really remember how she started. She was a very responsible individual; she could do practically anything, from hard physical labor to operating machinery or milking cows. She also enjoyed seeing to it that others did their work as well. So she, too, was a real contributor to accomplishing the never-ending work at hand.

I was next in line. In addition to being off the low end of the scale on mechanical aptitude, I couldn't get the hang of driving anything. I really didn't like physical labor or cold weather; therefore I didn't contribute much to the "outside" work. In the house, I didn't fare well either. I was not nearly as efficient in the kitchen as my mother, nor were my culinary products comparable in quality. That left routine household chores, like laundry, ironing, scrubbing and cleaning with some simple baking. I was helpful and felt useful but my work was not really what you would call "mainstream." In today's jargon, one would probably say that I did not possess the competencies that were critical to the business! But I did love school. I loved to read and could hardly wait for the next box of library books from the county library to arrive at our one-room country school. And I was never asked to miss school to help at home; my contributions weren't that essential. I doubt that I ever volunteered either!

My younger brother Bill's most obvious talent as a youngster was his musical ability. He started playing the piano "by ear" when he was four years old; he plunked out the melody of "Nearer My God to Thee" after attending a neighbor's funeral. He was a handsome kid with big eyes and a charming smile. He was an excellent student, too. While he worked in the fields and helped with the cattle and sheep, he never really demonstrated much interest or exceptional ability in those areas. Those who were a better "fit" for the work were more likely to be assigned the task and involved in the operations.

My youngest brother, Doug, came along several years later. Even as a baby, he was an observer. As a young child, he spent hours walking in the fields and pastures looking for (and finding!) Native American relics. Like me, he was not mechanical or physically motivated, but he was more investigative and detail-oriented. Whereas routine housework was my route to usefulness, there were relatively few work responsibilities that Doug was interested in or able to perform efficiently. He spent a great deal of his time looking for arrowheads and in later years, fishing with Dad, who was delighted to have his companionship.

How did the story end? Well, it continues. My brother Glenn took over the farming operations, bought additional land and is a cattle rancher. My sister Margie married a farmer and is still a very active partner in a successful operation that now involves their two sons. Brother Bill is an econometrician, a profession that combines mathematics (a discipline that is often selected by people with musical talent) and economics. Brother Doug is a soil scientist. My work has always been in some type of "school" or learning situation. I am still reading (and writing) books!

The moral of the story? The situation that I have described illustrates some basic dynamics of human behavior:

❖   Certain "motivated" abilities appear early in your life and appear to be enduring. The basic themes endure like the main trunk on a tree.

❖   These "motivated" abilities are irrepressible. Regardless of the environment or circumstances, your pattern will express itself somewhere in your life.

❖   Certain themes recur in activities that you both enjoy doing and feel you do well. These themes or "patterns" orient and direct your performance.

❖   The "fit" of your pattern to your life/work profoundly impacts your self-esteem, your relationships, your career and, most profoundly, your life.

"MOVING" VS. "STUCK" EMPLOYEES

When researchers Dalton and Thompson [15] studied the careers of knowledge workers,* they collected their data by asking employees and managers what seemed to differentiate employees who were "stuck" in their careers from those who seemed to "keep moving" throughout their lifetimes, steadily increasing their responsibilities, and yes, even their salaries. The responses from hundreds of such interviews had one recurring theme that is critically relevant to the "fit" concept: *Those employees who continued to "move" knew how to leverage their strengths.*

In the many years of working with career issues of knowledge workers, I have observed that these "movers" do more than leverage their strengths. They have a "fire in their

---

*The term "knowledge worker" refers to employees whose brains—rather than brawn—are central to their performance. Knowledge workers are not only doctors, lawyers, software professionals and teachers, but also all employees who serve customers, help solve problems, think of better ways to do things, and continuously learn (and share that learning) on the job. In short, most employees could be classified as knowledge workers in today's economy. Source: Recruiting and Retaining Employees, published by the American Society of Training and Development and the Society for Human Resource Development, June, 2000.

belly" (meaning a real passion for their work—not indigestion!) and they know how to keep it burning brightly. The "movers" also seem to realize from the very beginning that they are 100% responsible for the proper use of their talents and the management of their careers. They do not wait for their talents "to be discovered" by their management. They do not expect that others will manage their talents wisely, because they know that it is unrealistic to expect someone else to fully understand their passions. They do not wait to be "scheduled" for a career discussion. They know that no one else has nearly as much at stake in their career development as they do. The "movers" take the initiative to build a working relationship with their supervisor, to communicate the nature of their talents, and to present strategies for the best use of their capabilities in meeting the organization's needs. The "movers" simply do not rely on anyone else to manage their careers, regardless of what the organization has promised or offered. **And, most importantly, the "movers" seem to be more connected to their work. They accomplish their tasks with less stress. They seem to have an endless "appetite" for their work. They say they are happy when they are working.**

FINDING "FLOW"

Mihaly Csikszentmihalyi is a psychologist well known for his extensive research on determining when people are truly happy. [16] His research on motivation has focused on how people described an activity when it was going particularly well and they felt "motivated" to perform the task. His major contribution to the understanding of motivation was to identify, across widely diverse activities, a common experience that respondents felt was "autotelic" (rewarding in and of itself). Csikszentmihalyi calls this experience "flow." He defines "flow" as the effortless action people feel in moments that stand out as best in their lives. The dynamics of the flow experience that make enjoyment possible are the same, regardless of the culture or the nature of the activity. The activity can be play, leisure, creative pursuits—and yes, even work! According to Csikzentmihalyi, flow states appeared to exist when the person was performing an activity that in some way served to "fulfill their being." The range of activities in which people experience flow confirms the existence of a practically unlimited number of potential flow activities, in any age or in any culture. This is an important fact. If the potential opportunities for "flow" are practically limitless, then we can all be optimistic about finding "flow" (or good "fit") situations.

One can readily sense the feeling of "flow" in the descriptions of activities that the following individuals reported as providing fulfillment:

Shawn's Achievement

"In training as an instructor for the National Outdoor Leadership School, I was part of a 16-person expedition. We traveled over 100 miles crossing the Continental Divide and ascended a 14,000-foot peak. I was chosen to be part of a two-man team that escorted an injured individual out of the program. This required a 20-mile, 2-day expedition out of the wilderness territory and then rejoining the main group at a rendezvous point. I have never felt more comfortable in a high stress environment, where the goal sometimes was simply to survive. There were times when we were so lost that people would start to cry. At this point, I had to take control, calm the group and use the analytical skills of each individual to determine just where we were and where we wanted to go. Other times I had to make quick decisions on what would be safe and what would be deadly based on the abilities of the group. I excelled due to, I believe, my poise and skills. The whole trip was awesome."

Gene's Achievement

"I designed and built, with my own hands, my entire house, doing the design, framing, roofing, electrical, plumbing, finish carpentry, cabinetmaking, concrete floors and sidewalks, all my myself, even while working full time as an electrical engineer. Building this house with my own hands, and doing the best job I knew how, these things I found very rewarding and fulfilling. I took no short cuts; I persevered until it was done correctly. I am very proud of my accomplishments, the tackling and successful completion of a project of this magnitude . . . and I very much enjoyed doing every part of it."

Heidi's Achievement

"As a senior in high school, I knew I wanted to learn Greek someday. During my freshman year in college, I told my advisor of my desire. He advised me to wait at least a year because he thought Greek would be a struggle for me (my grades were mostly C's and B's). I felt a bit angry that my advisor didn't think I could handle it, so I registered for beginning Greek. I worked really hard at it and enjoyed it immensely. It soon became my favorite class, and I was tutoring my classmates. I decided to major in Greek along with my Theology major. Getting straight A's in my Greek classes was very satisfying—especially since I had gone against my advisor. It was also very satisfying to tutor others. But the greatest satisfaction was what had motivated me in the first place—the ability to read the New Testament in the original language."

Morgan's Achievement

"I solved an intermittent problem that showed up in very few computers and at very infrequent intervals. By solving this problem in the development stage, I saved the company significant dollars and avoided a field-service headache. I doggedly tracked down the problem, by not giving up until I had truly identified the root cause of the problem, then redesigned the printed circuit board and verified that it was fixed. I concluded this effort just one hour before the release to production meeting. The satisfaction came from figuring out a very complex and elusive problem."

Each of these achievements gives us a picture of what an individual is able to accomplish, when he or she is doing something that is truly aligned with their natural strengths. We can appreciate the power and thrill of their achievements; we can almost see the sweat on their brows as they engage their passions and pursue their purpose. We can share in their feelings of fulfillment and satisfaction from their efforts. We can recognize and appreciate the quality of the outcome that is created, when a person's job is aligned with his/her natural strengths. Shawn's talents saved lives. Gene's house was probably very close to perfect. Heidi's enthusiasm for the original language of the New Testament was surely evident in her sermons. And Morgan's problem-solving undoubtedly saved many computer users lost time and headaches! **The productivity AND fulfillment which come from the use of "giftedness" are powerful and compelling reasons why job "fit" is critically important to both employees and employers.** (Note also the perseverance and the doggedness that permeates the descriptions of people doing what they love to do. No need for a manager to be pushing these folks along. More dollars saved!) These are just four examples from the lives of very "ordinary" people, and we know that none of these outcomes would have occurred if these people were not "gifted" for their respective roles.

THE EVIDENCE FOR PATTERNS

In the past 40 years, analysts at People Management International LLC have studied the relationship of the "fit" of employees to their work. After examining the data of over 50,000 knowledge workers, their observations have led to the following characterization of "motivated" behavior—behavior that engages one's passions and purpose: [17]

When people describe achievements from their work and life that have been particularly satisfying and enjoyable, they reveal a consistently recurring pattern. The pattern emerges in early years, and while the individual continues to learn new knowledge and skill, his/her basic motivational "pattern" appears to remain fairly constant throughout his/her life.

Thus, the pattern reveals what the person really wants to do in life, what he/she gets excited about and receives satisfaction from. Most importantly, every time a person accomplishes a personally significant, enjoyable achievement, he or she repeats some or all of the same elements of this Motivational Pattern. Taken in this context, the word "motivated" refers to the manner in which a person uniquely perceives and attempts to perform his or her work.

To identify these Motivational Patterns, individuals are asked to describe in detail 5-8 achievements from their life/work activities that they have enjoyed doing and felt they did well. The following examples of life/work achievements from Margaret illustrate this "pattern" phenomenon:

✧ "At age 10, I created a haunted house in our garage, working with the kids in the neighborhood. I came up with the idea and got my friends to pitch in.

✧ "In high school, I participated in mock United Nations discussions and resolved major political/social issues—worked with teammates to develop resolutions.

✧ "Created a Girl Scout Troop for my daughter and her friends and was co-leader.

✧ "Participated in the creation of a business organization for women professionals.

✧ "Successfully administered downsizing in an organization while maintaining morale and integrity in treatment of employees.

✧ "Created a team that developed a strategic plan for information systems auditing.

✧ "Successfully mentored several high performing professionals and had them return to thank me for my counsel and advice."

To develop a complete pattern, one would need to know a great deal more detail about the role that Margaret played in each of these achievements. However, one can identify some themes by adding up the "recurring evidence" which appears even in this limited information. For example, Margaret is motivated to work with people, both individuals and groups. (Either individuals or groups are part of each of her selected achievements.) She also works with intangible subject matters, like concepts, strategies and policies. (Again, note the recurring presence of these subjects in her achievements.) There is evidence of motivation to influence and to provide leadership. (She organized the kids to do the haunted house, her teammates to work on political-social issues, started and was co-leader of a Scout troop, etc. Every example has some evidence of her influencing and leadership motivation.) While limited, it is the beginning of a "pattern" that provides evidence for why Margaret is moving rapidly as an executive in a large organization and is totally excited about her job and her career—and her life.

Every person has a unique pattern, so there are endless combinations and permutations of pattern elements to form the individual patterns. In other words, the examples of "passion and purpose" come in all flavors! I call these descriptions of selected work/life achievements "stories of passion." The following is one of my favorites:

Achievements of Brent, the Investment Counselor

Childhood Achievement:

"I acquired and sold bubble gum to classmates in middle school, making several hundred dollars in profits. One day I was offered 25 cents for one piece of bubblegum that I had taken out of my pocket. At the time, you could purchase an entire 5-piece pack of bubble gum for 25 cents. I noticed that the gum, which I had purchased in Pennsylvania, did not yet exist in Virginia. I recognized an opportunity to make a profit and before I knew it I had sold several hundred dollars worth of gum."

Adult Achievement:

"Providing my friends and family with attractive investment opportunities. I knew that I wanted to run my own business, and some friends and I tried to start many different businesses (which all failed). As a hobby, we began to actively manage our own personal retirement assets and did not even realize that there was a business opportunity in doing so. Then, after a year of actively managing our money, we realized that we could build a business of providing this service to clients. Our firm is now managing 80 million dollars. We have over 200 clients and do a lot of work for friends and family. Since we have started, we have provided our clients with excellent risk adjusted returns."

One can just see this kid making his moves on the playground—and sense his passion and calling for the financial investments world! Who knows where he will end up if he stays "on purpose"? At age 27, he is the lead counselor in a group of four investment counselors who manage $80 million.

WHY WE DO WHAT WE DO

A Motivational Pattern is actually an entire system of behavior, in the sense that it cannot be divided into pieces and still make sense. Each element must be perceived in the context of all the other elements described. In other words, the person achieves a certain outcome using certain abilities, working through and with certain subject matter, within certain circumstances and maintaining certain operating relationships with others. No part can be understood accurately except in relationship to other parts. The systemic nature of Motivational Patterns should make clear why it is erroneous and incomplete to describe a person's motivated work behavior in a sentence or two, much less in one word typologies.

Once you have identified the Motivational Pattern, you understand why people behave as they do. You see clearly, for example, why he doesn't tie up loose ends; why he gets the union mad; why she never plans before stepping out; why her sales record is sporadic; why two people continue to clash; why he always exceeds the budget.

As though looking through "motivational glasses," a person's perception of the requirements to perform a particular job or assignment is "colored" by her Motivational Pattern. Influencers will attempt to perform their tasks by influencing; analyzers will focus on analyzing; and collaborators will seek someone with whom to collaborate. Her approach to solving problems, her reactions to assignments, her needs for definition and recognition are all determined by her Motivational Pattern. She will consistently try to perform her work and live her life in accordance with her Motivational Pattern. For example, based on the achievement data previously reviewed, one can expect that Margaret will continue to accomplish her purpose by involving others. Brent will continue to initiate profit-seeking enterprises.

LEARNING ABOUT "NATURAL PATTERNS"

The long-term, broad-based studies on performance and career satisfaction done by People Management International LLC and the Gallup Organization are discussed in the Foreword to this book. Their advice to both individuals and organizations seems clear: *Recognize and use the natural patterns of behavior.* [18]

I first heard about *natural patterns* in 1974. I was working at the Lawrence Livermore National Laboratory in Livermore, CA. (LLNL is a national research laboratory that has approximately 9,000 employees, primarily scientists and engineers who work in national defense, bio-medical and energy research.)

In the process of developing one of the nation's first organizational career development programs, we invited Art Miller to tell us about Motivational Patterns. To help us recognize the presence of Motivational Patterns and the power of job "fit," Art did then what continues to be the best way to teach people about patterns. He collected data from individuals about life/work achievements that they believed they did well and enjoyed doing. From this data, he prepared the Motivational Patterns that described in detail the recurring themes in the individual's achievements. He also described the implications of those themes, given the individual's current work role and future career goals.

Then, just as they are now, participants (including top LLNL managers and Ph.D. researchers) were amazed that the review of such selective data would provide a comprehensive description of their "motivated" behavior. They were also surprised to see how powerful and pervasive the patterns were. They could see how their performance was controlled by these motivations and how they found ways to express their motivation, regardless of the circumstance or the job description.

Understanding their Motivational Patterns helped these knowledge workers to understand why, regardless of their strong personal discipline and intellect, they simply could not achieve desired performance standards in certain roles. It also helped them to see why their self-esteem suffered so dramatically in certain situations. In addition, they recognized how quickly performance AND self-esteem were restored when there was "fit" with their work.

Art Miller worked with 15 of LLNL's opinion leaders. Their positive responses gave support to using Motivational Patterns as the foundation for LLNL's Career/Life Planning Program for the next fifteen years. [19] Follow-up studies with program participants and their management reported very favorable impact on employee satisfaction, retention and performance. [20, 21] Some of these studies were published and presented at professional conferences. There was a tremendous response from other organizations that wanted to know more about our work. Taking my cue from their interest, I began my own consulting practice, providing career/life planning products and services to organizations like Bell Labs, The Aerospace Corporation, DuPont, Exxon, Merck and Monsanto. Some of these organizations have also conducted extensive follow-up studies that confirm positive participant outcomes. [22] Exxon, Merck and The Aerospace Corporation received national awards for their achievements in career management.

. . . to be both successful and fulfilled . . . we must be doing work that engages our innate motivations . . .

While many others have studied and written about the phenomenon of innate motivations, (Jung, Maslow, McClelland, Csikszentmihalyi, Drucker, Haldane, Hillman) Miller's work is unique in providing a process for actually identifying the nature of these motivations for a given individual and providing a taxonomy for understanding the respective patterns and their implications. Miller defines the behaviors in positive, performance-related language. *There are no "deficiencies" in an individual's pattern. There are only "fit" issues that are dependent on the match of the individual with the requirements of the work situation.* While this may seem like a subtle difference to the casual observer, it offers a distinctly different opportunity for the knowledge worker who is discussing performance and career issues with his or her supervisor.

After years of helping individuals to understand Motivational Patterns, I am totally convinced that to be both successful and fulfilled in our work (and in our lives), we must be doing work that engages our innate motivations. No one seems to be exempt from this fact. For those who, for whatever reason, are not in situations that are aligned with their innate motivations, there are costs to be paid. Dalton and Thompson's research (previously cited) reported that employees who don't "leverage their strengths" become "stuck" employees. Brian Justice, author of *Who Gets Sick* says *work without meaning is deadly.* [23] (A later chapter in this book provides excerpts from Justice's research, which tend to get your attention, especially if you are in a job that doesn't "fit.") But, if you are in a job or career that is not a good "fit," you probably do not need research studies to alert you to the problem. You are reminded every morning when it is time to go to work.

But you may need some help in determining the nature of your mismatch situation and in defining criteria for making more accurate job/career decisions in the future. (No more "out of the frying pan and into the fire" moves!) Read on.

WHAT IF YOU HAVE NEVER HAD THE OPPORTUNITY?

Every person has examples of activities that illustrate his unique motivational gifts. But not all of us have experienced the power and fulfillment that come with the full utilization of our giftedness. Some people, upon hearing or reading achievement stories and learning about the concept of innate motivation, will say: *But I never had the opportunity to…take music lessons, learn to ride a horse, go fishing or hiking, build anything, operate machinery, belong to a club* or just about anything else that one could think about wanting to do. What about it? How does "opportunity" impact the expression of our giftedness?

Probably the most important characteristic (other characteristics will be discussed later) **of innate motivation is that it is irrepressible.** This means, regardless of the environment or circumstances, your pattern will express itself somehow and somewhere in your life. Your giftedness will surface. As the research on identical twins separated at birth indicates, even significantly different (but "normal") childhood environments did not significantly alter the interests and abilities of the identical twins as expressed in their adulthood. (Circumstances that involve abuse and deprivation can have negative impact). [24] People seem to instinctively and actively seek out whatever it is that gets their motivational juices going.

Even in environments that do not actively encourage or support a particular motivation or interest, individuals will seek a way to exercise their motivations. For example, as a child on a remote farm in North Dakota, I felt isolated from the rest of the world. (With no electricity or telephone, and only a battery-powered radio that was reserved for news broadcasts, we actually were quite isolated!) I really wanted to know what people in the rest of the world were like. I read a great deal and looked at photographs, but that didn't seem to be enough. One day I spotted an article in the "*Weekly Reader*," a school newspaper, which listed students in other countries who were interested in forming "pen pal" relationships. At about age 12, I began corresponding with girls and boys from all over the world—all of this before e-mail! It was a terrific way to overcome my feeling of isolation. (Remember that not everyone would feel "isolated" in this situation. In fact, in a recent conversation, one of my brothers recalled nothing about my "pen pal" strategy or what prompted my efforts.)

The following are more examples that express the "irrepressible" nature of our innate motivation or "giftedness."

Irrepressible Achievement of a Successful Entrepreneur:

"After not being satisfied with past summers at home in New Jersey, I packed my car and spent my summer on Martha's Vineyard. I didn't have a job or a place to stay, but I found them both. I ended up earning a substantial amount of money and meeting many new acquaintances."

Irrepressible Achievement of a Professional Wrestler—His Father Had Prohibited Him From Participating in Team Sports:

"The PE teacher presented an award to students who could climb to the top of the rope. When I was 12, I had a goal: to do the 'rope climb' from the floor to the ceiling of the gymnasium using only my hands. I did pull-ups and push-ups regularly and tried the rope at every opportunity. Finally, I did it!"

Irrepressible Achievement of a College Professor:

"I struggled with doubt that I could go to college, because my family was poor, but I started with a community college and went on from there. I also got past some skepticism of intellectual pursuits that were part of our religious environment. I became the first one in my family to apply to and to be accepted at a university."

Repressing one's giftedness is like trying to keep an inflated raft under the water! You will search for ways to express your innate motivation somewhere in your life. Ideally, you will find or create a job/role where you can leverage and develop your talents. Whether or not this becomes a reality for you, you will express your motivations in your relationships with family and friends, in your avocation and religious activities, and in your volunteer work. (Volunteer work is an excellent example of how much effort people will expend to be able to do something they are motivated to do—without payment for their services!) Just for a moment, think about the people you know who spend hours performing in community theatre, campaigning to be the president of the condominium association, serving as a soccer referee, training to be an emergency medical technician or organizing family reunions. Now you know why they do what they do!

Chapter 2. What It Means to Be Motivated

Your self-esteem must come from doing the work itself, rather than from some hoped-for promotion, pay raise or other reward which may never materialize.

Richard Nelson Bolles

ORDINARY ACHIEVEMENTS TELL THE STORY

As you can tell from reading the achievement examples previously discussed, you do not need "Nobel Prize" achievements to provide insights about passion and purpose. Your daily experiences from throughout your life and work are packed with rich evidence about what you enjoy doing and feel you do well. However, to benefit from this information, you must take the time to reflect on your achievement experiences and think carefully about exactly what you did, as well as the nature of your satisfaction.

As a way of encouraging you to think about your work/life achievements, I would like to share some of my achievement activities from my childhood and early adolescent years. As you read my descriptions, pay special attention to the recurring "payoff" or "outcome" that I seek in each achievement.

Marlys' Achievements

Childhood achievement:

"I learned how to play pinochle when I was five years old. Playing pinochle (card game) was the main source of family entertainment in our pre-TV days. My sister and brother played nearly every evening with my father—but they needed a fourth and my mother was always too busy to play cards. And, with everybody else involved, I felt left out. So I decided that I needed to learn how to play pinochle. While I had not yet started school, my sister had taught me how to add and subtract. With a lot of help, I learned how to keep score and how to bid. I had watched the game for some time, while sitting on my father's lap. One night, he pulled out another chair for the card table, stacked up some catalogues for me to sit on and dealt me in! It was a tremendously satisfying moment. I can still remember looking at the cards and not being really sure what I had—but I would just hang in there and pretend that I did. I kept at it, constantly asking questions about what to do in certain cases. It was a tremendous achievement to have learned a very difficult card game, especially since I was the youngest person. It was also great to no longer feel left out of the action!"

High School—"Town Kid" Became My Best Friend:

"When I started high school, I moved by myself to a town about 20 miles away. I lived in a bedroom and prepared my meals on a hot plate. I was 13 years old. In today's world, it would probably be considered child neglect! There was a very strong clique of 'town' kids who distanced themselves from us "country" kids, or so it seemed to me at the time.

"There I was . . . an overweight 'country' kid with my homemade cotton print clothes and my laced-up brown oxford shoes. All this was topped off with a mop of frizzled hair, replete with the splendor of a new home permanent. To complete the picture, I didn't know any of my peers, having gone to elementary school in a one-room country school with five students, including my two brothers.

"However, I was not about to be written off. After sizing up the situation, I decided that my best (perhaps my only) strength was my academic ability, which became my bargaining chip. In those days, students were seated alphabetically. The girl who always sat behind me was a very attractive (one could say sexy) blonde with a truly fun personality. Schoolwork was neither a priority interest nor a motivator for her. I did notice how badly she felt when she would repeatedly get failing grades, while the teacher recognized me frequently for scoring the top grade. I offered to help her with her homework. Since she was rather desperate, she agreed to give it a try. She lived in the town (a 'town' kid, no less!) and it was a welcome break for me to walk to her house after school, instead of heading alone to my one-room existence. She needed lots of help; we spent nearly every evening after school together. Winter comes early and stays late in North Dakota. She would often ask me to stay overnight, rather than have me walk the half-mile back to my room when the wind chill was a minus forty or fifty degrees.

"We had lots of time to talk about other things. She cut the frizzle off my hair and put me on a strict diet. Together, we made some new clothes. We were a feature story in the school newspaper, pictured in our look-alike outfits—red blouses and leopard print skirts, with matching scarves for our blouses. Wow! A town and country duo, previously unheard of! It was very satisfying to be considered part of the 'town clique.'"

Overcoming Obstacles:

By now, you have no doubt identified the recurring outcome in these two achievements: to prevail over difficult situations—to overcome obstacles. Most of the time, this is a productive motivation with positive outcomes. However, this "overcoming obstacles" motivation, like all motivations, can be seductive. It causes people to think that they have to constantly prove themselves, to meet every challenge, to resist authority, and to "buck the system." Knowledge workers can be extremely vulnerable to this phenomenon, especially in workplaces where one is rewarded for "putting out fires." Because their broad and varied learning abilities are often coupled with an innate nature to overcome, prevail, meet the challenge or "pull it off," they often get off track and end up pursuing career/life goals that are really not a good "fit" for them. The attraction to them is just proving they can do it! For me, it took about ten years to get "realigned" after I took on yet another obstacle:

Became Typing Whiz Despite Teacher's Objections:

"In our small high school, there were only two electric typewriters; the rest were manual. The typing instructor's practice was to allow the top academic students to use the electric typewriters. Since I was a top student, when I entered the typing class, I seated myself at one of the electric machines. Soon the typing teacher was whispering in my ear: 'I know you are a top student, but we try to reserve these machines for those who could really excel in typing and, you know, your hand.'" (I have a congenital deformity in my right hand that restricts my typing to the ring finger and the thumb for the space bar.)

"I can still hear her voice as I write this. The bells and whistles went off in my head. The flag was up! I was very hurt and I was furious. My experiences in dealing with my mother had long ago convinced me of the futility of throwing a fit, so I said very little and just went on typing. She left me alone until the bell rang and then she came back to me with the same line. I just shook my head and told her that I had earned the right to use an electric typewriter, and I planned on using it. Like my mother, she was not persuaded.

"After thinking about the situation for the rest of the day, I decided to take it to the Superintendent after school. Without an appointment, I walked in and asked to see him. He was a very approachable man, so I told him my story. He called for the typing teacher to join us and was very diplomatic in seeking a mutually agreeable resolution. We talked about coming in at other periods, but I was taking a full load of classes and had conflicts. I suggested coming in at 7:30 a.m. every day. The teacher reluctantly agreed. She would have to be there to open up the room for me. She didn't like it, but she did it. I won . . . at least that's what I thought at the time.

"I worked like mad on my typing. I practiced with a vengeance. My reading and memorization skills helped to compensate for the limited number of typing fingers on my right hand. The teacher noticed my progress and administered all the usual timed tests. I was on a roll. No one else was half as determined as I.

"I won all the typing contests at our school and went to a state contest. I won first for three-minute speed and accuracy on difficult material. The Superintendent gave me my award at an all-school assembly. I must admit that the typing teacher was the first to stand and applaud. I can still see her standing there applauding. What a kick!"

WIN THE BATTLE BUT LOSE THE WAR!

The problem with taking on challenges (win or lose) that are not aligned with one's passion and purpose is that the outcome often takes one off course. My "win" had long-term implications—the story is a bit complicated, but there is an important message here!

I had always thought about going to law school when I finished high school, but I was now an accomplished and recognized typist. Since money was an issue as well, I solved the problem by heading off to a junior college to become certified as a legal secretary. The following year, I married a fellow student and worked as a court reporter to help him through engineering school. By the time he was a senior, I had started to have pain in my right arm and hand. While I didn't know that it was carpal tunnel syndrome, I did know that I was really overusing the ring finger on my right hand, as I spent hours each day transcribing court proceedings. I knew that I couldn't continue that pace much longer. Besides, the work was totally boring for me, as there was little interaction with people. I was just listening to proceedings and transcribing my shorthand.

With my husband's encouragement, I enrolled in a four-year college. Because I had taken my legal secretarial training at a junior college, I did have some college credits. By applying these credits toward a major in Business Education, I was able to finish my bachelor's degree in two years. My husband finished his engineering degree at the same time. We headed to Los Angeles, where he had a job in the aerospace industry, along with several thousand other Midwesterners! The LA schools were bulging, and teachers were in big demand. I secured a position teaching typing and shorthand at a prestigious high school. All was going well, until the parents of two students in my typing class complained to the principal that because of my handicap, I was not qualified to teach typing. After many discussions, I was assigned to a junior high school to teach World History. That was one battle I didn't win, at least not right away.

Later, I became involved in student counseling and earned my master's degree in counseling psychology. This opened the door for an entirely new career that is a much better fit. However, nearly ten years had passed since I insisted on proving that I could type competitively on that electric typewriter!*

Many knowledge workers share this persevering motivation to overcome or meet a challenge. For example, a frustrated chemist once commented that *my temptation has always been to count as my significant achievements those that are the most removed from my natural talents.* Some spend major parts of their lives getting a Ph.D. in a field that really does not interest them. Or, in order to maintain competitive performance, they work 70-80 hours a week in a job that doesn't fit them. They "knock themselves out" to accomplish their objective. It becomes difficult for them to achieve and sustain the performance they need to compete. They often become cynical and disgruntled employees, when their incredible effort does not seem to produce the rewards they seek. Unknowingly, they have failed to harness the real power that lies in aligning their passion and purpose with their work.

SEEING THE FOREST AND THE TREES

Some of us need help to recognize and understand our passions and purpose. Our own vision may be too clouded by the very expectations that initially impaired that vision.

For example, I think of a young computer scientist whom I met in a workshop. He was quite upset that his detailed descriptions of his most enjoyable and rewarding life/work achievements contained no evidence of working with and through others. There was no evidence of influencing and persuading others. Since he had his heart set on a career in management, he was trying very hard to find some evidence for these motivations in the descriptions of his achievements. But the evidence simply was not

---

*I am frequently asked if this "overcoming" motivation is more likely to be observed in individuals with physical handicaps and thus be the product of an environmental condition rather than innate motivation. Experience with thousands of individuals reveals the "overcoming" motivation to be as random as any other motivation, appearing in all types of individuals. It is also apparent that in certain situations, e.g., a primarily white male environment, the first women and ethnic minorities to break the barriers are often individuals with an "overcoming" motivation. It makes sense, doesn't it? Likewise, the individuals with physical handicaps whom we meet in organizations are also likely to be people who have "overcome" the obstacles and stayed the course.

there. Even though he had participated in a very "full" life with involvement in athletic, artistic, social and religious activities, all of his enjoyable achievements involved his personal performance on very technical subject matters. When I asked him why he was interested in management, he said he felt it offered more visibility, status, salary, and authority. After some discussion, he began to see that he was not really interested in the work of management, but in the perceived rewards for performing the role. We talked about how he might achieve status, salary and authority as a technical specialist. We discussed how difficult it would be to actually achieve those rewards as a manager who wasn't really motivated to manage. And what would happen to his passion for technical work? Would he be able to achieve his real purpose, which was to demonstrate his competence and proficiency? With no motivation to work through others nor to influence or confront others, management would be a nightmare for him and for any one else who might be involved.

After reviewing the recurring themes in the achievements he had selected from his life/work, this computer scientist decided to devote his efforts to developing his programming skills. A recent check of his progress found him very pleased with the many well-rewarded opportunities he has had to demonstrate his ever-expanding proficiencies.

Chapter 3. Work Without Meaning Is Deadly

To live well is to work well, or to display a good activity.

Thomas Aquinas

WHAT DOES THE WORK DO TO THE WORKER?

A few months ago I was giving a workshop in a large government agency. During the attendance procedures, it was determined that a military officer listed on the workshop register was not present. Another participant spoke up to tell the group that he had seen an ambulance take the Major out of the building on the previous day. I assumed that he probably would not be attending and continued with the session. But the Major appeared after lunch, looking a little worn but clearly interested in joining the session. I briefed him on the morning's activities and he joined us. He was a terrific participant and practically hung on my every word. He wanted to know everything I knew about innate motivations and job-fit. Later that day, I met alone with him for his feedback discussion. He started the conversation by telling me that I was probably going to save his career and his life. He had been experiencing extremely high levels of stress with his job; he had actually passed out in his office the previous day. When we looked at the descriptions of his life/work achievements, we saw he was highly motivated to make things work efficiently and effectively. He was currently in a staff assignment where he had little or no control over the results of his efforts, and he simply could no longer tolerate the stress of being unable to engage his passions to accomplish a meaningful purpose. But he had been blaming his superior officer for his stress, rather than the "mismatch" of a staff vs. a line position. He left with new insights about the situation and focused his efforts on finding a job/role that would work for him. He called a few weeks later to report that he had been re-assigned to a quality control project when he explained the serious nature of his situation and, most importantly, was able to suggest a mutually beneficial role.

Dr. Khalsa, the author of *Brain Longevity*, defines stress as *anything that causes us to believe that we cannot perform that which is expected of us.* This definition describes quite precisely the situation of a person in a job or role that is not aligned with his/her innate motivation, thus establishing a causal relationship between job "mismatch" and job stress. [25] In the United States, stress-related diseases, such as ulcers, high blood pressure and heart attacks, cost the U. S. economy $100 billion per year in absenteeism, compensation claims and medical expenses. [26]

But the question of what the work does to the worker is hardly ever asked. Managers and supervisors assume that workers will not only be willing to adapt to the needs of the business, but that they will also be able to make the adaptation. Employees recognize the organization's requirements and try their best to meet them.

. . . people literally do kill themselves trying to meet all those expectations!

Spouses and other family members think their breadwinner is crazy to turn down a job with more pay. Individuals choose to work overtime in order to make extra money and move into more responsible positions. Entrepreneurs are determined to make their business work. And people literally do kill themselves trying to meet all those expectations! As Rollo May describes it, *going out too far, dispersing one's self in participation and identification with others until one's own being is emptied, is the tragedy of the organization man.* [27]

If you are struggling to perform in a role that doesn't fit you, you will soon start to recognize some or all of the signals of a "mismatch" situation:

⬥   It takes you longer to accomplish the work than it takes some of your colleagues who seem to be a better "fit."

⬥   The performance of the work takes on a "hollow" quality; you start performing without thinking too much about what you are doing.

⬥   You find yourself making errors that seem small and unimportant to you, but others seem to have a different reaction.

- ✧ You have trouble getting up in the morning and hate to think about another day (week, month, year) of work ahead.

- ✧ You are absent from work more frequently and you are ill more often.

- ✧ You rarely read about, discuss or explore the content of your work on your personal time.

- ✧ You are less likely to speak up in meetings, to engage in discussion and debate with colleagues, to take on additional involvement in related tasks, or to offer leadership.

- ✧ You feel what you have to say or do will appear inappropriate, or even worse, just plain stupid. You become embarrassed when called upon for your opinion.

- ✧ Eventually, you start to think less of your abilities because you feel you are unable to meet expectations (both your expectations and the expectations of others).

- ✧ You are becoming more involved with interpersonal difficulties at work and in your other relationships. You find yourself blaming others for things they are doing or not doing.

- ✧ You begin to mentally "beat up on yourself" for not being able to sustain the level of performance that you achieved in other situations.

- ✧ Your self-esteem diminishes, because you are not being recognized and rewarded for who you are. Indeed, your image may become tarnished as you are viewed performing work/roles that do not engage your passion and thus your best energy and effort.

- ✧ Your overall health is suffering. Your headaches are more frequent and more severe; you consume more than your share of anti-acid medication. Occasionally, you awaken at night with what seems like an anxiety attack. Your blood pressure has increased. It feels like you almost have to "spit blood" to muster the energy to perform competitively in this role.

- ✧ You are thinking more about what you are doing with your life, where are you going, where there is to go.

The aspect of mental health that seems to be impacted most quickly when we are in situations that do not "fit" us is our self-esteem. If we are doing work that engages our innate abilities, we have the opportunity to express our passions. We have the opportunity to be positively rewarded for doing what we love to do! People see us performing every day in our "best suit." All of this serves to make us feel more worthwhile and valuable.

On the other hand, working in a mismatch situation is like coming to work in our gym clothes. We look very different in our gym clothes than we do in our best suit! **In a mismatched role, we don't get a chance to show off our talents; we only take the risk of being visible in an arena that is NOT best suited for us.** Others do not have the opportunity to see us demonstrate our best abilities. We increase potential for negative feedback and decrease the potential for positive feedback. We simply feel less worthy because we are not using our passions to meet our purpose. It's clearly not a good strategy. In fact, it's a terrible dilemma for many, many people.

No one seems to be exempt from this phenomenon. In fact, the more achievements individuals have experienced in their lives, the more vulnerable they seem to be in situations where they cannot sustain competitive performance and are not fulfilled by the activity.

Failure (which, in this context, means not achieving one's purpose) can be difficult to accept if one has only experienced success. The individual's dilemma is often complicated by his/her inability to recognize the problem. Emotions tend to interfere with perceptions. And how difficult it is for all of us to permit ourselves to see the truth of what is happening, especially when we (and our loved ones) are depending on our performance in this role.

LONG-TERM IMPACT OF JOB DISSATISFACTION

Work satisfaction has been found to be a powerful predictor of how long we live, as well as how likely we are to remain healthy. Conversely, dissatisfaction with not only work but also with life in general is associated with significantly higher risk of illness:

Research studies repeatedly show that employees who get sick most often are usually those who have high job dissatisfaction and related stress:

- ✧ "New Economy" knowledge workers (who have been dubbed "gold collar" workers because of their focus on money as a motivator) report higher levels of burnout and depression at earlier ages. [28]

- ✧ A research study of some 10,000 American workers—including professors, lawyers, farmers, accountants, printers, librarians, sales and clerical personnel—concluded that people at higher risk of myocardial infarctions go through life striving without joy, in the manner of Sisyphus, the character from Greek mythology, who was condemned to push a heavy stone to the top of a hill only to have it always roll back down. [29]

- ✧ A nine-year prospective study of 65 people who had experienced heart attack predicted which individuals in the group would suffer new myocardial infarctions, based on how much they tended to view life as a striving without satisfaction. [30]

✧ 20% of 416 air traffic controllers averaged more than 5 episodes a year of mild to moderate illness, mostly upper respiratory infections, asthma, viral disorders and gastrointestinal upsets. Another 20% had less than one episode per year. The frequently sick men had lower morale (which was determined in advance of their illnesses) and greater job dissatisfaction. [31]

✧ In a Swedish study of people who had experienced heart attacks, the post-infarction patients reported substantially greater work dissatisfaction as compared to matched healthy persons. [32]

Passion and purpose are necessary for our very health and survival. For each of us, our health is significantly impacted by the "fit" of our passion and purpose to our daily existence. To the extent that we are able to routinely use our innate abilities to accomplish a purpose in which we believe, we will feel satisfied and fulfilled in our efforts. If our daily existence and efforts do not engage these innate abilities toward a meaningful purpose, we will find ourselves increasingly frustrated and stressed by the situation.

One of the most impressive studies on the effect of stress on cardio-vascular health was done at a major aerospace company. [33] A disproportionate number of employees were having heart attacks in their late 40's. In fact, this was such a widespread occurrence that the medical staff in the community began to call the phenomenon "the Lockheed Syndrome." [34] The aerospace company decided to investigate. They randomly identified about 400 male salaried employees and administered tests to categorize them as "Type A" (behavior is aggressive, ambitious, task-oriented) or "Type B" (behavior is more collaborative, easy-going, focused more on relationships). The researchers also studied the nature of the job that each of these individuals held. The jobs were also categorized as Type A—a role that required more aggressive, ambitious, task-oriented performance, or Type B—a role that was less demanding, more collaborative and more involved with building and maintaining relationships. The study then identified the incidence of cardio-vascular disease that was reported in these populations. **The findings indicated that cardio-vascular disease was significantly higher in individuals who were in "mismatch" situations (Type A person in Type B job, or Type B person in Type A job) than it was for individuals who were in jobs that matched their personality type.** These data challenge the popular belief that Type "A" individuals are more prone to cardio-vascular problems. But it makes a great deal of sense to those of us who spend our lives counseling employees and know that one person's joy is another person's pain.

We can readily think of individuals whose job/careers are so poorly matched with their innate motivations that they are prime candidates for job-fit stress. Some common examples could include:

✧ An engineer who is motivated to investigate and analyze existing problems, working in a role where she is expected to create and design "from a blank sheet."

✧ A systems analyst, motivated to "troubleshoot" and meet difficult challenges, administering well-tested applications software.

✧ A computer applications specialist who is motivated to meet specific needs and requirements but is working in a loosely defined role without benefit of defined needs and requirements.

✧ An administrator who is motivated to get into new situations, learn how to perform the role, and then move on to another role, but he is working in a "maintenance" role where there is little opportunity to learn something new and demonstrate his proficiency in that new task.

✧ A salesperson who is motivated by response from other people, yet she is working in a behind-the-scenes role, perhaps on a computer terminal.

✧ A designer, motivated to work with tangible, defined subject matter, who has been moved into a strategic planning role.

There are countless examples of "mismatch" situations. In fact, employee surveys tell us that probably only 1/3 of all employees are engaged in work activities that use their motivated abilities at least 70% of the time. [35]

MISMATCH AND STRESS

Khalsa's definition of stress [36] as *anything that causes us to believe that we cannot perform that which is expected of us* describes quite precisely the situation of a person in a job or role that is not aligned with his/her innate abilities. Even if we are ABLE to perform the task, if we do not find the activity fulfilling to perform, it is difficult to SUSTAIN our performance without chronic stress.

Because so many people face stress from work/life situations that are not aligned with their passion and purpose, training people in techniques for coping with stress has become very popular, as well as profitable for those providing the training. Most of us do respond to chronic stress in ways that can cause health problems. We start smoking or smoke more, or overeat and become overweight. We may develop high blood pressure. We get sick more often and are sick longer. We show symptoms of premature aging, including disorientation and memory problems. While coping strategies of exercise, low-fat diets, meditation, talking out your troubles, and limiting caffeine may relieve the symptoms of stress, such strategies do not deal with the SOURCE of stress which is anything that causes us to believe that we cannot perform that which is expected of us.

Stress researchers like Khalsa, Justice and Sapolsky consistently report that a situation which one person finds stressful may not bother someone else. Most of us don't need a research study to tell us that! What the researchers have failed to report is that the conditions that each of us find stressful are directly related to our innate motivations.

Conditions that each of us find stressful are directly related to our innate motivations.

For example, a person who is motivated by handling logistics and arrangements could be thoroughly engaged and fulfilled as a conference planner. Individuals who do not have these motivations will be stressed by the expectation that they will have all the logistics and arrangements under control. A person who is motivated to listen, discuss and counsel others will be motivated and fulfilled by listening to the personal problems of others. Individuals without these motivations will be uninterested in this work; they will become stressed if they have a daily calendar full of individual counseling sessions. Michael Roizen, M. D., author of the popular book and website *Real Age—Are You As Young As You Can Be?*, recalls an interaction with a sales clerk that tells the *real* story about how job-fit reduces stress:

"In the midst of a Christmas shopping madhouse, I said to the clerk: 'You must be glad this day is over. Talk about stressful!'"

"The woman laughed and said, 'I love my job. In how many other jobs do you have people fighting over you?'" [37]

If you are experiencing symptoms of chronic stress, you will want to identify and eradicate the source. To do this, you will need to take the time to reflect on your life/work experiences that have brought you satisfaction and enjoyment. You will want to discover the recurring themes that appear in these achievements. Working with these themes, you will want to define the "best fit" scenario that will give you the opportunity to exercise your talents to achieve a purpose that is meaningful to you. You will want to take immediate steps to plan how you can remove yourself from situations that cause you to believe that you cannot sustain the performance expected of you. You may be thinking "But I have a family to support" or "I couldn't pay the mortgage." However, if you are indeed experiencing chronic stress from your current job, you will want to consider the potential long-term health and financial consequences of ignoring the warning signals.

Chapter 4. The View Is Worth the Climb

Of all psychology's sins, the most mortal is its neglect of beauty. There is something quite beautiful about a life.

James Hillman

BE ALL THAT YOU CAN BE

Some individuals are reluctant to believe that it is possible to achieve the kind of "fit" in their work that will truly engage their heart and their mind. They may be committed employees who have worked diligently to make the best of whatever their role, firmly believing that work is work. They may have never experienced a work situation that was sufficiently stimulating to convince them of the reality of the "fit" concept. Others may have had fulfilling experiences, but see no way to meet their financial needs/goals by working in their "motivated" occupation/profession.

Even you may be thinking: *How can I be sure that the next job/career will be any more satisfying than the present? Maybe this is good as it is ever going to be!*

One of the ways you can experience a sense of reality about the concept of job "fit" is by talking with individuals who are truly "gifted" for their work. I am referring to the scientist with a never-ending appetite for knowledge, the travel agent who always has just the right trip for you, the waitress who knows what you want before you even think of it yourself, or the investment counselor who picks the right stock in a down market. All of these are people who are in jobs that obviously utilize their "gifts." (Remember, all of us have unique "gifts," which are expressed as our Motivational Patterns. When these gifts or patterns are aligned with our jobs/careers/lives, we are able to express our "giftedness." Others are more likely to experience us as "gifted" because we are more confident in our abilities).

How do you find these individuals? Since only about one person in three does indeed occupy a job/career that fully utilizes their talents, you may have to do some searching. But these good "fits" do exist and you probably will be able to think of two or three of your acquaintances who seem to fit the criteria. *The one characteristic that differentiates these individuals is that they seem to be "gifted" at what they do. They have unusual aptitude and/or skills for their work, whatever it is. They appear to be efficient and productive in their work and perform with seemingly less effort and stress. They have a passion for their work.* They often enjoy special recognition from their peers as well as their supervision. When you think you have identified potential "gifted" candidates, ask them how they feel about their role. Listen for their "stories of passion"—stories about achievements they truly have enjoyed doing and believe they have performed well. Ask how they got involved in the activity, what they believe they "bring to the party" that makes a contribution, and how they know what to do. Ask them, too, to tell you what is most satisfying and fulfilling about this activity. If you listen carefully, you will hear very different responses but with a similar theme: the role really "fits" the individual. Each individual has a unique pattern of gifts and some are more highly valued by our society than others. **But the powerful, mutually beneficial dynamic of "giftedness" is set in motion when there is alignment of the individual to the task.**

As examples of what you might hear when you talk to people who are truly "gifted" for their work, I would like to share some "stories of passion" from two people who love their work and their life.

Achievement Data from Myler, Museum Curator

"I enjoyed searching for information on what was original for a '31 Chevy—went to car shows—subscribed to Chevy Club magazine—made contacts with others who had already restored a '31—enjoyed talking with them to gather info on details as to what the original parts looked like—made connections with old parts dealers—asked lots of questions about how they have done things so I would know how to restore my '31 when I have time—located parts in states all across the country—took two years to find original parts that I needed. Now I know the car in great detail—something very satisfying about returning car to original condition—sometimes there was a very small detail between the original and not original parts, such as the 150 S tag on the carburetor—had to find one with the tag to be complete and original—now have all original parts and ready to begin serious restoration."

Achievement Data from Jesse, President of Family Business

"Three key business segments of our family business went sour, our banking relationships became strained, and my father (company CEO) became ill. I stepped in as President and led the company through a brutal downsizing in order to pay down debt. Although it was very difficult personally at the time, I was the best person for the job. Short-term problem was cash flow, the mid-term problem was maintaining a viable business, and the longer-term problem was positioning to meet the myriad market challenges. This period was probably some of my best work. In 24 months, we developed and implemented a plan that paid down $25 million of bank debt and trade. We negotiated and settled two significant legal disputes in a manner favorable to the cash position and balance sheet of the company; we negotiated and completed the sale of four operating units; and we obtained a new banking arrangement. We met our targets in all arenas. During the middle of all of this, my wife gave birth to twins, a girl and a boy, now 13 . . . another interesting part of the story. My satisfaction came from being able to maintain things while in the midst of chaos. This was a particularly stressful personal time, with family illness, legal disputes and new twins!"

BIOGRAPHIES TELL THE STORY OF GIFTEDNESS

Another excellent way to learn about the patterns of giftedness is to read biographies of famous people. Almost without fail a comprehensive biography will identify a passion or giftedness that appears early in the individual's life and is pursued throughout his/her life. The authors of these biographies have most likely never heard a word about Motivational Patterns or giftedness.

An example is the life story of Jane Goodall, British ethnologist, world renowned for her research on wild chimpanzees in the African jungles. [38] Jane grew up in London in a quite ordinary lower-middle-class neighborhood. As a child, she loved to read—especially about jungle animals. She was also an ardent observer and asked her father to build a platform in a tree in their yard so she could observe what was happening all around her. Her mother reported that Jane spent hours on that platform. A pet dog and a stuffed toy gorilla were her favorite companions. Her passion for animals and observation continued into her young adult years; the famous Dr. Leakey became her idol. She worked her way to Africa as a waitress on a ship. She managed to arrange a meeting with Dr. Leakey and convinced him of her passion and ambition. Without formal training or degree, she went to work for Dr. Leakey. Of course, the rest of the story is history—and a great example of the power of passion and purpose! **It reminds us that the nature of one's gift is not always obvious at the beginning. It often takes a lifetime of pursuing the passion to fully nurture and develop the potential.** Jane Goodall—and many, many others—were not born famous. Their fame came through the utilization of their gifts.

Many other such examples of early evidence of giftedness abound in biographies. For example, Thurgood Marshall, Supreme Court Justice who was a critical player in American integration legislation, remembered bringing strangers of all races to his parent's house to eat and to sleep. His home became known as "The Friendly Inn." [39] Winston Churchill's favorite pastime as a child was playing war strategies with a cousin. They had rooms full of toy soldiers and equipment; Winston was the strategist. Thomas Edison's mother couldn't leave the boy without supervision or he would take apart anything within his reach. Victor Borge, Danish "clown" prince of classical music, made his piano debut in a concert at age 8, but was fascinated by comedy. After arriving in America penniless, he taught himself English by spending hundreds of hours in movie theatres. His biographer, Niels Kaiser, said Victor was *truly gifted. He was able to combine musicality and humor.* Borge, who died at age 91 with two more years of concerts already scheduled, was dubbed an "irrepressible" talent. But Borge's own comment is most revealing: He said: *We all do what we can; we all have limitations. Apparently, within my limitations, there is enough to go on and on and on.* [40] Like many other "famous" people, Victor's story is one of potential that appeared early and was fully exercised in his life's work.

SIMA® PATTERNS PROVIDE DIRECTION

The reflective process of prioritizing and then describing achievements leads to insights that surprise even the most introspective soul. Whether initially eager or reluctant to develop their achievement data, most participants report a renewed sense of self-esteem after researching their lived experiences. They report that they see themes they had not previously realized. They find connections and inter-relationships in activities that had seemed quite random to them. They begin to see and to value the potential in the patterns. They feel more confident about discussing their motivations and the "best-fit" scenarios for them. They have both language and a process for operationalizing their talents.

A recent hire in a computer applications company wrote the following comment following the identification of his Motivational Pattern:

I have always had the attitude that I can do anything I put my mind to. Although this may be true (at least in my eyes), I have learned from examining my Motivational Pattern that I could be 100x more effective if I focus my energy on what I really like to do. It was astonishing for me to see a pattern of my motivated abilities dating back to kindergarten. Can you believe that? I've had this pattern for the last 25 years and did not even know it! Maybe I knew about one-third of it, but it's the other two-thirds that really shocked me. And it gives me some real direction on what I should focus my energies on. I can see how I can save myself and my employer years of wasted energy and money.

The following is a letter from Ken, who had several "careers" and was again seeking a change:

I have achieved much in my career, partly because my interests are broad and seemed to be ever changing. My employment history is as varied as my interests. When searching for a new job, I was never comfortable being specific about what I was looking for because selecting just one thing felt too limiting. As you can imagine, I have had long job searches because people didn't know how to help me.

The Motivational Pattern assessment showed me that project management was more than just another one of my skills. It was actually my style of working. Everything I do follows a methodical process toward a tangible result. For the first time, I understand what ties everything together.

I have tried other interest assessment techniques. None of them succeeded. They could only highlight things that I already know. The benefit of your assessment is that it organized my experience and drew new insight from that.

Because of the assessment, I have a focused job search. This focus has given me new confidence and energy. My resume is clear and strong. I can discuss my vocational interests, style and history around a single theme. I may continue to have long job searches, but, at least, I know that when I do find the right job, it will be satisfying.

With appreciation, Ken

NO "NOBEL PRIZE" ACHIEVEMENTS?

Some people are reluctant to participate in the patterning process because they feel they do not have any achievements that are worth writing about. Sadly, this seems to be especially true for women who have had a "family" career. The good news is that these individuals are often the most impressed and excited when they do complete the process and see the "pattern" in their life/work. They see how their life's work with their home and family definitely has distinct achievement themes. For example, Carolyn's achievements during her 20 years as a homemaker provide significant insights into her motivations.

Carolyn's Achievements

Age 8: "Learned to cook and cooked many of the family meals thereafter."

Age 12: "Organized party, collected money from relatives and saved lunch money for a surprise birthday party for Mom's 31st birthday."

Age 14: "Helped underprivileged neighbor kids get proper clothes for school events."

Age 24: "Scrounged materials and remodeled home, landscaped yard . . . increased the value of the house."

Age 35: "Headed PTA project to address 'school skipping'."

Age 40: "Refurbished parents' home and gave dinner party for their 50th wedding anniversary."

Age 45: "Organized clean up and landscape project for cemetery where son is buried."

Carolyn's achievements are full of evidence of her motivation to initiate an activity, to oversee a process and to coordinate the efforts of others. All of her achievements focus on helping individuals or addressing causes. Before completing her Motivational Pattern, Carolyn did not know what to say in a job interview. She described her employment experience as "only a homemaker." Using her achievement data, she could cite with confidence explicit examples of organizing, coordinating, and helping others. She landed a "good fit" job as a coordinator of a FEMA (Federal Emergency Management Agency) project in her community.

Carolyn's stories illustrate how our individual motivations are expressed in the course of our daily work and lives. Carolyn, like everyone else with whom we have worked, found a way to express her "motivated" abilities to achieve a purpose that was meaningful to her. By looking at the patterns that emerged, Carolyn also realized why she always felt so fulfilled as a homemaker, even though she felt that others did not always respect her role. But now, as an empty nester, she needed to find a role that would provide daily opportunities to play key and central roles in helping other people and addressing causes.

Homemakers are not the only ones who may feel as though they have no achievements about which to write. Often even individuals with graduate degrees may report similar feelings. This is most likely if they are performing tasks and responsibilities for which they are not motivated, so they naturally feel there is little that they have enjoyed doing and felt they have done well. The good news is that, just like Carolyn, they will have found ways to express their motivation somewhere in their lives. Upon reflection, they will recall achievements from their youth, their scholastic or athletic activities, or their community participation. For others, it will be the deck they built on the house or the walleye they caught that summer in Minnesota. Maybe they will describe the cakes baked for the neighbors over the years, or they will remember how they enjoyed keeping the records at church. In doing thousands of patterns, we have found no shortage of achievement data, only hesitation to participate because of the feeling that the achievements are not sufficiently "worthy" to provide useful data.

WHAT'S IN THIS FOR YOU?

When you understand precisely how your Motivational Pattern impacts your performance and fulfillment, you will have the foundation for meaningful career discussions and joint planning with your supervision. No more asking the supervisor what he thinks you should be when you grow up! You will also understand why emulating "role models" (whose passion and purpose may be vastly different than yours) does not work. And you will recognize the folly of taking the standard route of "getting into management," unless you are truly motivated to oversee the work of others.

Most importantly, the comprehensive, analytical process of identifying your Motivational Pattern will prepare you to describe in specific detail the nature of your work-related passions and the purpose of your efforts. You will also be able to recognize the limitations of preference-based career inventories that you may have taken in high school or college, or even as part of a job-search or career development process. Almost all other assessment inventories use multiple-choice questions where one's responses are easily influenced by societal, financial or personal biases. For example, I may feel somewhat uncomfortable with the reality that I like to be the center of attention and fully enjoy almost any kind of recognition. Thus, I may be reluctant to select a multiple-choice response that indicates audiences and listeners are highly important to me. Instead, I may select an option that is more "socially acceptable."

By contrast, the Motivational Pattern is based on specific evidence of recurring behavior from lifelong enjoyable and satisfying experiences. Thus, if I select and describe several achievement experiences that involve audiences and listeners in some way, I have developed recurring evidence that I am more motivated to perform in a situation that provides this kind of recognition. I may also be relieved to learn that this is a common motivation and not a "deficiency." Furthermore, I will not be counseled to "grow up" and quit hogging the show! Instead, I will be encouraged to find or create work/life situations where I have on-going opportunities for audiences and listeners, because this is an important part of what I need to sustain my motivation and give me personal fulfillment for my efforts.

Because YOU develop the evidence, the process becomes somewhat like holding a mirror up to your life and looking for the recurring themes that are unique to you. *It is not a "black box" wherein judgments are based on how your responses compare to the responses of others—who, by the way, also have unique motivations that may have become distorted by attempts to generalize.*

One of the ways to assess your self-understanding of your passions and purpose is to test yourself on the presence/absence of critical motivations. Presented below is a list of questions addressing factors that contribute heavily to performance success (or failure), as well as to personal satisfaction from performing a given role. *Before continuing with this book, please take the time to carefully consider each of these questions.* By thoughtfully completing this exercise, you can determine to your own satisfaction whether you really need to spend the time and effort to get a more comprehensive understanding of your Motivational Pattern.

ASSESSING YOUR PASSION AND PURPOSE

Are you sufficiently clear about what "motivates" you to answer these critical "fit" questions? A misperception on any one of them could create significant performance and/or fulfillment issues, if it represents a critical requirement for your situation. As you respond to each item, think about situations that provide "evidence" for your response. Be careful of wishful thinking and common biases!

You may be thinking—"Why such a long list?" Remember that Motivational Patterns are unique, so there are many variations on the theme. If a short list of only the most common were presented, it might omit the very element that is at the core of your work/life fulfillment! And surely, getting a better understanding of what you really need to know about yourself justifies more than 20 questions! By doing a thorough self-assessment now, you will also create a tool for later measuring what you learned from completing your Motivational Pattern.

"Motivated" means that this is an activity which you both enjoy doing and feel you do well.

Yes   No   Do you know what it takes to get you started and actively interested in pursuing a task or activity?

Yes   No   Are you aware of how you go about influencing others?

Yes   No   Are you "motivated" to sell?

Yes   No   Are you "motivated" to plan?

Yes   No   Can you identify three objects or subjects with which you love to work?

Yes   No   Do you know whether or not you are at home in a politically-charged environment?

Yes   No   Do you quickly grasp the essentials of a subject that is not well defined?

Yes   No   Are you aware of how you would react to a job that was not well defined, in terms of what you were expected to accomplish?

Yes   No   Do you know whether you are "motivated" to start an assignment or a project from scratch?

Yes   No   Do you require ample time to prepare when asked to respond to an unexpected request?

Yes   No   Do you know whether you must have a standard or other way of measuring your performance?

Yes   No   Is exercising initiative a high priority for you?

Yes   No   Would you say you know how much and what kind of stress and pressure you can handle comfortably?

Yes   No   Would it bother you if you could never find out whether people used your work?

Yes   No   Do you have entrepreneurial tendencies?

Yes   No   Do you have specific goals? If not, do you know why?

Yes   No   Are you a person who recognizes an opportunity before it is apparent to others?

Yes   No   Is money important to you?

Yes   No   Are you a conceptual person?

Yes   No   Are you a creative person?

Yes   No   If you are creative, do you know in what ways and how original is your creative expression?

Yes   No   Are you a strategic person?

Yes   No   Are you "motivated" to make risky decisions where your reputation is on the line?

Yes   No   Are you comfortable confronting others?

Yes   No   Are you aware of the reasons you lose your cool (when you do)?

Yes   No   Do you know why you get depressed occasionally?

Yes   No   Are you a leader?

Yes   No   Is controlling others important to you?

Yes   No   Are you " motivated" to build relationships with others?

Yes   No   Do you sweat the details?

Yes   No   Are you good at probing others for information?

Yes   No   Are you good at solving problems?

Yes   No   Are you a results-oriented person?

Yes   No   Are you someone who could be trusted to get the job done, in spite of the difficulties?

Yes   No   Can you see how something will look in advance of it being made a reality?

Yes   No   Do you like to go beyond where other people are?

Yes   No   Do you worry about the bottom line?

Yes   No   Are you "motivated" to run an operation of some sort?

Yes   No   Are you a dealmaker?

Yes   No   Do you know how you would function if placed on a team of people?

Yes   No   Can you wing it when required? And not lose sleep over it?

Yes   No   If you have some management ability, could you describe how you get things done through others?

Yes   No   Are you "motivated" to teach?

Yes   No   If yes, do you know what kinds of people and learning situations you find agreeable?

Yes   No   Can you define what it is that you want to accomplish in your work—more than anything else?

If you feel that you have accurately and precisely responded to all these questions, please give this book to someone whose life/career may be more stuck in the weeds! However, it is our experience that most people cannot respond accurately to the majority of these questions about their behavior. They simply have not had the tools or opportunity to examine their "motivated" behavior with the precision and completeness that provides this depth of understanding. Without understanding the essentials of their own motivations, they will continue to misrepresent their talents and to make erroneous decisions about their work and their lives.

THERE IS MUCH TO BE GAINED—WITH LITTLE PAIN

Once you have completed your Motivational Pattern, you will more fully appreciate the potential that lies in fully understanding and utilizing your innate motivations. You will understand why it is critical to productivity and employee satisfaction that work is performed by individuals who are both gifted in doing the tasks involved and highly motivated to achieve the end result. You will also realize how unrealistic it is (for both employers and employees) to view an individual as "putty" to be molded.

It is my hope that this book will inspire you to investigate the nature of your own unique giftedness. The contents herein are a synthesis of many, many years of interaction with knowledge workers around career issues, and the examples provided are from real people in actual situations. Their positive feedback over the years has served to confirm my belief that while we can't be anything we want to be, there are tremendous rewards for being ALL that we can be.

ION B.
WHAT ARE YOU "MOTIVATED" TO DO?

Chapter 1. Develop Your Achievement Data

You will find your genius by looking in the mirror of your life.

James Hillman

RECALL YOUR ENJOYABLE AND SATISFYING ACHIEVEMENTS

Finding your true passion and purpose is the objective of this section. If you are like many of the knowledge workers who have participated in this process, believing yourself capable of experiencing truly fulfilling work (and life) may be a stretch. For now, you will have to take our word for it. Later you will believe because you will have proven it to yourself.

You have been endowed with a unique giftedness, and a passion to use your gifts in particular ways for certain purposes. Every time you do something you enjoy and believe you do well, you express this pattern of natural strengths and motivation.

Your purpose may be accomplished in several different ways, but to be fulfilling for you, you should have the opportunity to engage your unique strengths and motivations.

By completing the following three steps, you will be able to recognize central themes or patterns in your achievements that form the essence of your purpose and the ways in which you seek to accomplish that purpose. [41]

Step One	Identify and list chronologically your achievements from throughout your work and your life.
Step Two	Select at least five (preferably eight) of the most important achievements; describe these achievements in detail.
Step Three	Identify the Recurring Themes—Your Motivational Pattern

Important: It may be more convenient for you to access the following instructions and form (without charge) on our website www.motivationalpattern.com. Most participants find the task of describing their achievement activities in detail is more easily completed on the computer keyboard than it is by handwriting.

STEP ONE: IDENTIFY YOUR ACHIEVEMENTS FROM THROUGHOUT YOUR WORK/LIFE

The first part of the process involves spending some time reflecting on your life. You will need to recall (and to record) the things you've done in your work and life that you

✧   have enjoyed doing

and

✧   believe you have done well.

To begin the process, recall your enjoyable achievements:

✧   These achievements should span your life chronologically—think of yourself as a child—what did you do then that you enjoyed and did well? (We know this is often hard to recall now, but please try.) Think about your teenage years: what filled them? And after high school . . . was it college or work or both? Think about the jobs you held, the sports you played, the friends you made. Think of this exercise like drawing a word "portrait" from the totality of your life.

✧   Achievements can be drawn from any part of your life. If you've found great joy in study, put that down. If activities in your work have been the primary arena of your interest, include those. If you recall family, leisure, religious, sports or hobby activities that meet the two key criteria, include them. Your "portrait" must be built from information on every area of your life that has given you satisfaction.

TIPS ON COMPLETING THIS EXERCISE

✧   Take enough time to complete the exercises. It should take 3-4 hours.

✧   Don't worry about whether or not you can recall impressive achievements. Select any activity you can remember enjoying and doing well. Don't reject it because it seems silly, trivial or unimportant.

✧   Write what was important to you, not what was important to your family or to your friends. If some honor or recognition left you cold, leave it out.

✧   Don't be limited to narrow time frames. If you have enjoyed achievement activities that have occurred over a stretch of years, list them.

✧   If your activities occurred in a group setting, focus on what you did, regardless of whether it was the same or different from what others did.

✧   Don't try to analyze or evaluate your achievements; it is your detailed description of the achievement that is important to this process.

✧   Don't be modest. You are the key actor in every event. These are your achievements.

Remember— Something you DID, not just experienced.

NOT   I toured America with a friend. We loved the Rockies.

BUT   Planned and implemented a trip to the States . . . everything worked out to plan. We had a successful trip.

Specific activities, not milestone achievements.

NOT   Went back to school.

BUT   Researched and wrote my thesis, making original discoveries and presenting it well.

Activities you can support with examples.

NOT   I'm good with people.

BUT   Managed to talk to everyone in the dorm and got their assent to our plan so no one felt left out.

The following are some examples of achievements from childhood and teen years; these are usually the most difficult for people to recall.

✧   Dressing up the dog - getting a laugh.

✧   Reading 50 books in one summer.

✧   Building a usable raft from scratch.

✧   Learning to really speak French—three months in France.

✧   Getting adult wages when I was 14.

- ❖ Preventing my friend from dropping out of school.

- ❖ Building a stereo set from a kit.

- ❖ Got $50 in tips at Christmas—paper route.

- ❖ Stood up for a slow learner being ridiculed.

- ❖ Invented my own computer game.

- ❖ Picked more apples than the adults.

- ❖ Sailed alone to Mackinac Island.

- ❖ Our gang built a three-story tree house.

- ❖ Taught myself how to use watercolors.

- ❖ Got an A from a tough professor.

- ❖ Hiked the Mohawk trail—all the way.

- ❖ Our team finally had a winning season.

- ❖ I usually accurately complete N.Y. Times Sunday crosswords.

- ❖ I befriended a Russian girl—no English.

- ❖ I demonstrated practical life-saving techniques.

- ❖ I increased my route to 150 customers.

- ❖ My sister and I imitated all the big stars.

- ❖ We supported our whole family for two years.

- ❖ I lost 30 pounds in 3 months.

- ❖ My outfit that I made looked exactly like the one in the shop window.

- ❖ In spite of my size, I made the team.

Some examples from the adult years:

✧   Designed and presented a Sunday School class.

✧   Assisted friend in progressing hobby into small commercial enterprise.

✧   Organized a choir in church.

✧   Invented a gasoline-leak detector program.

✧   Developed team to run soccer tournaments.

✧   Won a long and difficult dispute with my condominium association.

✧   Set up own training department for company for the first time!

✧   Saved approximately $8,000 on material costs of each unit.

✧   Increased capacity of assembly line by 20%.

✧   Raised three children successfully.

✧   Discovered misappropriation of funds.

✧   Designed and built cabin, did major portion of manual work myself.

✧   Coordinated a meeting with several important clients

✧   Successfully led small unit through numerous missions in Vietnam.

✧   Became part of "think tank" group for promoting advanced strategies.

✧   Stayed within $32 of operating budget, though work load doubled.

✧   Learned how to knit.

✧   Discovered mutual funds and set a dollar goal to be invested regularly—never missed goal.

Please note that all these examples are:

✧   Specific achievement activities, not experiences.

♦   Specific activities, not significant milestones.

♦   Activities that are not vague generalities, but specific and particular.

Go to it ...

There is no time limit to this. Take as long as you like.

It is not a test.

There are no right or wrong answers ... enjoy yourself!

LIST YOUR ACHIEVEMENTS IN CHRONOLOGICAL ORDER

Note: You may not have four achievements for each period or you may have more than four . . . so please adjust this form as necessary. Do try to identify some achievements from your early years. You may also want to access this form on www.motivationalpattern.com.

CHILDHOOD:

1. _____

2. _____

3. _____

4. _____

TEEN YEARS:

1. _____

2. _____

3. _____

4. _____

EARLY ADULT:

1. _____

2. _____

3. _____

4. _____

ADULT:

1. _____

2. _____

3. _____

4. _____

LONG-TERM ACHIEVEMENTS:

1. _____

2. _____

3. _____

4. _____

STEP TWO: SELECT YOUR MOST IMPORTANT ACHIEVEMENTS

Having done a preliminary scan, look back at what you have just written.

✧   Are your descriptions like the examples given—specific activities rich in details about what you actually did?

✧   Do they span all of your life—childhood, teens, twenties, thirties—?

✧   On reflection, is there anything that you've missed or forgotten?

Put an asterisk next to those achievements (at least five, preferably eight) that you consider most personally significant. Depending on your motivation, you may find it difficult to select the most significant achievements. You may be tempted to ask others (like your parents) what they thought you did that was most significant. You may want to have more defined criteria for selection—like "Was the achievement fun?" or "Were you rewarded?" But the purpose of this exercise is to select the achievement activities that "stand out" in terms of meeting these two criteria: You enjoyed doing the activities and you felt you did them well.

(Please select at least one achievement from childhood and/or teen years.)

DESCRIBE YOUR ACHIEVEMENTS IN DETAIL

The next step is to describe those achievements that you have selected in greater detail.*

Creating good data is crucial to your discovery process, so consider these guidelines:

Take time to give details

It is unlikely that you have ever previously described your achievements in the kind of detail needed for this exercise. For that reason, you may not even believe that you can remember such details about events that happened so long ago! Trust us. You can and will remember exquisite detail if you will just give yourself the time and space to recollect.

Avoid generalities

Example: I really liked to be in school plays.

INSTEAD—describe the specifics of what you did and how you did it.

Use illustrations and examples

It is more useful for you to describe in detail how you were able to field 50 catches before making an error, than to say you were good at playing shortstop.

Describe how you convinced your boss through cost savings on the need for a new and larger press—it is not sufficient to just say that you were good at influencing management.

Describe an example where you recommended an off-the-wall but effective solution to a structural mystery, rather than that you were good at coming up with innovative answers to engineering problems.

Avoid conclusions (especially self-serving ones)

Example: I really believe in team play.

(So does my English Setter, but she still hunts alone.)

INSTEAD—describe the specifics of what you actually did and how you did it.

---

* If you are not "motivated" to write, describe and explain in detail, you may find this part of the process more difficult. An alternative to writing all the details is to be interviewed by a SIMA® analyst. If you are interested in learning about this alternative, please contact us at _mbanson539@aol.com_ or www.motivationalpattern.com.

Avoid judgments

Example: I'm not as good at it as my brother was.

(Maybe not, but so what?)

INSTEAD—describe the specifics of what you actually did and how you did it.

Avoid psychologizing

Example: I could have done better if my parents had supported me.

(Possibly.)

INSTEAD—describe the specifics of what you actually did and how you did it.

Avoid causes or reasons why or why not

Example: I do that because I'm such a perfectionist.

(So how come your car is rusting?)

INSTEAD—describe the specifics of what you actually did and how you did it.

You may find it helpful to review the achievements described in Examples A and B. Note the kind and amount of detail that is expressed in these examples.

In describing your achievements in detail, be sure to address the following:

- ◈ **How you got involved in the activity:** Were you asked to help? Did someone suggest you try it? Did you invite yourself? Did someone have a need? Did you perceive an opportunity?

- ◈ **The details of what you actually did:** Revisit the actual scene in your mind and remember the detailed things that you did, how you approached the tasks involved, whether you were especially noticed, what was important to you, what was going on in your head as you proceeded. Sometimes it helps if you think about describing what someone sitting on your shoulder would have seen you do. Like the proverbial fly on the wall, if someone were carefully watching what you were doing, what would they have seen you do?

- ◈ If the achievement involves an activity or series of tasks inherently complex or many faceted (e.g., rebuilding and racing cars), **pick out those aspects you did especially well and found most fulfilling.**

❖ In fact, this last point is useful in describing most any achievement. Don't write about what's involved in racing cars, flying, or putting a new process in place; **write about those parts you did that you believe you did well.**

❖ **When you were engaged in the achievement, what do you remember that you found enjoyable/satisfying?** It could be in the work itself, some effect you had on others, some result or outcome of the work, some way you or others measured the goodness of the effort, or some other payoff of significant personal value.

Example A: Detailed Description of Achievement

Achievement Activity: "Ski Lessons."

Summary Statement: "Took ski lessons and quickly progressed to expert level by skiing nightly at a local ski hill. Eventually became a ski instructor and was able to ski any terrain."

How I became involved: "Saw a television program showing somebody skiing down a very steep but beautiful mountain. I liked the idea of being in such beautiful scenery doing something that looked difficult."

Details of what I did (how I went about doing it): "I bought the latest ski magazines and planned the purchase of the proper equipment. I went to a local ski area and attempted to ski without lessons. It was much more difficult than I thought it was going to be. I fell almost all the time initially. After the falling tailed off, I noticed I had real problems turning the skis properly. I read somewhere that this could be caused by an improper boot-ski match, so I undertook to fix the problem. I spent some time in the workshop modifying the connection between boot and ski and tested each combination. Whether it was my adjustments or I was just getting better, I don't know but the turning improved quickly. Once I had the confidence to turn properly, I started to ski on more and more difficult slopes, falling a lot in the process. Within two years, I had progressed to expert status. A local ski area was hiring ski instructors and I applied and took a test. I was hired and taught all types of skiers, from beginners to advanced."

What was particularly satisfying to me: "I particularly liked planning the equipment purchase and fixing the problems with the equipment. The equipment is beautiful to look at and I like its high-tech feeling. I also like the feeling of being alone on a steep slope and getting to the bottom as quickly and as dangerously as possible."

Example B: Detailed Description of Achievement

Achievement Activity: "Team Design Procedures."

Summary Statement: "Leader of team developing design procedures for a novel oil-burning system for power generation."

How I became involved: "I was made leader of a small team that was part of a project team of about 40 people."

Details of what I did (how I went about doing it): "The first step was to optimize the design concept for a full-scale power station. I was given the job of developing a design procedure using a computer simulation. I identified the experimental data required and proposed a test program. I set up a system for processing, analyzing and reporting the data, writing the computer program myself. I trained a subordinate to run the system and handed over day-to-day responsibility to her. I identified the need to build three new test facilities to obtain data on detailed features. I prepared design specifications, operating procedures and data processing procedures. When the rigs were completed I was allocated five staff to operate them. I trained them and made sure that they understood what we were trying to achieve. Then I delegated authority to plan and carry out the work. I visited them at least once per day to encourage them and to look at the new experimental results. I then concentrated on interpreting the data and developing a computer simulation. I decided the overall principles and a subordinate did the details and computer programming — he was more able than me in this area. The entire project was a success, both the software that my team established and the hardware that the other teams developed. I publicized the work by giving many technical presentations."

What was particularly satisfying to me: "Seeing what was required and making it happen. Finding solutions to problems."

FORMAT FOR DESCRIBING YOUR ACHIEVEMENTS IN DETAIL*

Directions: Use this outline to describe in detail at least five but preferably eight of your achievements. Be sure to provide the kind of detailed description that is expressed in the examples.

Achievement Activity:

One line summary statement:

How you got involved:

Details of what you did (how you actually went about doing it):

What was particularly satisfying to you:

---

* You may want to complete this information by accessing the SIMA® Form on www.motivationalpattern.com.

All finished? Congratulations! Often just the experience of sitting down and reflecting on your achievements is truly valuable as well as enjoyable, but the best part is yet to come! It may be that just by completing this reflecting and writing exercise, you have been able to recognize some of the themes that recur in your achievements. These themes are the basis for your Motivational Pattern, your pattern of giftedness. These themes are not inconsequential, for they:

✧ Describe what triggers and sustains your "motivated" behavior, which is the source of all excellence.

✧ Determine whether and why you get stressed.

✧ Control how your job/role is perceived and performed.

✧ Present the foundation for any effective and lasting development efforts for you.

✧ Govern the effect of incentives/rewards on you.

Chapter 2. Add Up the "Evidence" for Your Motivational Pattern

Even in the sciences, we only begin to see the phenomenon in the sky or under the microscope if someone first describes that which is in front of the squinting eye.

James Hillman

HOLD UP A MIRROR TO YOUR WORK/LIFE

James Hillman's [42] observation about needing to know what we are looking for is "right on" when applied to Motivational Patterns. While we may be aware of some aspects of our recurring motivations, we usually do not recognize the complete pattern until it is described for us. Most people have simply not been made aware of the existence of these patterns nor have they had the opportunity to identify their own pattern. Innate patterns probably have been present since the beginning of humankind, yet scholars who so completely understand and report their nature and power have presented little evidence of the existence of these patterns. But the evidence is all around us. **Every single person manifests concrete evidence that we are born with a defining image.** Our life stories are filled with episodes rich in the intricate details of how our unique pattern is expressed, beginning in early childhood. We can *see* this pattern in full display if we will only take the time to reflect on our life experiences. We can identify the pattern if we will only *look backwards* over our lives for the events that brought us satisfaction and fulfillment.

To prepare you to identify your Motivational Pattern from the achievement data that you have developed, you must first learn more about the nature of patterns and how to utilize the "evidence" to identify the recurring themes. In my experience, the most effective way to learn how to identify these recurring themes is by working with examples or case studies. Let's start with Shane, a researcher at a biomedical laboratory. Shane has prepared the following descriptions of achievements from his work and life that meet the two criteria for the Motivational Pattern analysis: These are achievements that Shane **enjoyed doing and felt he did well**. As you read these achievements, identify the recurring themes in the data.

Shane's Achievement Data

Childhood:

"Read about everything I could get my hands on, interested in invertebrates . . . always looking for different types of worms, etc. Fascinated to see particular organism . . . always looking for new types . . . fascinated with finding unusual types. Did experiments, made cuts in worm, grew two heads, two tails."

Age 22-25:

"Conducted an extensive research project for a class . . . Physiological Changes in Limpets in Response to Escape Eliciting Substances. Worked on project two months beyond course despite lack of cooperation from professors. Very interesting . . . fascinating complex of behaviors. Figured out some kind of experiment . . . animals showed these very interesting responses. Some were quite absurd . . . nobody really looked at the physiology of this thing. Fascinated by the whole subject . . . presence of the extract resulted in increase in heart rate and respiration."

Age 31-35:

"Discovered two mechanisms involved in response to simulated jet lag in monkeys. Discovered during analysis of data . . . looked for something that was cohesive. Discovered different pattern in data of one monkey. Pursued it to point where I got this presentation . . . took data and explained . . . fascinating in that I had discovered this and didn't expect to see this—really interesting."

Identifying the Motivational Pattern involves examining the achievement data for "evidence" in the actual words the achiever used to describe what he remembered about this achievement experience. For example, in examining Shane's achievement data, the following evidence and related themes can be observed:

Evidence	Theme
read, interested in, looking for	Investigating
did experiments, made cuts, figure out	Analyzing
really look at, discovered	Observing
took data and explained	Experimenting
invertebrates, worms, organisms, physiological, limpets, animals	Physiology
(There is no mention of following procedures or specifications. He "worked on the project two months beyond the course despite a lack of cooperation from professors.")	Freedom to Experiment
(The researcher doesn't mention working with or through others to achieve his purpose. He only describes his own "individualist" efforts and the results of his efforts.)	Individual Contributor
fascinated to see, looking for new types, excited to find, discovered two mechanisms, discovered different patterns, fascinating that I had discovered this, didn't expect to see this	Discovery

THE MOTIVATIONAL PATTERN®: A SYSTEM OF BEHAVIOR

The analysis of thousands of Motivational Patterns has revealed five distinct aspects of motivation that are present in the achiever's description of his/her achievement activities. **These five parts of motivation are interdependent, thus it is important to think of the pattern as a system of behavior, each part enabling as well as restraining the other parts.** The five parts listed are described below, and examples of each are provided. These five parts are also used to create a framework for the evidence identified in Shane's achievement data.

Five Basic Parts of the Motivational Pattern

1) **Motivated Abilities**—Among your abilities are some that are **motivated,** which means you never get tired or bored using them. You use these abilities repeatedly in activities that you find rewarding and enjoyable. Most of us have a longer list of abilities we can perform, but "motivated" abilities are the ones that continually recur in our achievements that we enjoy doing and feel we do well. **Shane's motivated abilities include investigating, analyzing, observing and experimenting.** (Others may be "motivated" to construct, assemble, sell, convince, design or write.)

2) **Subject Matter**—This is what you are motivated to work with or through. It may range from something very concrete to something that is highly abstract. **Shane's subject matter is very focused; he is primarily interested in physiology.** Many people have 3-5 areas of "motivated" subject matter (e.g., tools, numbers, people, concepts, structures, methods, strategies).

3) **Circumstances**—There are certain factors that trigger your motivation and certain environments that transform you into a highly motivated person. For example, some people need clear objectives in order to function. Others develop direction as they go. Some people function in stress, in emergencies, or in problems that would render another immobile. **Shane is motivated by circumstances that provide him freedom to experiment.** (Others may be motivated by competition, projects, causes, results, profit, recognition or a host of other circumstances that will be presented later in this book.)

4) **Operating Relationship**—There is a particular way you like to relate to others in a work situation. Your Operating Relationship has nothing to do with whether you are sociable or not, or whether you are *introverted* or *extroverted*. Your Operating Relationship only describes your preferred relationship to others when you are performing activities that are most satisfying and rewarding for you. **Shane is motivated to work as an Individual Contributor.**

People who are motivated to relate to others in their achievement activities as *Individual Contributors* want to occupy a well-defined role and to be able to secure results through their own efforts. People who are motivated to accomplish their work as individualists may at times involve others in their work, but they are not a good "fit" for jobs that require them to have overall responsibility for others. This is a "fit" issue; it does not mean that individualists have a deficiency. This is an important difference between the SIMA® assessment method and other methods that seek to identify and correct "deficiencies." In fact, the majority of highly rated knowledge workers who command "expert" status roles and hold patents and copyrights are motivated to work as individualists. If the nature of their work involves being on a team or project, their productivity will be enhanced if they are given a specific assignment that is later integrated into the work of the team. While this may sound directly contrary to the current training on "teamwork," effective supervisors know this is how it really works best.

People are motivated to relate to others in a variety of ways when achieving their purposes (e.g., team member, spearhead, trainer, enabler, coach, facilitator, director, manager or leader). A person may be motivated to perform in more than one of these Operating Relationship roles, but only about 25% of knowledge workers are motivated to seek overall responsibility for outcomes and to oversee the work of others on a daily basis. [43] This means that while there are many knowledge workers who are truly motivated to be managers or leaders, it does take some investigation to determine which individual truly has the motivation for the job.

Because our society values management careers so highly, this is probably the most common "mismatch" that we find in the careers of knowledge workers. *Individual Contributors* accept (and seek) management and leadership roles because of the success, prosperity and power (real and/or perceived) that these roles involve.

5) **Motivational Payoff**—At the core of your motivation is a singular, uniquely characteristic outcome that you seek in order to feel a sense of accomplishment and satisfaction. This payoff is not simply a pleasure-seeking outcome; it is the fulfillment that comes with performing activities that achieve your particular purpose. The payoff can be achieved from any kind of activity, e.g., with your family, in school, in a job, a sport, religious organization or volunteer activities. The joy and fulfillment that comes with achieving your payoff keeps you "coming back for more of the same" throughout your entire life. **The outcome or payoff that Shane seeks is the discovery of something new. He is also "motivated" when he is involved in the discovery process.**

Some people are motivated when they are able to excel, gain recognition or in some way differentiate their performance from others. Yet others want to exert dominance and willpower, be in charge or overcome obstacles. Many people feel particularly fulfilled and satisfied when they meet a goal, need or challenge. Others want to effect a change on a person, object or situation, as in gaining a response or making an impression. Usually only one of these "payoffs" dominates an individual's achievement data. Other payoffs may be present but are more likely to be the means to the end, not the end in itself. **It is this end point, or Motivational Payoff, that individuals are least likely to recognize and understand.**

STEP THREE: IDENTIFY THE "EVIDENCE" FOR RECURRING THEMES

<u>Now it's your turn!</u> After learning about the five basic parts of Motivational Patterns and how to recognize and "add up" the "evidence" provided in the detailed descriptions of achievements, some readers will be ready to identify their own Motivational Pattern. Individuals who have Motivated Abilities to analyze will obviously be a better "fit" for this task.

If you are a person who learns by doing and would like an additional opportunity to "practice" this analysis process, or if you are motivated by challenge and want to "test" your analytical abilities, turn to the Appendix and complete the Practice Case. If you find this "do-it-yourself" analysis process is simply not a good "fit" for your motivation, you may want to have a SIMA® counselor review your analysis. If you would like assistance in identifying your Motivational Pattern, please contact us at www.motivationalpattern.com or mhanson539@aol.com.

To identify your Motivational Pattern, simply "add up" the evidence in your achievements for each of the five parts of the Motivational Pattern. Directions for identifying each part of your Motivational Pattern are presented below:

IDENTIFY YOUR MOTIVATED ABILITIES

Motivated Abilities <u>recur</u> in your achievements as you describe how you went about *doing whatever it was that you did.* You never seem to tire of using these abilities. Day after day, year after year, you will use these skills to accomplish your purpose—throughout your life! There may be other things that you "can do" but these are the abilities that you are "motivated" to use. Motivated abilities are not always impressive but they do stand out, not always because of what they accomplish, but because they allow you to accomplish so much with so little effort.

Motivated Abilities are reflected in the **VERBS** (action words) that you used in the detailed description of the actions in your achievements. These actions are usually **observable** (e.g. walk, write, design, advise, sew, sell, fix, research) OR **represent an action** that achieved a demonstrable result (e.g. formulate, plan, strategize, analyze).

Motivated Abilities are organized in the following categories:

Learning	Organizing
Evaluating	Overseeing
Planning	Influencing
Creating/Developing	Doing
	Performing

Abilities: *The abilities that recur in your achievements.*

Directions: REVIEW your achievement data and CIRCLE all the verbs (action words). SELECT the Motivated Abilities below when there is "evidence" in 2-3 of your achievements. You will probably not have Motivated Abilities in all of the main categories. You may have evidence of more than one item within a category.

Learning
How did you go about learning how to do or understand what was involved?

Did you read about it?

- ☐ Reading, studying
- ☐ Listening, discussing
- ☐ Probing, inquiring
- ☐ Observing, examining
- ☐ Doing, trying
- ☐ In-depth researching

Evaluating
How did you go about evaluating or deciding about something?

Analyze detail?

- ☐ Analyzing, dissecting
- ☐ Comparing against a standard
- ☐ Assessing worth or value
- ☐ Weighing pros/cons
- ☐ Figuring, calculating
- ☐ Empathizing, discerning

Motivated Abilities (continued)

Planning
How did you go about planning what needs to be done?

Propose a strategy?

☐ Strategizing, charting a course
☐ Setting goals
☐ Drafting, laying out
☐ Defining the tasks to be done
☐ Arranging details, scheduling
☐ Anticipating, preparing

Creating/Developing
How did you cause the new to emerge?

Adapt or modify what exists?

☐ Adapting or modifying what exists
☐ Originating ideas or concepts
☐ Inventing or innovating
☐ Growing or building up
☐ Constructing, crafting
☐ Designing, processing

Motivated Abilities (continued)

Organizing
How did you go about preparing to get the work done?

Providing structure?

- ☐ Building a system
- ☐ Classifying into categories or units
- ☐ Providing structure, definition
- ☐ Preparing by rehearsing and practicing
- ☐ Integrating, gathering

Overseeing
Did you work with / through others?

Managing the talents of others?

- ☐ Facilitate the work of others
- ☐ Directing the detailed work of others
- ☐ Checking and monitoring the work of others
- ☐ Coordinating the work of others
- ☐ Leading/inspiring the work of others
- ☐ Managing the talents of others

Motivated Abilities (continued)

Influencing

How did you influence others to respond?

Encouraging others?

- ☐ Teaching, presenting
- ☐ Convincing, persuading
- ☐ Explaining, describing
- ☐ Initiating, suggesting
- ☐ Counseling, advising
- ☐ Involving, getting participation
- ☐ Encouraging, nurturing

Doing

Did you take a "hands-on" approach?

Manually, physically?

- ☐ Manually, physically
- ☐ Operating something, running it
- ☐ Maintaining, keeping in condition
- ☐ Overseeing a process

Performing

Do you seek an audience?

Performing for an audience?

- ☐ Athletically
- ☐ Academically
- ☐ Musically
- ☐ On stage

IDENTIFY YOUR SUBJECT MATTER

The test for identifying your "motivated" subject matter is *passion*. You have certain subjects or objects on which your motivation thrives. It is what you gravitate toward and emphasize in your work/life. It is what you are interested in, what you think about after work, what you work on late into the night. Motivated subject matter can range from concrete (mechanical devices) to that which is intangible and abstract (concepts or ideas).

The **NOUNS** that you used in the description of your achievements provide "evidence" of the subject matter that you are motivated to work with and through. For example, you may write about playing *sports,* or building *forts,* or writing *letters,* or reading *stories*, or organizing a *club*, or proceduralizing a *system*, or brainstorming *strategies*, or calculating *numbers*.

The Subject Matter is organized under the following headings:

DATA: Includes numbers, symbols, words, language, details, facts, arrangements, logistics, and money. Individuals motivated to work with data want to compose, compile, evaluate, process or communicate one or more of these kinds of data.

INTANGIBLES: Intangible subject matters have no physical substance. Includes ideas, concepts, thoughts, expression, principles, philosophy, values, ethics, spiritual, knowledge, information and personal goals.

TANGIBLES: Objects that are perceptible by touch and have a definite shape (e.g., structures, tools, machines, animals, plants and materials). Tangibles include physical or manual expression, those activities that involve the extensive use of the hands or body.

MECHANISMS: Processes or techniques by which something works or produces an action or effect (e.g., systems, angles, techniques, methods, procedures, strategies, roles, stories and literature).

SENSORY: Involves concern and sensitivity for elements, features and characteristics that appeal to visual, audio, taste and touch senses (e.g., graphics, pictures, music, colors, textures, feel, design).

TECHNICAL: Pertains to having or dealing with to a specialized knowledge or skill (e.g., engineering, science, math, finance or other specific technologies).

PEOPLE: Involves working with people in some way—in relationships, with specific individuals, in groups organizations, with behavior, society or culture.

Subject Matter: *What you are motivated to work with and through.*

Directions: REVIEW your achievement data and UNDERLINE all of the nouns. SELECT the Subject Matter below when there is "evidence" in 2-3 of your achievements. You will probably not have Subject Matter in all of the main categories. You may have evidence of more than one item within a category.

Data?

- ☐ Numbers, symbols
- ☐ Words, language
- ☐ Details, particulars, facts
- ☐ Logistics, arrangements
- ☐ Money, dollars

Details?

Intangibles?

- ☐ Ideas, concepts
- ☐ Thoughts, expression
- ☐ Principles, philosophy
- ☐ Values, ethics, spiritual
- ☐ Knowledge, information
- ☐ Personal goals

Knowledge?

Subject Matter (continued)

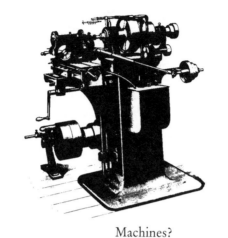

Machines?

Tangibles?

- ☐ Physical/manual things
- ☐ Structures
- ☐ Machines, vehicles
- ☐ Tools, devices
- ☐ Animals
- ☐ Materials, plants

Mechanisms?

- ☐ Systems
- ☐ Angles, techniques
- ☐ Methods, procedures
- ☐ Strategies
- ☐ Roles, parts
- ☐ Stories, literature

Systems?

Graphics, pictures?

Sensory?

- ☐ Graphics, pictures
- ☐ Sound, music
- ☐ Colors
- ☐ Textures, feel
- ☐ Design

Subject Matter (continued)

Technical?

- ☐ Engineering
- ☐ Science
- ☐ Math
- ☐ Finance
- ☐ Technology

Science (Archaeology)?

Working with groups?

People?

- ☐ Individuals
- ☐ Groups, organizations
- ☐ Behavior
- ☐ Society, culture
- ☐ Relationships

IDENTIFY YOUR MOTIVATING CIRCUMSTANCES

There are certain Circumstances that will trigger your motivation and sustain your "motivated" behavior. You will perform your best when you can function in circumstances (or environments) that are motivating to you. The more you understand about the circumstances that trigger and sustain your motivation, the more accurately you will be able to select (or create) the right work environment for yourself!

Circumstances are organized under the following headings:

✧ **What triggered your motivation . . . How did you get involved in the activity?**

Were you confronted by a problem—almost forced to deal with it—or did you choose to respond to a problem? Maybe you were asked to get involved—or simply decided to initiate the action?

✧ **How well structured was the activity?**

Was there an established goal to reach? Did you have clear requirements or standards? Maybe the situations were unstructured—perhaps you brought order.

✧ **What conditions/environment recur in your achievements?**

Is there always competition, or projects, or something new and novel? Perhaps you require plenty of time to learn and prepare—or you want to work in a team or group—or be entrepreneurial or attack problems.

✧ **Did you seek recognition in your achievements?**

Is there recurring evidence of audiences, listeners or viewers? Awards? Maybe you are motivated by reputation or visibility—or you could prefer to work behind the scenes and support others?

✧ **What was the end use or result of your activity?**

Do you seek an outcome that is measurable or visible? Or want profit or gain? Perhaps seeing the finished product is critical—or having application or use? Some want precise and exact results; others want efficiency or effectiveness.

Circumstances: *Themes that trigger motivation and/or sustain your "motivated" behavior.*

Directions: REVIEW your achievement data and IDENTIFY words/phrases that describe your working conditions and environment. SELECT the Circumstances below when there is evidence in 2-3 of your achievements. You may have "evidence" of more than one item within a category.

What triggered your motivation?

Others asked you?

- ☐ Others asked you to do something
- ☐ Confronted by a test or problem
- ☐ Personally initiated action
- ☐ Responded to a need or problem
- ☐ Engaged by cause, mission

How well structured was the activity involved?

Clear requirements?

- ☐ Clear requirements or standards
- ☐ Well ordered and defined
- ☐ Very fluid and unstructured
- ☐ Established goal to reach
- ☐ Brings structure, order

Circumstances (continued)

What were the conditions/environment?

- ☐ Plenty of time to learn
- ☐ Entrepreneurial
- ☐ Difficulties and obstacles to overcome
- ☐ Participative
- ☐ Competitive
- ☐ New, novel, different
- ☐ Project
- ☐ Outdoors, nature

Entrepreneurial?

Did the person seek recognition in his/her achievements?

- ☐ Audiences, viewers, listeners
- ☐ Awards, badges, trophies
- ☐ Notoriety, reputation
- ☐ Personal recognition
- ☐ Status settings, positions
- ☐ Visibility
- ☐ Behind the scenes, support

Personal Recognition?

What was the end use or result of the activity?

- ☐ Profitable outcome
- ☐ A measureable or visible result
- ☐ A finished product, project
- ☐ Improvement in efficiency
- ☐ Greater effectiveness
- ☐ Application, use
- ☐ Precise, exact outcomes

Profitable Outcome?

IDENTIFY YOUR OPERATING RELATIONSHIP

There is a particular way you like to operate with others in a work setting or activity. When you examine your enjoyable achievement experiences, you will find that you have repeated specific kinds of relationships with others as you move about your achievement activity. This information will indicate how best to manage yourself and whether you are motivated to manage others.

Operating Relationships are organized into three categories:

✧ The INDIVIDUAL CONTRIBUTOR does not depend on others to take action—he/she consistently does things alone and does not mention involving the efforts of anyone else in the achievement activity.

✧ The INFLUENCER influences others to take action, but doesn't seek continuing overall responsibility for managing others. Examples may be teaching, counseling, advising, facilitating, selling, or politicking.

✧ The MANAGER/LEADER works through others in accomplishing an end, and seeks overall responsibility. Examples include team leader, project leader, manager, leader, director or commander.

Operating Relationships: *How you operate with or relate to others in your achievements.*

Directions: REVIEW your achievement data and IDENTIFY how you related to others in these achievements. SELECT the appropriate Operating Relationship when there is "evidence" in at least two of your achievements. You may have evidence in more than one of the three main categories.

1. Individual Contributor: Effort does not depend on others for action.

☐ **Team Member.** Wants to operate in the company of others whenever possible, views contributions as merged with the efforts of others.

☐ **Individualist.** Content to operate with others or alone, but occupies a well-defined role, and wants to be able to secure results through his or her efforts.

☐ **Key Contributor.** Enjoys filling a key role whose contribution is critical to success of overall project; likes to step in with advice or expertise.

☐ **Star.** Seeks out performer-audience relationship with others; views his or her efforts as being observed by others.

2. Influencer: Influences others to take actions, but does not seek continuing or overall responsibility for managing others.

☐ **Trainer.** Focuses on developing the capabilities of others through his or her influence. Prefers to work through programs/structured group activities.

☐ **Enabler.** Prefers to work on a one-to-one basis, helping others develop or attain goals in a highly personalized, rather unstructured way.

☐ **Coordinator.** Coordinates the activities of others in a participatory fashion, but prefers not to confront or use hire-fire authority; often causes others to take action who are not under his or her immediate jurisdiction.

☐ **Spark Plug.** Relates to others as the communicator and promoter of a new idea, vision or activity. May spark successive new thrusts within an activity, but generally moves to some other role after impact has been made.

3. Manager/Leader: Involves others in accomplishing an end, seeks overall responsibility.

☐ **Team Captain.** Participates with subordinates in the action, influences their action by his or her example or expertise. Leads by performing so as to inspire, show the way, take the lead.

☐ **Director.** Directs the action of others to perform in exactly his or her way; gets involved at the level of detail and maintains close control. Utilizes the efforts of others as if they were extensions of himself/herself.

☐ **Manager.** Brings about results by actively managing the talents of others; consistently delegates to others. May or may not maintain close control, but confronts others on their performance when necessary.

☐ **Engineer.** Controls others in precise ways by devising a plan of action for them to follow and then feeding them into it. Relates to others primarily through the medium of the plan as opposed to relying on personal direction or administration.

☐ **Leader.** Causes others to follow, on a sustained basis, his or her proclaimed mission, ideology, or values. Concerned with grass roots support and commitment. Readily wins confidence and respect. Is inspirational and futuristic.

IDENTIFY YOUR MOTIVATIONAL PAYOFF

Serving as the integrator for all the parts of the Motivational Pattern is the overall result called the Motivational Payoff. This is the result that you seek from all of your achievement activity. This is what you hope to get out of all your efforts. This describes the objective of your quest and zeal. Motivational Payoffs are organized under the following headings:

✧ **Focus on personal performance, comparison with others.**

Look for comments describing you as the only one in the class, the tallest, the first, the best, the champion, outstanding, better than your sister, unique in your style, the key player. Whatever the situation, you will find a way to be recognized and visible—and to measure your performance against others as a way of confirming your standing.

✧ **Focus on dominance or power.**

This Motivational Payoff is about exercising power or influence over people or things. It is about owning, mastering, comprehending and overcoming. Look for comments where you were in charge, overcame the problems or obstacles, controlled all the variables, set the direction, bought, collected or acquired several items or read everything on the subject and then wrote a paper.

✧ **Focus on object or effect on the object.**

This Motivation Payoff is about leaving your mark in some way. Look for comments about how you repaired the clock, made the process work, improved the situation, had a major impact, made a difference, got the child to respond, recognized the potential or made things more effective.

✧ **Focus on defined effort, purpose, and goal.**

This Motivational Payoff is about reaching a target or goal, passing the test or meeting expectations. Look for comments on how you met the challenge, pulled it off, fulfilled a need or special request, made the team, made the grade, fulfilled the requirements or brought it to completion.

✧ **Focus on the process.**

The process of performing the activity engages people with this Motivational Payoff. Look for comments on how you learned how to drive the car, developed a product or process, pioneered a new effort, discovered something previously unknown, took on a new job and performed it quickly, realized a lifelong dream of being like Uncle Harry, continued to advance in your work or raised a great garden.

Motivational Payoff: *The recurring theme that describes the outcome or result that the individual seeks from his/her achievements.*

Directions: REVIEW your achievements; IDENTIFY what was most satisfying. SELECT one of the following five main categories that is evidenced in all of your achievements. You may have evidence of more than one item within a category.

1. Focus on Personal Performance, Comparisons with Others

☐ **Be Best, Excel**
Wants to be fastest, first, longest, earliest, most thorough, biggest, better than others.

☐ **Be Unique, Outstanding**
Seeks opportunities to demonstrate qualities, accomplishments, skills, products which are distinctive, unique in some way.

☐ **Gain Recognition, Attention**
Centrally interested in gaining the attention of others; wants to be known; be in the spotlight; appear in the paper; wave at the cheering crowd. (Should be evident in the body of the achievement, not merely at the end of it.)

☐ **Be the Key Person, Prime Mover, Be Central**
Wants to be the person who makes things happen; the person who is needed and vital. Seeks visible, central role in any group, organization or situation - not necessarily the boss.

2. Focus on Dominance or Power

☐ **Be in Charge, Command, Be in Control**
Wants to be on top of people and situations - in authority - in the saddle - where he or she can determine how things will be done.

☐ **Overcome Obstacles, Prevail**
Wants to come up against and prevail over bad guys, other experts; entrenched status quo; personal handicaps; opposition; lack of experience, etc.

☐ **Acquire, Possess - Exercise Ownership Over**
Wants to get and have; exercise ownership over a variety of things including money, positions, operations, family, others.

☐ **Master or Perfect**
Goes after rough edges, complete domination of a technique, control over all the variables, wants to master a subject or skill, perfect a system, method, process.

☐ **Comprehend and Demonstrate, Reduce to Expression**
Wants to understand complex ideas, skills, processes and things; strives to figure it all out, get at its essence and demonstrate comprehension by reducing the essence to some form or by explaining, showing, or otherwise communicating it.

3. Focus on the Object or Effect on the Object

☐ **Improve, Make Better, Enhance**
Makes what is marginal, good; what is good, better; what is working adequately, work more effectively.

☐ **Make Work, Make Effective**
Fixes what is broken, changes what is out-of-date, redesigns what was poorly conceived, restores what is not working.

☐ **Extract, Achieve Potential**
Unearths potential in a person, or market, or object, or idea, and exploits it; when not apparent to others, sees a hidden potential, a giant talent, a hot product, a promising market, and makes use of it.

☐ **Gain Response — Influence Behavior**
Wants people and groups (and perhaps animals) to react to his or her touch, influence, action; to function or respond as the achiever intends.

☐ **Impress — Impact on — Make Mark — Shape**
Wants to leave a mark, to impress others; finds satisfaction in making a visible impact on policy, object, organizations. Seeks a position where shaping influence can be exerted.

4. Focus on Defined Effort, Purpose, Goal

☐ **Bring to Completion — Reach the Objective**
Wants to complete project, step back and see the finished work; complete the assignment as planned or envisioned; realize the intended purpose.

☐ **Make the Team, Grade**
Wants to achieve a pre-determined mark of having "arrived"; wants to "make it" in terms of grades, rank, status; gains access to the inner circle, varsity, the sorority. Eagle Scout rank, the country club, the executive dining room, the honor roll.

☐ **Meet the Challenge — Pull it Off — Meet the Test**
Meets difficult deadlines, solves problems; comes up shining under demanding circumstances; wants to accomplish specific tasks, pass specific tests which are challenging.

☐ **Meet Needs — Fulfill Requirements — Satisfy Expectations**
Rises to the occasion when need is announced or becomes obvious; works hard to meet stated requirements, follow specifications, follow instructions, perform to meet expectations placed on him or her by others (or even by himself or herself).

5. Focus on the Process Involved

☐ **Build — Develop — Form**
Wants to make something where there was nothing; or carry to a higher or more advanced or useful state; structures, technical things, formulations, organizations, relationships.

☐ **Realize Concept — Fulfill Image, Role**
Wants to make concepts come alive in real life, to make what is seen in the mind's eye become tangible, to flesh out an image, live out a role, live up to a model.

☐ **Become Proficient — Demonstrate Competence**
Learns "how to" in a variety of fields. Shows adaptability to new situations. Develops knowledge and technique to point of demonstrable competence, then seeks new avenues for learning, demonstration.

☐ **Pioneer — Explore**
Moves in to new realms, virgin territories, presses beyond established lines, knowledge, boundaries; hungry for "new" knowledge, techniques, experiences.

☐ **Advance — Progress — Move Up, On, Forward**
Receives satisfaction from his or her own, or organization's, or project's forward movement, through ranks, stages or levels of productivity, knowledge, skills, influence.

YOUR MOTIVATIONAL PATTERN APPROXIMATION*

Directions: Take the time to transfer each of the items that you have checked to the following form. This will provide you a quick reference of your motivations. This listing will also serve to remind you of those items that you are NOT motivated to perform.

I. Motivated Abilities:

Learning by _____   Overseeing by _____

Evaluating by _____   Influencing by _____

Planning by _____   Doing by _____

Creating/Developing by _____   Performing by _____

Organizing by _____

II. Subject Matter:

Data _____   Sensory _____

Intangibles _____   Technical _____

Tangibles _____   People _____

Mechanisms _____

III. Circumstances:

What triggers your motivation? How do you get involved in an activity? _____

What degree of structure/definition do you need? _____

What working conditions or environment motivate you? _____

What end use or results do you seek? _____

Do you seek recognition? _____

IV. Operating Relationship:

How do you work best with people? _____

Individual Contributor? Influencer? Leader/Manager? _____

V. Motivational Payoff:

The primary result you want to achieve: _____

---

* If a certified SIMA® counselor prepares a pattern after an interview with the individual, it is a Certified Motivational Pattern. If the pattern is prepared from written achievement data or in a workshop setting, it is called a Motivational Pattern Approximation.

IMPLICATIONS OF YOUR PATTERN

After you have identified all the elements of your pattern, take a few minutes to think about how your pattern has expressed itself in your work and life. For example, you might want to think about how you are motivated to learn. Did you love to read as a kid and take to school like a duck to water? Or was reading a chore and a bore, and your school years a bad memory, but you loved to actually get your hands on something and learn by doing and trying? Or maybe you learned by participating in an activity first and getting some experience in it?

Maybe you have always had trouble selling your ideas. Is there any evidence in your pattern of motivation to sell? Maybe you have always done a super job when you knew what was expected of you, but you would procrastinate if you weren't sure of what you were supposed to do. These are just a few examples of the many, many experiences that we can have in our work/life that can be explained by examining our Motivational Pattern.

Motivational Patterns provide insights that allow you to maximize your talents and to be more aware of how to manage any limitations.

Understanding Your Motivational Pattern

Directions:

Identify at least two or three areas of talent you have enjoyed in your work/life and note the elements of your patterns that give evidence of these talents. Likewise, identify two or three limitations that you may have experienced and note what elements (either present or absent) might be responsible. Then press on to learn more about maximizing motivations and managing limitations!

TALENTS and related Motivational Pattern Elements (present).

1. _____

2. _____

3. _____

LIMITATIONS and related Motivational Pattern Elements (present or absent).

1. _____

2. _____

3. _____

Chapter 3. Recognize the Power of the Pattern

Know thyself...and become who you are.

Socrates

CAN WE REALLY BE ANYTHING WE WANT TO BE?

A School for Animals

Once upon a time the animals decided they must do something heroic to meet the problems of a "new world," so they organized a school. They adopted a curriculum consisting of running, climbing, swimming, and flying; and to make it easier to administer, all the animals took all the same subjects.

The duck was excellent in swimming, better, in fact, than his instructor. He made passing grades in flying, but was very poor in running. Since he was slow in running, he had to stay after school and drop swimming to practice running. This was kept up until his webbed feet were badly worn, and he was only average in swimming. But average was acceptable in school, so nobody worried about that except the duck.

The rabbit started at the top of his class in running, but had a nervous breakdown because of so much make-up work in swimming.

The squirrel was excellent in climbing until she developed frustration in the flying class, where her teacher made her start from the ground up instead of from the treetop down. She also developed charley horses from over-exercise and then got a "C" in climbing and a "D" in running.

The eagle was a problem child and was disciplined severely. In the climbing class, he beat all the others to the top of the tree, but insisted on using his own way of getting there.

At the end of the year, the queer abnormal eel, that could swim exceedingly well and also run, climb, and fly a little, had the highest average and was valedictorian." [(44)]

This fable characterizes the enduring nature of our motivations and the struggles associated with trying to do something that we are not naturally suited or "motivated" to do. Like the animals, we find that it takes great effort to perform in areas that are not a good "fit." Because we are trying so hard to adapt to the difficult situation, we often miss the opportunity to shine in situations that would really "fit" our unique talents.

CHARACTERISTICS OF MOTIVATIONAL PATTERNS

To help understand how central Motivational Patterns are to your work and life, consider the following characteristics that explain how these innate motivations really work. To provide examples of their impact, elements from Shane's (the researcher) Motivational Pattern are used to illustrate the power of the respective characteristics.

Irrepressible

As previously discussed, Motivational Patterns are irrepressible. It is literally impossible to keep your giftedness from expressing itself ("bubbling up") somewhere in your life. Even if you want to repress a "motivated" behavior, it will surface in some way.

As demonstrated by Shane's early examples, he found a way to express his interest in science and in research by collecting and examining worms. This was neither a position held nor a request made by someone else. The event took place well before his years of education in the field. As a boy, he simply found a way to express his motivation to do scientific research.

Controlling Your Job Performance

You will try to perform your work in accordance with your pattern; e.g., an innovator will change things; an overcomer will find or make things to overcome; a doer will continue to perform the details, regardless of what is wanted, expected or necessary.

You will view the world through your own "motivational glasses," and then you will address what you see. **You will try to make the job into what it is you are motivated to do.** If you are motivated to create, you will attempt to perform the requirements of the job by creating. If you are motivated to influence, then influencing will be key. Shane, the analytical researcher who is motivated to discover, "worked on the project two months beyond the course despite lack of cooperation from professors." Shane was motivated by the analysis and investigation so he "shaped" his job and continued with his research.

We can see how "fit" problems are created. Shane is not motivated to meet goals or to bring projects to completion. What if Shane were on a tight delivery schedule and there was a new project to start? How would he feel about closing down the project and foregoing the opportunity to discover? **People redefine their tasks not because they are rebellious or stubborn or self-willed, but because they cannot do the tasks well any other way.** They are driven to express their giftedness, striving to do the thing to which they were born. Circumstances can encourage or impede the expression of one's giftedness but do not prohibit a "motivated" behavior from its expression, as long as the circumstance or environment fall within a "normal range," e.g., no abuse or severe deprivation. [45]

Explanatory of the Past . . . Predictive of the Future

Your motivation is expressed again and again—over your lifetime. Once identified, the pattern will explain why you perform as you do. You will see clearly, for example, why you are always confronting authority, why you take on more jobs than you can possibly do. You will understand why you spend more time than you should talking to your co-workers about their personal problems, why you are prone to talk too much and not listen enough. You will always try to perform in accordance with your pattern. It will appear in your future as surely as it has appeared in your past.

Our achievements from childhood help to give credibility to the predictive nature of this phenomenon. For most of us, the childhood achievements contain precious "nuggets" of our patterns. These childhood achievements often present our pattern more clearly, as these are achievements that are more likely to be "designed" by us and are less likely to be "biased" by constraints, pressures or rewards from others. Shane's childhood example of collecting and examining worms is a great example of his early interest in investigation and science. The sense of the lasting nature of discovery is also clear. Discovery was motivating to Shane in the past and will be motivating to him in the future.

You may be thinking...*but I have changed a great deal over the years. When I was in grade school, I was interested in dinosaurs and fossils. Then in high school it was electronics and computers. But I ended up getting a law degree—and I love my work as a lawyer. I just don't see a pattern here.* One would have to look at all your achievement data to be sure, but it is quite possible that learning something new and then demonstrating your competence is the underlying pattern. Your subject matter could involve a range of knowledge and information—and your role as a lawyer might give you an on-going opportunity to exercise this motivation as each new case requires you to learn and then demonstrate your knowledge. The way you express the motivation may change, but the basic Motivational Pattern remains the same. If you cannot identify the pattern, it is probably because you are not aware of the common denominator.

Because participants frequently ask whether or not Motivational Patterns change, one of our clients (a large aerospace company) initiated a longitudinal test-retest study to establish the consistency of patterns over time. The basic research question: Do patterns change? In this study, the Motivational Patterns of 15 subjects were selected from the SIMA® files of People Management International LLC. These 15 individuals were again contacted (about six years later) for another SIMA® interview and pattern. Dr. John Crites, internationally recognized vocational psychologist who conducted the study, reported that the patterns showed "marked stability" when these participants were re-patterned after the six-year interim period. While the study involved a relatively small number of subjects, it did confirm what appears to be true for every person who has been patterned: The pattern remains stable yet continues to develop. *All that really changes is the maturity of the functioning as the person develops through more complex and demanding achievement experiences.* [46] The builder seeks new experiences in building—maybe houses and decks, or relationships or even teams. The "comprehender" keeps learning—about airplanes and motorcycles, then about cars and as an engineer, about rocket engines. The entrepreneur starts new enterprises—a paper route, a baby-sitting business, and later, an investment counseling service. The teacher continues to teach—her siblings, her students, her children, and then her grandchildren—at home, in school, in church and at play with her granddaughter.

> *You will always try to perform in accordance with your pattern. It will appear in your future as surely as it has appeared in your past.*

Deals With What, Not Why

There is no attempt to determine the reason WHY you are motivated to do what you do, or to understand the causes of your motivation. The recurring themes in Shane's pattern describe the kinds of behavior and performance that can be expected from him. The assessment does not explore why Shane likes to work independently, why he is interested in invertebrates, or why he is so motivated to discover new things. It does not seek to explain or ascribe psychological causation. This focus on action as contrasted to psychological issues makes the process more acceptable and enjoyable for participants. They feel affirmed by the attention given to their achievements and frequently report an increase in their self-confidence as they become more able to articulate the nature of their talents.

In summary, Motivational Patterns appear early in your life; they are irrepressible and predictive of future activities. There is a "deepening of interests" but the basic themes endure like the main trunk on a tree. There is no attempt to get at your underlying psychological make-up. Your pattern deals with WHAT you are motivated to do.

THE POWER IN THE PATTERN

Achievement data provides evidence on which to base job/career decisions.

We need to consider the implications of our patterns for decisions about job-fit and career direction. For example, let's review Shane's Motivational Pattern in terms of "match" to possible career situations.

Shane was working on a research project in a biomedical laboratory. His performance had been outstanding on his research responsibilities. In many R&D organizations, such an employee is likely to be promoted to supervise other researchers. Knowing that Shane is truly "motivated" to work as an individualist in physiology research, is this the best decision for:

✧   The employee?

✧   The organization?

✧   Those employees who now report to their new supervisor?

Rather than offering subjective guesses as answers to these questions, we can look at Shane's achievement data for evidence on which to base our decision.

Is This the "Best Fit" Decision for the Employee?

This employee is motivated to discover new knowledge about animate objects by independently analyzing and experimenting. There is no indication of motivation to work with or through others or to coach and monitor the work of others. There is no indication of interest in issues of an administrative nature. The new supervisory role, if performed effectively, could remove the employee from the work he most enjoys doing and does well, the work he is most "motivated" to do. Not only his productivity and creativity would suffer, but his sense of fulfillment and eventually self-esteem would be impacted.

Is This the "Best Fit" Decision for the Organization?

Probably the organization will lose an outstanding researcher and gain a supervisor who is not motivated to do the work of supervision, not motivated to confront poor performance, to coach, to arrange for resources for others, to advocate their ideas, or to leverage their talents. The employer will likely be paying more but getting less in terms of overall contribution. And, most importantly, the organization will lose the opportunity to develop a truly motivated researcher.

Is This the "Best Fit" Decision for Employees Who Report to This Supervisor?

As employee surveys repeatedly show, supervisors who are not motivated to do the work of supervision get very low scores from their employees. At worst, these mismatched supervisors compete with their employees for the best assignments or micromanage the work of others. At best, they are mediocre supervisors and contribute little leadership in addressing the complex tasks of managing today's diverse workforce in a highly competitive environment.

THE REAL REASON FOR THE "PETER PRINCIPLE"

Most people are familiar with concept of the "Peter Principle," which simply stated, says that everyone is eventually promoted to a level of incompetence. In most of these situations, the poor performance is not because the person has reached a "level" of incompetence. The performance is poor because **the nature of the work is no longer a good "fit" for the individual.** Most of us can think of many of these "Peter Principle" situations that are really examples of poor "fit." For example, remember:

- ✧ The outstanding teacher who was promoted to school principal and was a disaster in her new role, overspending the budget and alienating the school board?

- ✧ The caring, thoughtful nurse who, as the nurse manager, simply could not confront the poor performance of her colleagues?

- ✧ The pioneering scientist who could not make a decision as the laboratory manager?

- ✧ The successful dentist who could not get along with his colleagues in their new venture where he now served as office manager?

In my own experience, I have found that individuals who are in mismatch jobs/careers are most vulnerable to layoffs. During the period of heavy corporate downsizing that began in the mid-1980's, I was often contracted to provide outplacement counseling for employees who were being terminated. Almost all of the participants in these outplacement workshops were currently in a mismatch situation. Because their performance was not competitive, they were the most vulnerable to layoff. It was a sobering realization for all who were present, including me.

DOING WHAT YOU ARE DESIGNED TO DO

Most individuals are only partially aware of the presence of innate motivators; even fewer are aware of the influence these motivators exert on their behavior and performance in both their careers and their lives. They may recognize that it is more difficult to get up in the morning when they have certain duties to perform. They may notice a great surge of excitement when they finish a project or get a letter of commendation. But few people can accurately describe in the necessary detail the kind of work situation that best "fits" their talents. Even fewer recognize how central their Motivational Pattern is to their feelings of self-worth, self-esteem and their overall feeling of fulfillment in their lives. They simply do not realize they possess innate "intentionality," meaning *intending to do something.* [47] This is the potentiality by which the acorn becomes the oak or each of us becomes who he or she truly is.

The concept of an "innateness" that energizes and orients one's behavior is hardly a new idea. Classical humanism voiced an understanding of life that has been lost to recent times:

> *The concept of this individualized "soul-image" has a long and complicated history; its appearance in cultures is diverse and widespread and the names for it are legion . . . image, character, fate, genius, calling, daimon, soul, destiny, pattern. Only our contemporary psychology and psychiatry omit it from their textbooks. The study and therapy of the psyche in our society ignore this factor that other cultures regard as the kernel of character.*

David Norton [48]

Most people think of these Motivational Patterns only as something each of us have, but they are not fully aware that these patterns also form an important part of who we are. Maslow [49] described motivation as desire for *self-actualization, a need to discover one's potentialities and limitations through intense activity and experience.* We want to be understood, known, and appreciated as the person who possesses these unique and specific abilities.

It boils down to this: If I am not able to express, use, display, and generally activate my Motivational Pattern, I will suffer greatly. As a person, I will feel diminished. My self-esteem will suffer and I will "beat up on myself" for being unable to perform and meet expectations in roles that are not a good "fit" for me. If I stray too far from situations that utilize my unique pattern, my own being will be emptied. In addition, blocked instinctual powers within me will turn into resentment, self-hatred, hostility and aggression.

The process of bringing one's potentialities into action is the central dynamic and need of life. It takes real courage to *know thyself and become who you are.*

Chapter 4. Why We Run Out of "Motivational Gas"

One more time: how do we motivate employees? Not by improving work conditions, raising salaries or shuffling tasks.

Frederick Herzberg

IS THERE AN EXPLANATION FOR LAZINESS?

One of the frequent questions that people ask when they learn about innate motivation is: *If these innate motivations are so powerful that they orient and direct our behavior at all times, why then do so many people appear to be "unmotivated" or lacking in motivation? And that probably includes almost everyone at some period in his life!*

Harold asked me this question as he left the room following a two-day workshop. I had noticed that he looked perplexed at times during the session. But even when prompted, he was not forthcoming with whatever was on his mind. I also noticed that he was very absorbed in his new hand-held computer.

Harold is a civil engineer and at the time headed a group of about 25 engineers to form the Facilities Engineering function for a large organization with several facilities. When I started to respond to Harold's question, he continued his comment by disclosing that he was really talking about himself. He told me that he had been in his current position of Facilities Manager for about 10 years. During this time, but not before, he had been treated for depression several times. Recently, he had been diagnosed as having Attention Deficit Disorder (ADD).

To further introduce Harold to you, I am going to share some descriptions of his life/work achievements, so you, too, can better understand the nature of activities that Harold reported as having been satisfying and enjoyable throughout his work/life. As you read Harold's achievements, look for evidence that would help to explain his lack of performance in his current role as Facilities Manager.

Harold's Achievements

Childhood:

"I was very good at basketball. Practiced continuously to improve various shots; beat my brothers two on one, well known at school for my short shots and dribbling. Proud of being able to shoot left-handed even though I am naturally right-handed.

Age 12-15:

"Loved fishing. Learned how to fly-fish and took the time to teach myself how to tie flies. Spent many hours in the library researching fishing techniques and finding new ways to tie flies. The flies were nearly perfect.

Age 21-24:

"Maintained, without any training, an Austin Farina sedan. Rebuilt engine, transmission, carburetors, brakes, etc. Spent time in library researching details and teaching myself about the combustion engine. Spent many hours finding junkyard parts. It was a finely tuned machine when I got through.

Adult:

"Bought a house while I was getting my Master's Degree. I designed and landscaped the yard, built a raised deck, patio, garden. It was beautiful . . . not a stone left unturned.

Adult:

"Built a cradle from a design . . . then designed and built three large dressers. Learned many wood working techniques and how to use the industrial size machines in the company wood shop. Learned how to sharpen the planer blades myself because they were always dull.

Adult:

" I was in charge of remodeling kitchens in Family Housing. I developed a plan that allowed construction to occur in occupied housing units. Made many unique design elements and turned it into a very functional and easily maintained kitchen.

Adult:

"When the volcano near the base where I was stationed erupted, I took action to establish a support system for evacuees. Was the representative in the logistics center, identified roofs subject to failure, moved people in danger and established damage assessment and reporting after the eruption. I had it all under control in a very short time."

Now compare Harold's motivations with Harold's role as Facilities Manager:

Harold is motivated to master a skill or a subject; to perfect a system, method or process. He goes after all the rough edges and wants complete domination of a technique and control over all the variables. He is motivated to work with tangible subject matter: materials, structures, design, logistics, and methods. He wants to be able to secure results through his own efforts, or to control others in precise ways by devising a plan of action for them to follow and then feeding them into the plan. He relies on the medium of the plan as opposed to personal direction for influencing others.

There are some aspects of Harold's job as Facilities Manager that sound like a good "fit" (structuring activity, defining the tasks to be done, some civil engineering), but there are several critical requirements of the role that are not in Harold's pattern. Harold has not given any evidence of motivation for

✧   Overseeing others by actively managing their talents, influencing others, including convincing, persuading, confronting, coaching, monitoring, communicating, negotiating.

✧   Working with people, both individually and in groups.

✧   Working with budgets.

✧   Long-term strategic planning.

Like many people with similar limitations who find themselves in mismatch situations, Harold did not act to correct the situation. He, like many others, felt constrained by other circumstances. (In Harold's case, his wife was adamant about his staying in the management role and "making it work.")

But Harold just couldn't make it work. The gap between what Harold is motivated to do and the critical requirements of his job was just too wide and too deep to transcend. Therefore, Harold simply performed less and less of his job. He became more and more depressed and dysfunctional. His interactions with his peers and with management turned from positive to negative, as everyone became disillusioned with Harold's performance. Harold felt like everything he did seemed to be wrong—so the less he did, the easier his life became. Gradually, he became so disconnected from his management role that his manager came screaming into his office and insisted that he avail himself of the company's Employee Assistance Program. The EAP counselor provided the diagnosis of Attention Deficit Disorder. (After watching Harold's fascination with his hand-held computer, I seriously question that diagnosis.)

After understanding his need to master and perfect a skill or system, Harold decided to approach his management. Using examples from his achievement data to illustrate his points, he was able to explain to his management WHY he was not performing in his current role. Harold was transferred to an emergency-planning project where he was responsible for implementing high-level emergency evacuation procedures. A recent check on his progress found a very contented and productive employee. He told me that the change in his mental attitude and sex life had even convinced his wife that management wasn't for him!

Beatrice, the Human Resources Administrator

Beatrice is another interesting example of the powerful negative impact of mismatch to one's job/career. Beatrice is middle-aged and worked as a human resources administrator for a large organization. She had been in this same role for about fifteen years. When I met her in a career workshop, she appeared to be very shy and would not look at me (or others) when she spoke.

Beatrice had provided only very sketchy written data prior to the workshop. But the achievements she listed from the early part of her life were quite adventurous. To get more detail about how she had become involved and exactly what role she played, I interviewed her during a break in the workshop.

Beatrice's Achievements:

Age 19: "Moved to Pakistan."

Age 20: "Learned to belly dance."

Age 23: "Moved to the Philippines."

Age 29: "Moved to Northern Ireland."

Age 30: "Helped to get a review for a person on death row—we were successful—he was released."

I asked Beatrice to tell me what I would have seen her doing in these achievements. She talked about caring for sick children in one country, picking them up off the street and taking them to a shelter, getting food and medical care for them. She talked about caring for very young pregnant girls in another situation, providing counseling and encouragement as their tiny bodies grew. As Beatrice talked about her work, she began to look at me. Her eyes became intense, her voice forceful and her expressions animated.

While all achievement data is unique, Beatrice's achievements do get one's attention, especially because a person who appeared to be so shy described these achievements. I asked Beatrice how she got involved in each of these achievements; she said that all of her travels and adventures had been with a cousin. And then her cousin got married and Beatrice was on her own.

She came back to the mainland and took the job in human resources, thinking that at least it would be a "people-related" job. She was wrong. It was a paper-pushing job; she rarely talked to anyone. She disliked the job from the beginning but she was self-supporting and had a health problem that impacted her ability to get insurance. She said she really missed her cousin's direction and decisiveness. She also said she watched her confidence erode with the monotony of each day's routine. As she put it, *I totally lost my nerve to do anything to get myself out of the situation.*

As her story unfolded, Beatrice became very emotional. It had been a long time since she had even thought about who she really was. She had devoted her energy to trying to be what she wasn't. Finally, she had "emptied her tank." There was nothing she could give and so she gave nothing. She spent her days looking out the window at the flower garden.

I found out later that Beatrice had been "sent" to the workshop because her performance had fallen below an acceptable level. Luckily, her supervisor was concerned about her and suspected there was more to this situation than met the eye. (The supervisor later told me that his interest in Beatrice had been triggered by her near "genius" level score on an assessment instrument that HR administrators were asked to take as "guinea pigs.") When Beatrice shared the nature of her mismatch situation, her supervisor arranged a transfer to a community outreach project sponsored by the organization. About a year later, I picked up the company newsletter and found her picture on the front page. She was ushering an elderly couple into their newly repaired and painted home—and she was the recipient of the annual "Best Performer in HR" award!

So how do talented and ambitious people like Harold and Beatrice get so far off-track? What happens to their powerful innate motivation that orients and directs their behavior? Based on my discussions with hundreds of people in all walks of life, I offer the following observations:

People are not "motivated" if they are in situations that do not engage the essence of their innate motivations. They may be able to perform at some level for a period of time, but if they remain in such a situation, they risk eventually becoming "unmotivated." They find themselves not only unable to sustain their performance on the "poor fit" tasks, but also unwilling to take any action to rectify the situation. If they remain in the mismatch situation, some will descend even further into what appears to be a doldrums-like state-of-mind.

WHY SOME PEOPLE STAY IN MISMATCH SITUATIONS

When our activity does not provide sufficient fulfillment or rewards to fill our motivational gas tank, we literally *run out of gas*. Some people, like Harold and Beatrice, simply "stop in their tracks." Others continue at low levels of performance but seek escape in other ways, especially by participating in sports and hobbies. The reasons why some individuals remain almost permanently "stuck" appear more complicated. Again, some observations:

1. They may have tried to perform, sometimes in several different roles, but they have only experienced failure, negative results and rejection. They simply do not want to go through it all again, so it is easier to do nothing than to risk doing something else that, for whatever reason, probably will not work out.

2. They may be "paralyzed" by conflicting criteria (i.e., finding a job that is good money vs. doing something that they really like to do).

3. There are strong external forces that constrain their options. They feel like they absolutely have no choice but to keep this job so they can support the family in the style to which they have become accustomed. They need to live in a certain geographic location because their family is there. Knowledge workers are also especially vulnerable to "golden handcuffs," those retirement benefits that keep us shackled to our long-term employers.

4. They may have never been in a role that they enjoyed doing and felt they did well. Their self-confidence is so damaged that they don't even think about a better "fit" scenario. Like the individuals who have been in a mismatch role for an extended period, they lose sight and understanding of what does motivate them.

5. They have placed the blame for their problems on some other aspects of their situation. They may feel it is a problem with co-workers, their boss, their spouse, or the company in general. Because they have not identified the correct reason for their difficulties, they are not able to address and solve the real problem. They become cynical, discouraged and unmotivated when they are not able to change their situation.

Like the proverbial lobster that doesn't notice that the water is heating up, many individuals stay in their mismatch situations until they are no longer able to initiate a move.

The motivational uniqueness of individuals who become trapped provides some insight into why these individuals tolerate the gradual breakdown. Many individuals who end up "unmotivated" are strongly motivated to meet the needs and requirements of a situation; thus, they will keep on trying until they literally "spit blood." In my years of preparing Motivational Patterns for individuals who seem to be "stuck," I have noted most of these individuals were NOT motivated to:

❖ Initiate change.

❖ Confront others.

❖ Plan strategically.

❖ Set goals and develop action items.

❖ Assess the risks of change (i.e., they are fearful of the change but fail to accurately assess the risk of not changing).

The good news is that all of these limitations can be remedied. For example, basic goal-setting programs can be life-changing experiences for these individuals.

Eventually, individuals in mismatch situations also share another characteristic: low self-esteem. When we are in a role that does not fit us, we are unable to fully demonstrate the strengths that are important to our self-concept; thus we are not going to receive confirmation and respect for being who we really are. In fact, we are really being observed as we perform activities that we are not motivated to perform. We also lose the opportunity for feedback and recognition for using talents that are central to how we see ourselves.

CAN THIS HAPPEN TO YOU?

While no one seems to be exempt from self-esteem problems, it has been my observation that high-achieving knowledge workers are more impacted by this phenomenon. They have strong track records of being able to do almost anything they set their minds to do; they are accustomed to achieving at top levels. Then, if they find themselves in a situation in which they cannot achieve or sustain the top performance, they start to "beat up" on themselves for not being able to make this an achieving situation. They start to think: *What's wrong with me? Why can't I make this work?* They have never experienced this kind of failure before and it is often devastating.

I first encountered this phenomenon when a prestigious research lab asked me to work with their engineers and scientists who were ranked in the bottom quartile of performance. This organization hired only the top graduates from top-level schools, thus it was a traumatic experience for those who found themselves in the bottom quartile. As I interviewed each of them, I was struck by how demoralized and cynical they were. Were these the same recruits the organization wined and dined just a few short years ago because they really had the "right stuff?" What had happened to these men and women to render such dramatic changes in such a short period of time?

After doing interviews and preparing an analysis for each person, I began to see a common theme: Many of these individuals were highly motivated by situations that provided clear requirements and expectations as well as measurable results that defined the level of their success. Given these criteria, their college courses were a great "fit." Structured subject matter, textbook problems, tests with grades, grades for each course, overall GPA, etc. were present in their academic "work environment." Then they moved to the research environment and worked with managers, many who were not motivated to provide structure and definition. They worked on research projects that were quite unstructured and fluid. The subject matter was often more conceptual, abstract and less defined than their course work. There were few measures by which to establish the level of their achievement, except the dreaded performance ranking that put them at the bottom of the heap. No wonder they were demoralized and cynical! (We were able to revive some simply by putting them to work with managers who were "motivated" to provide structure and recognition; others were reassigned to better "fit" roles.)

High achievers often find their self-esteem dramatically impacted by job/career mismatch.

The next time you are tempted to say that someone is "lazy," think again! Perhaps "unmotivated in their current situation" is a more descriptive term. At least this approach prompts a different course of action—one of seeking understanding and solution as opposed to rendering judgment.

SECTION C.
UNDERSTANDING INNATE MOTIVATION

Chapter 1. The Nature vs. Nurture Controversy

I am not developing...I am.

Pablo Picasso

"INHERITED BIOLOGY" VS. "PERSONAL BIOGRAPHY"

The idea that nature in any way determines the potentiality of an individual has not been a popular concept. Scientists send shock waves through the culture whenever their new theories of what is biologically inherited (as opposed to socially learned) confronts the popularized ideas about the self.

Many people still prefer to believe that they are born with blank slates and are purely the products of their environment. They want to believe that they can remake themselves into anything they want. Even when their attempts repeatedly fail or when they find no fulfillment or satisfaction from performing the role they once passionately desired, they still tell themselves that they can do this if they try hard enough.

The work of Carl Jung, [50] noted psychologist, has long recognized both our "inherited biology" and our "personal biography." According to Jung, our inherited biology contains the instinctual system of our species. We are governed and determined by this inherited biology; it has permanent features and is the ultimate shaper of our talents and lives. It also contains fundamental processes that have remained constant and universal throughout history and humankind's occupation of the earth. In computer language, this inherited biology could be thought of as our "hard-wired" part.

On the other hand, our personal biography, which could be called our "software," programs us via our life experiences, the beliefs, assumptions and myths of our culture.

More recently, the emerging science of molecular biology is telling us that genes are the single most important factor that distinguishes one person from another. The latest research in genetics, molecular biology and neuroscience provides compelling evidence that many core personality traits are inherited, and that many of the differences between personalities are the result of difference in genes. One researcher put it this way: *We come, in large part, ready-made from the factory.* [51]

Probably some of the most definitive research on the influence of Nature vs. Nurture is the research on twins. Some of the most well known examples include:

✧   University of Minnesota (more than 8,000 pairs).

✧   Virginia Commonwealth University (15,000 twin pairs plus their siblings).

✧   Veterans Administration (all twins who served in World War II and Vietnam).

✧   Pennsylvania State University (Black Elderly Twin Study).

In addition, there are major twin registries in Kansas, California and Kentucky and smaller ones all over the country. In Holland, Denmark, Sweden, Norway, Finland and Australia, nearly every twin in the country has been identified.

Lawrence Wright, author of *Twins and What They Tell Us About Who We Are*, summarizes the outcome of these research findings:

> *The genetic idea has had a tumultuous passage through the 20th Century, but the prevailing view of human nature at the end of the century resembles in many ways the view we had at the beginning. That is that people are largely responsible for their station in life, and that circumstances do not so much dictate the outcome of a person's life as they reflect the inner nature of a person living it. Twins have been used to prove a point, and the point is that we don't become. We are.* [52]

While each study offers volumes of data, the general conclusion from the research on twins is that:

✧   Identical twins reared apart turn out to be about as much alike on most measurements of personality, interests and intelligence as twins reared together and

✧   Genetically-unrelated siblings who are raised in the same family will turn out to be more like their biological parents than their adopted ones.

These findings challenge deeply held philosophical, political and religious ideals. Some people still refuse to believe it. In fact, Wright says *the bitterness over the battle of twin studies has rarely been matched in the history of academic warfare. It just didn't seem possible that two people who had never met could be as similar as two people raised as brothers or sisters in the same home.* [53] But the evidence was strong and based on very large numbers. It showed that genes not only help determine how we look, but how we act, feel and experience life. Genetic differences cause individuals to respond differently to similar rearing conditions. (*Behavioral geneticists joke that people with one child are believers in the "nurture" or environmental concept; those who have raised more than one child are "nature" or genetic advocates.)* [54] Even young children are genetically programmed to create certain experiences for themselves:

> *We propose that development is indeed the result of nature and nurture, but that genes drive experience. Genes are components in a system that organizes the organism to experience the world.* [55]

Like most controversies, this is not an either-or situation. The genes are not fixed instructions. Indeed, as Hamer [56] points out, *the key is the interplay between the hardware we are born with and the software we add. It's not nature or nurture, it's nature AND nurture. While all the wiring is present when we are born, not all of it is switched on.* Therein lies the critical role of nurture, especially in the very early years of childhood. The knowledge of one's nature must be used to create more effective nurture. By learning more about our nature, we can select and design "nurture" that is going to have more lasting and positive impact.

CONFLICTS WITH OTHER MOTIVATIONAL THEORIES

Twentieth Century investigators began to acknowledge that each animal species, including humankind, inherits a preparedness to learn and perform particular behaviors. But the impact of Freud was still felt deep and wide in the schools of psychology and psychiatry. Motivations were generally attributed to conflicts over sexuality, acquired in the family over the first decade of life.

Behaviorist theories (Ivan Pavlov, B. F. Skinner) came under more scrutiny as studies of the child's acquisition of intellectual talents revealed *that reward and punishment were unable, alone, to account for either the time of emergence or the substantial variation in language, memory and thought.* [57] But, nevertheless, the concept of behavior modification was more in keeping with what people wanted to believe. This theory supported their idea that *you could do anything you wanted to do if you worked hard enough.*

The battle is still being fought. For example, large organizations typically identify a set of "competencies" determined as necessary in order for the organization to be successful. Employees must demonstrate these "core competencies" in order to be "valued" by the organization. Much time, money and effort is expended in identifying, describing and communicating these core competencies. Many organizations use these competencies as "yardsticks" for measuring employee's performance and development. Thus, much like Pavlov's dogs or Skinner's children, employees are expected to develop these highly-valued competencies. **Competencies have become the "golden rules" in today's organization change and career management systems.**

Chapter 2. Innate Motives: The Core of Competencies

David McClelland's research [58] on motives has helped to integrate the concept of innate motivation with contemporary developmental psychology. He recognized the foundational role of "motives" and described their critical relationship to competencies. McClelland developed a graphic useful in illustrating the profound nature of "motives." (See Figure A)

Figure A

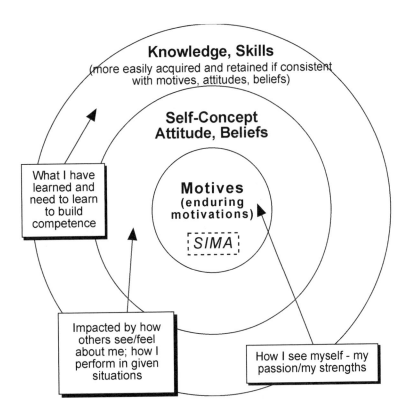

McClelland identified "enduring motivations" or "motives" at the core of one's competencies. These appear early in life and seem to endure throughout our lives. Motives are the basis of our passions for various kinds of work activities . . . art, writing, researching, mechanical interests, working alone, working with others, etc. Motives also form the purpose of our efforts, e.g., helping others, winning, gaining recognition, completing a goal, or overcoming difficulties. McClelland said that motives are *intrinsic self-starting master traits that predict what people will do in their work, long-term, without close supervision.*

In other words, a competency requires that the individual must have an innate motivation to perform this competency. Competencies are built upon innate motivations.

In the second ring of McClelland's competency model are Self-Concept, Attitudes and Beliefs. These are formed by the feedback we get from others and the cultures in which we live. For example, if a young man is highly artistic but grows up in an athletically focused home, he may feel differently about his talents than a peer who is admired and supported in his artistic efforts. McClelland pointed out that Self-Concept, Attitudes and Beliefs can be changed, but it does take awareness and consistent effort. Self-Concept, Attitudes and Beliefs can impact how we express our intrinsic motives.

Knowledge and Skills comprise the outer ring in McClelland's model, representing what he believed were the most readily learned aspects of competencies. But he also pointed out that Knowledge and Skills will be most readily acquired and retained if they correspond to the foundational motives as well as to one's Self-Concept, Attitude and Beliefs. For example, if one has natural motivation for music, piano lessons will produce more lasting competency to play the piano. There will then be more passion for learning this skill. There will be more interest in practicing and more willingness to sustain the necessary effort. On the other hand, learning and fulfillment are dramatically reduced if there is no corresponding motive to perform the task.

Knowledge and Skill can predict what someone CAN do, not what he or she WILL do. To learn more about what a person will do, we need to examine his achievement data to understand more about his motives—his Motivational Pattern.

Chapter 3. Is Money a Motivator?

By now we ought to face the troubling fact that manipulating behavior by offering reinforcements may be a sound approach for training the family pet, but not for bringing quality to the workplace.

Alfie Kohn

WILL WORKERS PRODUCE MORE IF THEY ARE PAID MORE?

This is a long-debated question, but the unprecedented compensation packages so prevalent in the current "war for talent" make the topic a suddenly urgent issue. In

1962, prominent industrial psychologist Frederick Herzberg presented the concept that money is NOT a motivator, but it can be a "dissatisfier." That is, in itself, money is not an incentive for performance. But, according to Herzberg, if employees perceive inequities or unfairness in their compensation, then the money-related issue could create dissatisfaction and thus reduce productivity. [59] Industrial Age management bought the concept and for many years, compensation systems sought to establish at least the image of equality with across-the-board and seniority salary increases for respective employee populations.

Beginning in the mid 1980's, global competition created a scurry of re-engineering and focus on cost-cutting efficiencies. Massive downsizing in major organizations was accompanied by new philosophies for compensation. In most organizations, a "pay for performance" approach provided compensation increases only for gains in individual productivity. It was a concept taken from sales and production functions where workers' productivity could be more readily quantified. Many organizations with knowledge workers continue to struggle to establish criteria for measuring their workers' individual contributions, making it difficult to determine whether the "pay for performance" approach is equally effective with different employee populations. Indeed, noted authorities on the subject don't mince words about its shortcomings:

✧ Alfie Kohn, noted critic of rewards and incentives, says the bottom line is that any approach that offers a reward for better performance is destined to be ineffective. [60]

✧ W. Edwards Deming, legendary statistical consultant, called the system by which merit is appraised and rewarded *the most powerful inhibitor to quality and productivity in the Western world.* [61]

But keen competition for top talent makes this a critical question. Money (in many forms) is used to both attract and attempt to retain employees, as well as to stimulate performance. But will financial incentives get people to do more of what they are doing? Will they do it better, more creatively? Can you buy imaginative thinking about how to solve problems that didn't exist yesterday? If you lure employees to your organization with money, will they stay—or will they be constantly on the lookout for more money elsewhere?

As early as 1962, David McClelland [62] had published reports from research studies showing that offering monetary rewards to individuals who were intrinsically high in achievement motivation did not increase their striving. In fact, introducing *extrinsic* incentives to people who were *intrinsically* motivated for achievement may have caused them to work less hard. However, McClelland also acknowledged that some research studies had demonstrated that subjects with a strong achievement motivation want a more difficult achievement to be recognized by a larger monetary reward. This was not true of subjects with a weaker achievement motivation. That is, subjects higher in achievement motivation tend to see money as a measure of success, rather than as an incentive.

McClelland also reported that money can be the means to the end. Money makes it possible for many individuals to get whatever it is that is motivating to them. They learn that the possession of money is the means of gratifying many different needs and that the lack of money may mean bearing many uncomfortable situations, such as living in a low rent district or inability to fund college for your children. McClelland believed that with the number of different drives supporting the need for money, it would be a rare occasion when the individual would be without any motivation to activate his or her need for money.

DIFFERENT STROKES FOR DIFFERENT FOLKS

Much like the extensive research of W. Edwards Deming and Alfie Kohn, examination of achievement data from thousands of individuals challenges the conclusion that everyone can be motivated in some way by money. In one People Management International LLC study, approximately 1200 Motivational Patterns of knowledge workers were analyzed and tallied. [63] Only about 30% of the population studied showed evidence that money was a motivator. As you read through the achievement data in the different case studies in this book, notice how many knowledge workers do NOT mention money in the descriptions of their achievements. An excellent example is Shane, the researcher, whose achievement data is used as an example is several situations.

In another People Management International LLC study [64] the Motivational Patterns of 453 upper and mid-level managers at a large hi-tech manufacturing company were prepared by certified SIMA® analysts. In that management population, the evidence for money as a motivator appeared as follows:

Money as a Subject Matter	12%
Money as Profitability, Gain	7%

By contrast, other outcomes were considerably more prevalent for this managerial population:

Growth Potential	33%
Overall Effectiveness	36%
Efficiency	18%

In this case, the lack of interest in (and attention to) financial matters led to overspending and mismanagement that eventually resulted in a buyout from a competitor. However, it is not uncommon to find similar data in other engineering and scientific management personnel. The individuals who are promoted to managerial positions are generally those who have done outstanding technical work and are less motivated by financial issues. This, of course, creates problems for many such organizations, just as it did for the hi-tech manufacturer.

IS THERE EVIDENCE THAT MONEY IS A MOTIVATOR?

When we look for "evidence" of motivation for money in achievement data, we can find it in these arenas:

✧ Money as a Measure for Comparing Success of One's Performance.

✧ Money as a Material Object to Acquire, Possess, Exercise Ownership.

✧ Money as a Subject Matter (the person enjoys working with money itself).

✧ Money as a Measure of Profitability, Gain Involved or Entrepreneurial Activity.

Let's look at some examples of each of these ways that money can be a motivator.

Money as a Measure for Comparing Success of One's Performance:

Comparing their personal performance to the performance of others motivates many knowledge workers. They may be motivated to surpass the requirements of their work. They want to excel at, or at the very least, do their best as they exceed the performance or expectations of others. They may be motivated to distinguish themselves from others by displaying some distinctive talent. They look for the contrasts they can create with other people.

Money is a very quantifiable measure with which to establish excellence or uniqueness. The things that money, especially unprecedented large amounts of money, can buy are also very useful in distinguishing oneself from others.

Tony's achievements reflect his motivation for money as a means of demonstrating excellence:

"Sold books—remember two things—I sold and I made money—sold 50 to 100 books at $4 to $5 each. No one else in the class even came close to the amount that I made.

"Worked at the supermarket carrying out groceries—hated the job but found out that I could even earn tips with extra effort and smiles. No one else was getting a dime!

"Had a super time at my class reunion—only one driving a Porsche—and wearing a Rolex. Talk about a kick!

"Got the system implemented on target—worked days and nights. Management rewarded me with a bonus that was out of sight."

Money as a Material Object to Acquire, Possess, Exercise Ownership:

The nature of this motivation is expressed through efforts to acquire what you want and to exercise ownership or control over what is yours. If this is your motivation, your goal may be to gain money, a position, status, specific material goods, skills, knowledge or even a family. Your greatest satisfaction and sense of achievement comes when you are able to get what you are after.

There might be a competitive side to your nature. Perhaps you thrive in an environment where others value and seek the positions to which you aspire. Your success in acquiring them may give you a sense that the position you occupy, the responsibilities you possess, the results you obtain or the things you own in some way establish or reflect your personal merit.

Your success might be founded on a special wisdom in financial matters, a nose for profit-making opportunities, or skill at clever bargaining or negotiating. Acquiring money may also come as a result of dogged determination and hard work.

Andre's achievements illustrate money as a motivator in Acquiring, Possessing, Exercising Ownership.

"Collected comic books—went to all the stores who sold them—went to flea markets—traded with my friends. Talked my mother into buying metal storage cabinets to store them. Never let my friends read them, though. My collection is worth a great deal of money—I have had several assessors tell me that.

"Got interested in antique dishes . . . especially pink depression glass. Found out that some designs were extremely valuable. Looked in many, many antique stores and bought very selectively. Had about 100 items when I was offered a very large amount for my entire collection. I sold it because I think the value of these dishes will diminish when the Depression generations have passed on.

"Didn't have a lot of extra cash to invest but wanted to learn about the stock market—so I created a paper portfolio and calculated the impact of my "buys" and "sells" over a year's period. Convinced my husband that I really had the expertise to do it for real!

"Got promoted to division manager—25% salary increase plus bonus incentive. Have oversight of both marketing and sales. Means putting in many more hours but I love my job . . . and the bucks."

Money as a Subject Matter:

Some people are simply interested in activities that involve dealing with money in some way. Dollars and cents issues and money matters interest them. Investing corporate funds or their own money may be some ways in which they express their motivation. Or perhaps they are interested in budgetary planning and management or in accounting procedures. Negotiating wage or price agreements or credit terms might be an outlet for their interest in money matters. In any case, their achievements reveal that money is an important concern for them.

Excerpts from Nancy's Achievement Data show money as a subject matter:

"In a 2 1/2 month period, working part-time and with a capital investment of less than $5, I was able to generate $3,000 needed to pay off a loan.

"Always did all fund raising and financing for the Jr-Sr Dance—organized magazine sales campaigns—was in charge of running the school store and concessions—we ended up with loads of money.

"Discovered mutual funds—did extensive study of best ones—recognized value of compound growth of invested dollars. Achieving this insight into financial security made life more fun.

"I did collections—my parents operated a grocery store and gave credit. Losses from credit were excessive. I went after the creditors—there was satisfaction when collections were made and you could see the numbers add up."

Money as a Measure of Profitability, Gain Involved:

Individuals with this motivation want to be involved in endeavors and ventures in which there is an opportunity for them to profit. They like to be in situations where they have a clear opportunity to gain in a material way by investing their money, time or effort or by trading, bartering or making deals. Risk may be exciting to them.

Some examples from Ralph's achievement data reveal an interest in money as a measure of profitability or gain involved:

"I was four years old—recovered 50 cents under the grate of outdoor laundry—it became a regular source of money for us—watched —tried poking sticks—didn't work—figured out how to get underneath.

"Knocked on doors of places that looked like they needed help—talked them into letting me mow their lawns—earned $1.15 one day—thought I was rich.

"Designed logo—started with image—drew 3 designs—got a check for it - $100 more because I asked for a bonus for exceptional quality.

"Debate contest—given envelope with topic—five minutes later discussed—figured out how to answer—talk to people, not at them—Won $1000 award.

"My marketing strategy turned out to be a winner—I documented 40% increase in profits in one year's time—with very limited capital investment."

Money as a Motivator in the New Economy:

According to the Bureau of Labor Statistics (Department of Labor), changing jobs has reached a record high. The average employee changes jobs every three or four years. But for younger people, the numbers are far more dramatic. A 22-year-old college graduate will average more than eight different employers before age 32. That means every 15 months, it's on to a new job!

A survey by Exec-U-Net, a Connecticut career information service, found that the five major motivators for changing jobs are money, personal development (including job "fit"), location, company reputation and job security. In a strong economy where the demand for workers far exceeds the supply, money has become a strong bargaining chip. Unprecedented opportunities for top salaries, stock ownership and bonuses are strong enticements, especially for the younger workers. They may feel as though they can do anything for 10 to 15 years, while cashing in on the big bucks. Then, by the time they are 30-35 years old, they will be financially prepared to do what they really want to do with their lives.

Some knowledge workers have reported such dismal success in finding and keeping a good "fit" situation that they have decided they might as well be working for the big bucks because they do not find their work satisfying anyway. They also report frequent reorganizations, overwork, unqualified management, continuous travel, and other factors that detract from their work satisfaction. (Remember, Herzberg said that extrinsic or external motivators become more important when intrinsic or internal motivators are not fulfilled.) [65]

But if you are tempted by monetary enticements, think carefully about the associated risks: If your work is not a good "fit" for you, and if money is truly not a motivator for you (and it is not for about 2/3 of the knowledge-worker population), you are facing years of stress with potential long-term negative impact on your health. You are also sacrificing the satisfaction and fulfillment that comes with doing work that you are truly motivated to do. You will lose many opportunities and years to develop the performance strengths that are truly motivating for you.

When the supply of talent is less than the demand, employers will tolerate "less than stellar" performance because there are few choices for replacement. But in an economic downturn, individuals who are in mismatch situations and unable to sustain competitive performance will be most vulnerable. The massive layoffs of mid-level managers in the mid-1980's economic crunch are examples of this phenomenon. Organizations took the opportunity to clean house, terminating many individuals with outdated technical skills and less-than-stellar track records as managers. A recession in the dot.com and Internet industry could have similar consequences for those employees who bring the least talent to their jobs.

In an economic downturn, individuals who are in mismatch situations will be most vulnerable.

Bartolome and Evans, researchers who have explored many aspects of career decision-making, found there were four main reasons why individuals found themselves in the wrong job: [66]

✧   The strong attraction of external rewards.

✧   Organizational pressure.

✧   An inability to say "no."

✧   A lack of self-knowledge.

Basically, it all comes down to self-knowledge. **If you don't understand your unique Motivational Pattern, you have no internal criteria for deciding what is right for you.** You are unable to assess the appropriateness and "fit" of any job, role, assignment, organization or career. You are vulnerable to enticements or organizational pressures. You have little basis on which to form enough conviction to say "no" to a seemingly attractive opportunity. You have no rudder; you become the proverbial "cork" in an organizational "whitewater."

PART II
LEVERAGING YOUR PASSION
AND PURPOSE

Section A.
Finding (or Creating) Work That "Fits"

Section B.
Managing Your Career

Section C.
Recognizing the Talents of Others

SECTION A.
FINDING (OR CREATING) WORK THAT "FITS"

Chapter 1. Understanding "Potentiality"

The afternoon knows what the morning never suspected.

Swedish Proverb

HIGH POTENTIAL . . . BUT FOR WHAT?

The ultimate challenge in managing our careers (and our lives) is to understand the true nature of our "potentiality." (Funk and Wagnall's Standard College Dictionary defines *potentiality* as "the inherent capacity for development or accomplishment.") **The critical point, frequently not understood, is that potentiality requires time in order to manifest itself. Therefore, potentiality may be present but not currently expressed in a recognizable manner.**

Potentiality is not a new concept. The Greeks used the word *daimon* to describe potentiality, which they termed *the inner will*. According to the Greek philosophy, each person's primary responsibility was to discover the *daimon* within and thereafter to live in accordance with it. One's worth was manifested only by living in accordance with their *daimon*.

The Greeks recognized the power of potentiality, and the concept has occupied philosophers to this day. Modern theater continues to depict the classic encounter, the collision of two forces:

✧　Fate or some variation of the will of the gods

　　and

✧　The force of the human character.

The *hero* is required to demonstrate *undeviating consistency of behavior* deriving from the unity within himself. The hero must be true to himself, for then we know what he will do. [67]

The Greek philosophy of *being true to oneself* recognizes man's freedom, through exercising his choice and will, to deviate from his own true course. But as Western civilization evolved, other philosophies gave different interpretations. The enfranchisement of the individual with the *right* to choose one's destiny became a central issue. In keeping with the political issues of the time, *becoming anything you wanted to be* had much greater appeal than *becoming who you are*, especially if you were a member of a lower caste. The struggle continues to this day as we endeavor to *become* whatever we believe to be more valued. The case of Keith, described below, illustrates that struggle.

CASE STUDY OF CAREER MISMATCH

At a career workshop sponsored by his employer, I met Keith, a 23-year old computer scientist who had worked for about a year in a computing services organization in a very large company. Keith was feeling very bored with his current work as a systems analyst. He thought if he went back to graduate school for an advanced degree in computer science, he would get into more interesting work. He also had been doing a good deal of "extracurricular" activity in his church and professional society and realized there were things that he enjoyed doing a lot more than working with computer systems. Keith provided the following detail about his life/work achievements. As you read about his achievements, ask yourself: What is the nature of Keith's potentiality?

Keith's Achievement Data:

Age 9:

"I saved enough money to buy my mother some Reebok tennis shoes without the help of anyone. My grandfather would always give me money to go to the movies, etc. I would always wish that I could get the kind of gifts for my mother that the grown-ups gave her. So I took the money that my grandfather gave me and bought her a $40 pair of shoes. It felt good to surprise my mom and make her happy."

Young adult:

"I came up with a way to help my friends solve their problems. I specifically listened to their problems, and did not offer advice. I just talked with them. I was the person that everybody called for their problems. Some people called me the resident psychologist. I feel a sense of purpose in helping my friends with life situations. I feel like I am needed and I feel like I am well respected."

Young adult:

"I coordinated a citywide party during Christmas for the United Negro College Fund. I got in touch with the UNCF office to see if they could get a free ballroom from one of the local hotels. They negotiated with a local hotel and got the room free of charge. Then it was up to me to gather enough people at the function to make a considerable amount of money. I asked a couple of friends to help me with the promoting of the party. I also arranged to be interviewed by two of the local radio stations to drum up support. I got one of the local radio station DJ's to DJ the party so that his following would be there. The night of the event we expected maybe 300 to 400 people but over 650 showed up. I enjoyed talking with and communicating my ideas for the party with people. I really enjoyed helping UNCF raise money. I liked being able to coordinate such a large-scale event for such a good cause."

College years:

"I ran for and won the office of President of the largest chapter of the National Society of Computer Engineers. My first priority was to make our chapter more family-like. I felt that there were too many cliques in our chapter. One of the main things I did was to make our general body meeting less businesslike and more fun. I felt if I loosened everyone up we would actually get more business accomplished. I also felt that the executive board, which is composed of 16 members, should have more responsibility with chapter programs. I loved the respect that was given to me as the president. I liked fighting for the people in my organization on campus. I felt like I was everyone's big brother and I had to look out for my little brothers and sisters. This is one of the best things that I have ever done."

Keith's other achievements include:

- ✧ "Gave a seminar to the seniors at my high school on getting scholarships.

- ✧ "Taught a junior achievement economics class. When I did my last day in class, the students told me that I not only taught them about economics, but also about life.

- ✧ "I am one of the first people in my family to graduate from college. I made my mother proud."

Keith's Motivational Pattern and "Potentiality":

All of Keith's achievements describe situations where he has impressed or impacted people, either individually or in groups. In describing all of his achievements, he did NOT mention computer science, data systems, numbers or computer language. He has not mentioned customers, applications, or designs—only people and his ability to influence and impress them. Even though the company may want to invest in additional computer training for him because he has leadership potential, there is no evidence that Keith can sustain sufficient interest in computerized information systems to perform sufficiently well to be promoted to a leadership position. (Note: When I asked Keith why he had chosen computer science as a college major, he said it was because he could then qualify for a NASA scholarship.)

Keith's "potentiality" does not seem to be connected to computers or computer systems. His potentiality is related to his interface with people. He wants to have direct impact and get direct response from them.

Potentialities are difficult to identify empirically; that is, by observing what is happening. Potentialities can only be recognized and observed through viewing behavior retrospectively, and then by inferring that past behavior is predictive of future behavior, a principle with which most psychologists do agree:

> *Past behaviors, not past exposures (e.g., education and experience) are the best predictors of future behaviors. The more long-standing the behavior, the greater its predictive power.* [68]

CASE STUDY OF CAREER "FIT"

To continue this discussion of potentiality and career "fit," let us examine the achievement data of Leo, a computer information systems major with education and experience similar to Keith's. As you read Leo's achievement data, think about the nature of Leo's potentiality and how his achievement data differ from Keith's achievement data.

Leo's Achievement Data:

Childhood:

"I built a wooden coffee table with smoked glass. We got to choose what we wanted to build. The instructor gave us an overview of what would be involved. I began by selecting the type of wood to use. I would assemble some of the pieces with glue and while waiting for the glue to harden, would work on another part of the table. Once all the pieces were assembled, I sanded and applied varnish to the table. I repeated this step three times. Then I applied a coat of linseed oil to the wood. After a day I waxed the table with bees wax and buffed the table. Once all this was done I laid the glass that I had ordered weeks before on the table. I was able to create a finished product that far exceeded my expectations. The table was all the more surprising considering that I made mistakes in the design but was able to correct them and turn one of them into an improvement on the design."

Early adult:

"Wrote a computer application to keep track of expenses for the State University Center for Laser Research. It saved the staff assistant from manually consolidating and reporting hundreds of charges each month. To determine what kind of software to use, I began reading computer magazines and talking to different people. Learning that another department on campus had a somewhat similar application in use, I met with the user to review what they had done. I developed a prototype and periodically met with them on the status of the project. It was absolutely critical that we all had the same understanding of what needed to be accomplished and what the finished product should look like and do."

Leo's other achievements:

❖ "Wrote a computer application to pay and invoice crude oil purchases and sales, and book the appropriate accounting entries. The application redesigned how the crude oil section did their work by combining numerous steps into one.

❖ "Solved the Rubik's cube without taking it apart.

❖ "As Treasurer of the Student Association, financially organized how we were going to take our weeklong trip to San Antonio. We received the funding necessary and the trip became a successful reality."

Leo's Motivational Pattern and "Potentiality":

Leo is motivated to identify a need, design and develop a product and interact with the customer to make sure his product meets their needs. He works with design and detail. He seeks measurable results. He gave specific examples with extensive detail of his work that almost mirrors that which he was expected to do. He also shows some leadership ability that could help him to serve as a successful team leader, mentor or project leader. A career in computer applications could be a rewarding and fulfilling opportunity for Leo to maximize his potentiality.

SQUARE PEG IN A ROUND HOLE?

While Leo's potential appears well matched for his career, Keith has a problem. By reflecting on his work/life achievements, Keith recognized that his true "potentiality" lies with working with individuals and groups around issues that have significant impact on them. The struggle continues for Keith, as he is reluctant to give up a well-paid position with a major organization to pursue a less defined career path. He did make the decision to continue his graduate education in the organizational development field, with the hope that he could eventually apply his computer background in a different arena. He also continues to pursue leadership roles in his church and professional societies, and to work in youth programs as a way to express his passion for working with people and cultural issues.

Keith's plan all sounds logical. He may be able to "integrate" some aspects of his true potentiality into his current career. But there are some very significant trade-offs in Keith's decision to, at least for the present, stay with his career in computer applications. **Keith's decision is very typical of how we try to make ourselves "fit" a role that we desire. We fail to assess the loss of opportunity to realize our true potentiality.**

Why is it so difficult to make these compromises really work for us? Probably the simple explanation is the correct one: We simply are not putty. We cannot change our innate motivation.

In Keith's situation, as well as in many others, he felt leaving his position in a large organization to seek a career that he was still trying to envision was just too risky. **What Keith and others fail to fully assess is the risk of staying in a career that does not really "fit."** This is especially true in a large organization where employees are annually ranked according to their performance contributions. Each year some percentage of the employee population finds themselves part of a "performance improvement planning" process. This is a process to help the employee improve his/her performance and to terminate those individuals whose performance does not meet the established goals. Most of the people in these programs are individuals in "mismatched" jobs/careers. Most "performance improvement" plans do not involve moving the individuals into better "fit" assignments. After all, these individuals have already been identified as low performers, so what supervisor would want them? Most of these employees are eventually terminated. In the last 15 years, Keith's organization has cut its employee population by about 40%, both with large-scale layoffs and aggressive individual performance evaluation systems. There is considerable risk that Keith will not be able to sustain sufficiently competitive performance to maintain his position with this organization.

It is risky to continue in a job/career that does not "fit."

An even more devastating scenario is also quite common: Keith will manage to "hang in there" until he is about 40 or 45. Then, he is really running out of "motivational gas" and it is even more difficult to think about beginning a new career. Besides, he now has a large mortgage, payments on at least two vehicles, and youngsters exploring their college options. You understand the picture, I'm sure, because we all seem to either go through this ourselves or have several acquaintances who fit the scenario. Our society often passes off these situations as "mid-life" crises, but the origins are often in a misguided career choice in the early twenties.

> *Nothing extraordinary is ever accomplished unless the work is performed by an individual who is "motivated" to do that work.*

The most compelling reason for *knowing ourselves and becoming who we are* is the fact that nothing extraordinary is ever accomplished unless the work is performed by an individual who is "motivated" to do that work. This may sound like a wild claim but think about it. Does one really have a chance of sustaining superior performance over the lifetime of a career if he is really not "motivated" to do the work?

In fact, outstanding performance by any employee, in any function, at any level, is directly traceable to the use of certain strengths possessed by the employee. **There is no outstanding performance, no innovation, no major improvement, no bright idea, no important product development, no well-conceived strategy, no sound business decision, and no big sale—unless and until strengths are engaged in the tasks involved.**

Many studies have attempted to provide tangible proof of this claim. The occupation that offers the most conclusive and consistent connection between "giftedness" and success on-the-job is sales. The main reason for this is because the results in sales positions are tangible and quantifiable. Most of us know that people can either sell or they can't. It's very difficult to "learn" and, unlike many other roles we play, it quickly becomes very obvious when it is not our potentiality.

In their book *Competency At Work*, Spencer and Spencer [69] reported:

> *A recent survey of 44 Southeast firms found that superior salespeople (earning an average of $41,777) sold on average $6.7 million and average performers sold on average $3 million. The superior group sold 123% more than the average salespeople, a difference worth not 123% but 8,857% (or 89 times) the average employee salary.* (The Spencers use competencies as a way of differentiating the superior from the average performers. They define competencies as an underlying characteristic of an individual that is causally related to criterion-referenced effective and/or superior performance in a job or situation. Innate motives form the core of the Spencers' definition of competency.)

The Spencers further state that depending on the complexity of a job, the value of one standard deviation of performance above the mean is 19 to 48% of output for non-sales jobs, and 48 to 120% for sales jobs. Thus, a minimum estimate of economic value of superior performance can be calculated by taking these percentages multiplied by the average salary per year for the job. They add that this global estimate approach seriously undervalues jobs that leverage significant revenues or assets.

Employee "giftedness" is the literal lifeblood of any organization. The development and use of one's potentiality is, as Nietzsche tells us, *the true purpose of one's life.* [70] *And what is true for you is also true for your employer, who can attain and sustain a competitive advantage ONLY through employees who are both gifted at their tasks and passionate about securing the results desired.* [71]

Chapter 2. How to Identify Management Potential

According to our polls of 80,000 managers, 30 years of research and in-depth interviewing, being skilled at something does not correlate to being a good manager.

Gallup Organization

DO I HAVE POTENTIAL FOR MANAGEMENT?

This is probably the most frequently asked career-related question, both by individuals who are seeking such a role and by those who are currently occupying the role. Before we look at an example of achievement data for evidence of management potential, assess your own management potential by rating yourself on the following behaviors. Remember that your achievement data should provide EVIDENCE of each of these behaviors if indeed you are "motivated" to perform the respective item. It is not enough to simply believe that a particular item is characteristic of you!

Predicting Your Potential in Management

Directions:

The following "motivated" behaviors are relevant to managerial effectiveness, based on People Management International LLC's analysis of pattern elements and correlation to managerial performance as reported by superiors, peers and direct reports.

Score yourself on a scale of 1 to 5 (with 5 being the highest) on each item.

___ 1. Initiative: I can recognize and act on perceived opportunity before it is obvious to others.

___ 2. Definition and Structure: I am able to operate in the face of ambiguity and fluid circumstances.

___ 3. Depth and Certainty of Fact-Finding/Learning: I do not require exhaustive data/knowledge before acting on a matter.

___ 4. Risky Decision-Making: I am able to make timely, complex and risky decisions.

___ 5. Planning: I am a visionary; I can set a new direction for the organization in the face of other likely possibilities.

___ 6. Confrontation and Accountability: I readily deal with unacceptable performance and hold people accountable for their promises.

___ 7. Perseverance: Somehow I will get the job done.

___ 8. Business Orientation: I am motivationally concerned with bottom-line results and generating profits.

___ 9. People Person: I get involved with people; I am accessible to them. I like to work with others.

___ 10. Influencing: I am able to convince others one way or another. (Give yourself an especially high score if you can negotiate a complex deal without alienation.)

___ 11. Communications: I am able to work the communications systems (formal and informal) to control and disseminate information, and to build and maintain an effective network.

___ 12. Spokesperson: I am generally impressive in presenting and defending an issue/program; I come across well in public arenas.

___ 13. Leads: People follow my direction and leadership.

___ 14. Manages: I am good at running the organization. I get things done through people. I build a compatible team. I focus on established goals and monitor the activity and the results.

Interpretation:

Assuming scrupulous honesty and reasonable self-knowledge, if 4 or above represents competence, consider the management ladder if you scored 50 or higher on the 14 competencies illustrated. To the extent your score is lower than 50, doubt the wisdom of that career direction. Especially question that direction if you scored in the lower numbers on 4, 6, 7, 9 and 14.

Achievement Data for Chris, the Manager

Let's begin our examination of the managerial motivations by reviewing the achievement data of an individual who has performed "successfully" in a management role. (Chris was identified by his superiors, his peers and his direct reports as having successfully performed his management responsibilities.) He has provided evidence of and fulfillment in the "work" of management by reporting achievements that have evidence of "management" motivations.

As you read Chris' achievement data, look for "evidence" that is related to working with and through others and to taking responsibility for the outcome in a situation.

Childhood—Playing Rugby:

"Set out to play rugby at school. I could see certain areas that I could learn fairly quickly—picked those areas—like learning to kick well. Became proficient at kicking. I picked someone that I knew fairly well and we worked together. If you can become proficient, it's a big asset to the team. Watched my friend's strengths and weaknesses. I'd say 'you point out what I'm doing wrong and I'll point out what I see you doing wrong.' We would gather together before the game and say 'They've got international players, they're much stronger than we are . . . but we can control in a certain way' . . . and we would play how we were going to control the game. The most satisfying part was seeing the fruition of it all . . . a lot of fun."

Ages 23-26—Started a Biochemistry Testing Lab:

"Got interested in certain aspects of biochemistry and wanted to try out some novel testing ideas. With a friend, we came up with some unique ideas for testing enzymes. Set up a testing company and had a lot of satisfaction in running all aspects of the business . . . realizing that one had to be economical as well as research and development oriented. We developed a theory together . . . he was stronger theoretically—I'd produce the testing results. We married the two together. Most satisfying to see I could do it . . . face problems, confront somebody, but you can always get around them. One of the most satisfying things was developing this young friend who had the idea . . . he had no education—I talked management into sending him for a master's degree. Got the ideas working and his career launched."

Age 40-47—Developed a Unique Sampling Method and Insisted on Its Successful Use:

"A technical thing I saw could be developed—part of my job was to select technical ideas for development. I had to fight with our own people and with the contractor to get that idea accepted. After the sampling program got going, I put together a presentation and gave it to upper management. Would have been foolish to give up on that idea—satisfaction was pushing that through and seeing that idea implemented."

To help you "add up" the evidence in Chris' achievement data, we have selected some key words and phrases that are relevant to management motivation. To emphasize the interrelationships within the components of the Motivational Pattern, the evidence is presented for each of the five parts:

Evidence	*Theme*
MOTIVATED ABILITIES:	
Could see certain areas . . . picked areas . . . picked someone . . . watched friend's strengths/weaknesses	*Evaluating*
you point out—I'll point out . . . confronted . . . talked management into . . . insisted on use . . . had to fight	*Influencing*
set out to . . . gather together . . . before the game . . . how are . . . we going to	*Planning*
friend's strengths and weaknesses . . . married the two together . . . picked someone I knew . . . he was stronger theoretically	*Overseeing*
if you can become proficient . . . wanted to try ideas . . . developed a theory together . . . developing this young friend.	*Developing*

SUBJECT MATTER:

someone I knew, friend, team company (individuals and teams)	*People*
we can control in a certain way . . . if you become proficient, it's an asset to the team	*Strategies*
biochemistry . . . novel testing ideas . . . developed theory together	*Technology*

CIRCUMSTANCES:

I could see areas that I could learn quickly . . . seeing that ideas were implemented	*Growth, Potential*

OPERATING RELATIONSHIP:

if you can become proficient, it's big asset to the team . . . watched my friend's strengths and weaknesses . . . set up an interesting company . . . running all aspects of the business	*Team Leader, Manager*

MOTIVATIONAL PAYOFF:

seeing the fruition of it . . . got the ideas working . . . friend's career launched . . . seeing that idea implemented	*Bring to completion, Reach the objective*

Chris' Motivations:

Chris is motivated to work with and through others to reach objectives. He assesses and develops the talents of others. He influences others by strategizing and confronting as necessary. He wants to get the job done. He wants to reach the intended objectives. He appears to be excited by and interested in technology.

To help you appreciate the difference in motivations, please review again the achievement data of Shane, the researcher who was motivated by physiology, discovery and experimentation:

Achievement Data for Shane, the Researcher

Childhood:

"Read about everything I could get my hands on . . . interested in invertebrates . . . always looking for different types of worms, etc. Fascinated to see particular organism . . . always looking for new types. Fascinated with finding unusual type . . . did experiments, made cuts in worm, grew two heads, two tails."

Age 22-25:

"Conducted an extensive research project for a class. Physiological Changes in Limpets in Response to Escape Eliciting Substances. Worked on project two months beyond course despite lack of cooperation from professors. Very interesting . . . fascinating complex of behaviors. Figured out some kind of experiment. Animals showed these very interesting responses . . . some were quite absurd. Nobody really looked at the physiology of this thing. Fascinated by the whole subject . . . presence of the extract resulted in increase in heart rate and respiration."

Age 31-35:

"Discovered two mechanisms involved in response to simulated jet lag in monkeys. Discovered during analysis of data. Looked for something that was cohesive ...discovered different pattern in data of one monkey. Pursued it to point where I got this presentation . . . took data and explained . . . fascinating in that I had discovered this and didn't expect to see this—really interesting."

Imagine that Shane and Chris have both applied for the first-level management position in this research group. Which employee is more motivated to do the work of management? Which employee would be more likely to develop his employees, support their ideas, see that they are recognized and rewarded? Which employee would you choose as your supervisor, given that both are reasonably ethical and competent individuals?

Look again at the achievements of both candidates for evidence to support your conclusion. Shane has given no evidence of interest in working with and through others; his interest is the discovery of technical knowledge. Chris' achievements show evidence of interest in "teaming" abilities even as a teenager. While Shane may demonstrate more technical expertise, Chris' past behavior indicates that he will function as a manager and effectively lead this research team.

In many organizations, the issue of technical or subject matter expertise is often the deciding factor in selecting supervisors. Employees who are ranked highest for their technical performance are typically among the top choices for team leader and management roles. The operating belief is that employees will not "follow" leaders who are not technically competent themselves. However, data collected from employees in many organizations refute that belief and indicate that the highly respected manager is one who equitably utilizes and develops the talents of others. [72]

CAN THIS EMPLOYEE BE TRAINED TO BE A MANAGER?

Let's go back to the question of training Shane to manage others. Can Shane be "trained" to become interested in involving others in his research, in developing the talents of others, in addressing the cost and budget issues? Will those responsibilities be the best use of Shane's talents? Will Shane feel fulfilled and stimulated in his new career as a manager? Will Shane be able to sustain over time the new skills that he learns in management training? Will Shane continue to do the research he loves—or, more likely, will he return the headhunter's call?

In 40 years of studying achievement data of over 50,000 individuals, analysts at People Management International LLC have found no evidence to demonstrate that Motivational Patterns change in response to any external stimuli. Of course, each of us can (and do) learn new skills and knowledge, but what we actually DO with the learning is highly dependent on our innate motivation. Most of us recognize this phenomenon from our own experience. If we are interested in the subject, we learn more readily and retain the learning more completely. **If we are neither interested in the subject nor motivated to perform the skills the role requires, it is difficult to retain the learning and sustain the new behavior.** We can watch this phenomenon in operation by observing our colleagues who have done very well in one role but have not succeeded—or perhaps have failed—in another role. We all know stories about individuals who fail to make the transition to management (e.g., the drafting supervisor who "took his table with him.") We also see notables like Rosabeth Moss Kanter, internationally famed author, speaker and management guru who was terminated in less than a year when given actual management responsibility for the *Harvard Business Review*. [73] There is also the story about a national laboratory director who had detailed sketches of site sidewalk construction on his board when the President of the U. S. came to visit. The director (I should say ex-director) had just finished a full week's high-level briefing on developing a vision for national labs. The rumor was that the President was furious; he was expecting a lively discussion on Lab mission and instead got a detailed briefing on the Lab's physical plant. The fact was that the director was relieved of his position within the month.

Today's new managers have even less time to learn their jobs and start contributing. Edward Betof, co-author of *Just Promoted*, surveyed 1,000 new managers and their supervisors. He found that, in the 1980's, a new manager could expect a honeymoon period lasting anywhere from six months to a year. Now, Betof says, the honeymoon lasts only a couple of weeks, if they get any grace period at all. And about 40% of managers and executives receiving promotions or winning new positions fail within the first 18 months in their new job! One of the most frequently cited reasons for management failure is that the learning curve is too steep. It takes too long for managers and executives to learn the elements of their jobs. [74]

> *One manager went through three companies before realizing it wasn't the company he needed to change–it was his work!*

Recent data from Challenger, Gray and Christmas (outplacement consultants) support Betof's study:

It's a tough time to be the top dog. Managers are under more pressure than ever to produce strong numbers every quarter. They are constantly being second-guessed and scrutinized. If it were baseball, they would be expected to hit .400 month after month. Management is a precarious perch. [75]

In an article entitled "Easing Burnout by Doing What You Want," the *New York Times* News Service reported that the stress among new managers is so prevalent that a new brand of career counseling is evolving: *This counseling helps managers afflicted by the early stages of burnout to find new jobs that they love rather than ones dictated by their resumes.* [76]

Given the cost-consciousness in today's economy, will it be cost-effective to spend time and money trying to train Shane to be a manager? Would you want to be accountable for making the decision to spend $10,000 for a week's management training for Shane? Losing the performance of a superior researcher? Risking the loss of other researchers who become frustrated with Shane as their manager?

BUT I'VE NEVER BEEN A MANAGER....

By now, you might be thinking: *Well, how do I know if I'm motivated to be a manager if I have never been one?* Again, the evidence of 50,000 Motivational Patterns examined over the past 40 years says that if people are motivated to do something, they will find a way to express that motivation somewhere in their lives or work.

Achievement data from thousands of individuals demonstrate that people will find a way to express their motivation to manage others, even if they are not in a formal management or leadership position. For example, in Chris' rugby achievement story, Chris demonstrates some leadership/management motivations (assessing abilities of others, working together as team, strategizing to reach the objective) even though he had no formal authority or role to perform such tasks.

Typical illustrations of management motivation often come from childhood and family situations. An administrative director in a major medical center provided a classic example. One of her achievements described how she organized her siblings around their household chores, made a chart to record their "performance" and then talked their mother into letting her dispense allowances based on quality of task completion. She did all of this when she was eight years old and the youngest sibling! Another achievement from a mid-level executive recalled how he had started raising chickens on his parent's farm when he was about 10. He continued to develop the business until he left for college at age 18, using the money he earned raising the chickens. The abilities he used in arranging for feed, caring for the chickens, dealing with disease and disaster, and getting his siblings to help were (not surprisingly) repeated in several of his adult achievements as a manufacturing plant manager.

MANAGEMENT VS. LEADERSHIP

Volumes have been written in attempts to explain, compare and differentiate these terms. Funk and Wagnall's Standard College Dictionary defines *leading* as "to go with or ahead so as to show the way; to guide or conduct." By contrast, *managing* is defined as "to direct or control the affairs or interest." While Leaders and Managers may have motivations in common, they also appear to have some important differences in motivation. In their study of Motivational Patterns, analysts at People Management International LLC have discovered that there are distinct differences in Motivational Patterns between a "Manager," a "Leader," and someone who exercises "leadership." To provide knowledge workers with a useful distinction between these behaviors, the following behavioral contrasts are offered: (The third category—leadership with a small "l"—is discussed later.)

Managing Behaviors	*Leading Behaviors*
Starts with a defined objective	*Starts with a vision of what is seen as possible*
Structures organization and builds operating strategy	*Proactively gets involved and envisions a way forward*

Seeks to influence/align others through participative but focused discussions

Seeks to catalyze and empower others with open collaboration on issues deemed critical by the group

Actively manages, making critical decisions on emerging problems and needs

Probes and persuades as both leader and doer

Keeps subordinates focused on common priorities, holding them accountable for agreed-upon results

Converges group efforts toward desired outcomes

Achieves objectives(s)

Achieves desired vision(s)

*Generated by self and others

Recognizing Leadership Potential

It is important to recognize the differences between managing and leading because some individuals who are not motivated to manage may be motivated to lead. Many individuals (and organizations) do not recognize or understand the less-structured leadership talents. Therefore, People Management International LLC has attempted to define this motivation more fully:

> There is a certain forthright quality in the way leaders act, speak, and express themselves that people respond to. People generally enjoy being around leaders. They like to serve, support and follow their lead in a voluntary way. Their charisma might also cause people to enthusiastically fall into step with some vision or idea they have in mind or a cause or policy that they personally endorse. Although leaders may like to work in the context of definite projects and programs, their leadership of others is ongoing and independent of defined structures. Leaders do not necessarily identify with any particular group or lead a group simply because it is their responsibility to do so. It is likely, in fact, that leaders frequently cause people who are not under their formal jurisdiction to take action. The nature of their leadership is characterized by the personal effect they have on others, rather than by the official power of any position or title. [77]

Achievement Data for Sierra, a Leader

The following excerpts from Sierra's achievement data illustrate her motivation as a Leader:

Organized a Network of Women at My Company

How I got involved:

"Several of the engineers in our area were having coffee one day, discussing how oppressive the company environment was for women. We decided that maybe we could weather it out better if we were more supportive of each other . . . it would be easier to survive."

Details of what I did:

"I organized a breakfast session over at a hotel across the street and invited a bunch of people and asked them to invite whoever they felt would be interested. I helped the group to build a process cycle . . . and the meeting revealed that there was suffering; that some people had experienced tremendous, horrifying harassment and had been trying to weather it alone. In that meeting, we all got to see that we were not alone and from that came some reassurance that we were not to blame for what was happening. It was not right and we had the power to control and change it. The meeting grew into a desire to organize and contribute to help make the workplace more humane. So, as the organizer, I set up the next meeting and the next and the next. I never offered any retribution for not attending or not participating. I accepted lots of input from people on how to change the meeting, etc. I helped the group organize into project work and to change the nature of the meetings to meet the needs of the particular project. We all built relationships with others that were not there before. I helped the group to put together the presentation to top management and to select the right people to make the presentation. In the end, we got management's ear and the opportunity to develop an action plan to address the issues."

What was particularly satisfying:

"I was uplifted by the human kindness that I found in all these women and the need and desire to support me and each other. I was proud to play such an important role in the creation of the network. I was pleased with my ability to go with the flow of the group and the individuals. I loved the relationships that this created for me with peer women outside my own organization and with women I would not have known otherwise, who are now my friends. I know they would not hesitate to help me or to ask me for help. The women's organization is still going strong—without me."

Led the XXX Technical Excellence Project

How I got involved:

"The project was a mess. I just rolled up my sleeves and started in."

Details of what I did:

"I spent the first three months getting the team on the same page . . . getting them educated about what a quality program was . . . acknowledging the problems of lack of interest and appropriate staff. I helped the five experts build relationships with each other and with our clients. I used a great deal of humor and it helped us to get to know each other as people, not just as technical experts. I had huge meetings with all the technical supervisors and managers. I organized and facilitated the meeting and helped the respective teams to take ownership and lead certain parts. They really responded to the organization, the interest in their work, the standards that I helped them to define. At our last meeting, I got a standing ovation and the technical standards we developed are used throughout the organization."

Established Job Posting System

How I got involved:

"I noticed that we generally only offered people one position, after 'we' had decided which one they should have. There was not much choice left to the individual."

Details of what I did:

"I started with one person, whom I gave a choice as to which of two jobs they might prefer. The corporate human resources system went crazy and I had some pretty senior people mad at me. After much conversation with several of the 'powers,' I convinced them that Job Posting was empowering to individuals and helpful to us in filling jobs. There was mutual benefit in having people actually interested in the jobs for which they applied. I gathered some information from other companies to help dispel some of the concerns about everyone changing jobs every month, hundreds of people applying for every job, and hundreds of people being disappointed when they didn't get the job. Corporate Human Resources came around and supported me. After more than a year of working with others to conduct 'pilot' tests, facilitating meetings, and organizing task forces, etc. the process was instituted in the company and is still in operation today."

In reading these excerpts from Sierra's achievement data, we can practically see Sierra in action. We can see through the details in her descriptions of her actions how she functioned as a Leader. Sierra:

✧ Initiated action even though she did not have a formal role or authority to act.

✧ Caused others to respond to her, to follow her lead, even though she did not have formal or positional authority over them.

✧ Had a strong personal effect on the actions of others. They wanted to be aligned with her and to help or serve her.

✧ Reported that the effort continues even after she was no longer the center of the action.

DIFFERENTIATING BETWEEN "LEADERS" AND "LEADERSHIP"

Obviously, not all of us have the innate managerial motivation to work through others, to actively manage, oversee and coach the work of others, or the leadership motivation that causes others to follow and align themselves with our direction. In fact, in analyzing the thousands of Motivational Patterns that have been prepared over the last forty years, People Management International LLC reports that only about 25% of the 50,000 individuals patterned had evidence of being motivated as either a Manager or a Leader. [78]

The analyses of hundreds of patterns have also revealed that an individual is most likely to display some level of "leadership" when that individual is engaged in activities that are aligned with his/her Motivational Pattern. For example, the researcher who is very focused on the theoretical concepts of her research will take more initiative when working on her favorite research topic. The individual who is highly motivated by guidelines and instructions might be having a terrible time offering leadership in an unstructured situation, but he is a tremendous resource to the local soccer club. But this kind of "leadership" is connected to the individual's own expertise and involvement. While it is crucial that we tap into the "leadership" that each of us can provide if our work engages our motivations, it is also important not to confuse this kind of "leadership" with the kind of influence that is provided by the person who is truly motivated to be a Leader. As individuals and organizations, we tend to trivialize the nature of true Leaders by failing to fully understand their talents. Leaders offer much more than "leadership" as defined above.

Chapter 3. Mismatch Issues for Knowledge Workers

I cannot regulate the tending of my truths to others, nor can I allow them to go untended.
David Norton

HOW TO IDENTIFY AND RESOLVE MISMATCHES

While it is dangerous to generalize about the innate motivations of individuals, there is much to be learned from the analyses of Motivational Patterns of several thousands of knowledge workers over a period of 40 years. **A Motivational Pattern is always unique for each individual; yet there appear to be specific motivations for individuals who select a particular profession.** For example, while every scientist is not motivated to evaluate by analyzing, that particular motivation appears much more frequently in Motivational Patterns of scientists than it does in Motivational Patterns of sales personnel. On the other hand, the motivation to influence by selling is much more likely to appear in Motivational Patterns of sales personnel than it is in the patterns of scientists. As one might expect, it is also true that scientists who are motivated to analyze are more likely to progress in their scientific investigations than their colleagues who do not possess that innate motivation. Sales personnel who are not innately motivated to sell may be removed from sales responsibilities relatively early in their careers, because their "mismatch" situation is easily recognized by their lack of sales. By contrast, some scientists may struggle in their careers for a lifetime without fully understanding the cause of their performance and career problems.

These kinds of "mismatch" situations can be very frustrating for the individual, who frequently does not comprehend the powerful impact that innate motivation has on his ability to sustain competitive performance in the given role. It is equally frustrating for those who supervise "mismatched" employees. **It is probably a fair statement to say that the manager who truly understands the presence and impact of innate motivation is clearly the exception, not the rule.** Many managers are simply not "motivated" by the subject of human behavior, so they spend little time or effort investigating the subject. Likewise, management training courses are more likely to present the employee as "putty" and assign to the manager the responsibility for "molding" these individuals to meet the organization's needs and wants. But, alas, the manager's experience is that it is VERY difficult to "train" a person to be analytical who is not so motivated. Likewise, if a person is not motivated to influence by selling, or by convincing and persuading, or by confronting, repeated exposure to even the best of the "Positive Power and Influence" courses seems to have little lasting impact in terms of sustaining an employee's performance of these skills. As previously discussed, this is an especially frustrating situation for knowledge workers and their management, most of whom have strong learning motivations and believe that learning to convince, persuade and confront should be a piece of cake compared to some of the subjects they have conquered. Many are truly angered (at themselves and others) when they begin to recognize that while they can learn the concepts, they cannot learn and sustain an effective performance of the desired behavior.

One way to help knowledge workers and their managers to more fully understand the "power" of the Motivational Pattern is to examine the achievement data of an individual when there is a problem situation. Almost without fail, such an examination will help the individual to understand the root cause of the problem and to develop a strategy for resolving the situation. The following case studies present two "mismatch" problems frequently identified in performance and career issues of knowledge workers. Each case study is followed with a brief commentary on the individual's motivational themes plus recommendations for the individual and his/her supervisor for dealing with the situation.

MISMATCH ISSUE #1: DESIGNER MOTIVATED BY MEETING NEEDS/EXPECTATIONS

When I met Sally in a career workshop sponsored by her employer, she was a very frustrated designer for an engineering project. She had recently been "promoted" from a field project. As you read through her achievement data, look for the specific "evidence" that tells you why the first stages of design are proving to be difficult for her. Compare your thoughts with the recommendations offered at the end of her achievement data.

Sally's Achievement Data:

Made wooden plant holder in wood shop:

"For some crazy reason, I decided to take wood shop in high school. There were two requirements in wood shop: (1) Make a plant holder and (2) make something else. Most of the students made three or more things. I only made the required. I liked working with the other kids . . . some really knew a lot about woodworking . . . and it felt really good to finish the plant holder. It was not a particularly nice looking one but my mother still has it hanging on her wall. It was great to finish the thing."

Went to Africa and climbed Mt. Kilimanjaro:

"I was looking for an adventure vacation before starting work full-time. From a booklet on Outward Bound, I decided that I would go on their African trip. With Outward Bound, it is required that you go on the trips alone so you do not know anyone in the group. So I signed up and flew to Kenya, the first time I left North America. It was a very exciting and nervous trip. My stay in Kenya was for three weeks. There were 20 people in the group from all parts of the U. S. . . . and they were really a great group to be with. The first week and a half was spent on safari. We then went to the base camp to prepare for the mountain. The hike took 6 days . . . 4 days up and 1 down. The most difficult part of the journey was the summit day hike. It started out at 1:00 a.m. with flashlights and a lot of warm clothing. By sunrise we were at the top 19,300 ft. Reaching the summit was so emotional! It was the most challenging thing (emotionally and physically) I have ever done. The sad thing is you spend so much time and effort to get to the top, only to stay for a few minutes."

Graduating from the Colorado School of Mines:

"While I was in high school, it seemed impossible for me to attend CSM. The school is very highly regarded and very difficult to be admitted to in Colorado. To me it seemed so far out of reach. I didn't even apply there while in high school. I went to Fort Lewis College in Denver for the 1st two years. CSM and FLC had a program where you spent two years at FLC and if you did well, you could go to Mines. I did well my first two years so I applied to Mines, fully expecting them to deny my application. To my surprise, I was accepted. A dream come true! I went to Mines and loved every minute, even the hard work required to graduate. The other students were great, too."

Completed my first 10K run in the middle of the Colorado winter:

"I really did not train much for the run. The run was in Denver in late November. There was snow and ice on the ground and it was cold. I made the entire distance without stopping. I remember that after I finished the sweat in my hair started to freeze. I was so cold! I finished even though my time was not as good as my friend's. This was my first big athletic event. I have since completed three other 10K runs."

Was lead designer on a Waste Water Plant . . . was assigned to the project:

> "Originally, it was just a set of boxes on a piece of paper . . . as we progressed, we gave those boxes shape, form, purpose. My job was to give input to the Offsite Design Team who actually did the design. I spent a lot of time getting their input . . . and with the Singapore people, getting their input on water quality regulations . . . I put together the requirements for tanks, piping, values, etc. There was a lot of concern about putting emissions into the air . . . many hours spent on how to reduce or eliminate emissions . . . trying to come up with solutions. Involved interaction with a lot of people . . . on-site design team, environmental people, Singapore refinery people . . . spent a lot of time getting clear on requirements and finally came up with something everyone could agree to. I think I brought my knowledge of equipment and processes that can be used to contain vapors . . . also my knowledge of Singapore people and their problems, since I had worked for the Singapore refinery. The most rewarding part was coming out with completed design specifications that were moved on to a contractor and knowing that it was going to be built."

Comparison of Sally's Motivational Themes to Her Current Job:

Sally is motivated to meet difficult and challenging goals but she needs some sense of application or meeting requirements in order to be motivated. She likes to work in a group or team setting; however, she wants independence and to see the results of her own efforts. She is motivated to work with tangibles (physical expression, equipment, mechanisms) and to see concrete results.

Her present role in the corporate office involved working on earlier stages of design; the designs were more abstract and less well formulated. Requirements were not yet established as they had been in the design work in her field assignments. She also did not have opportunities to interact with necessary people to define the requirements more precisely. She was more frustrated than some people might be in this role because she is so determined to reach the goal, however difficult it is. But in this staff role, the solution was not in her control.

Recommendations for Sally's Supervisor:

Most organizations would expect Sally to finish this assignment successfully or her future career opportunities will be diminished. Encourage her to get input to define requirements from whomever she needs. Make it "okay" for her to talk to others; she is afraid you will read this as a deficiency. Work closely in helping her to understand the kinds of roles that will be best for her and which assignments she should avoid. Don't isolate her with early-stage, more abstract designs. She should also avoid research roles with no concrete application.

Recommendations for Sally:

You need to be candid with your supervisor about what you need in order to be motivated to perform. If you need more defined requirements, then tell him that. You might also suggest that one way to obtain these requirements would be for you to put together a "straw" plan that you could use to gather input from relevant sources as well as from your management. If you can get your supervisor's input first, you will be more confident in sharing your ideas with others.

Footnote: Sally did share her motivational needs with her supervisor. He was most understanding, liked the idea of starting with a "straw" plan and worked with Sally until she was clear on the needed direction. He also recognized that long term, this was not the job for Sally. They discussed openly what she needed in an assignment; within three months, she was in a new role. A few months later, I received an email from "Sally."

> *"Hello! I am writing to let you know where I am and what I have been up to since I changed assignments. I am on a loan assignment to XXX Project Services. This is the project development team for the Russia Exploration project. So far I really like what I have been doing and I feel like I can make a home as long as I continue to work projects. This project has been very interesting and it has allowed me to travel to Russia many times. What an interesting place! It is pretty inspiring to find yourself standing in the middle of Red Square or be off flying on a Russian helicopter! I am the Oil Spill Response Coordinator for the Project. I support the drilling operations by making sure there are oil spill resources available on the island. The thing I like the most about this job is the level of responsibility. No one is standing over me or giving me small pieces of the pie. There is a lot of pressure to get things done but I really love the freedom to make decisions and to work the issues. My results are actually concrete and not just some report that few people are going to read. Well, I must get back to work!"*

If you had met Sally when she was frustrated with her design role, you would have never guessed that she was the woman that went to Africa alone and climbed Mt. Kilimanjaro, or that she successfully ran marathons! She, as do many people who are fighting mismatched situations, appeared drained and defeated. I was delighted to learn of her new assignment and to feel that sense of personal courage in her words that is so essential to her self-esteem and her sense of well-being.

MISMATCH ISSUE #2: A "BE THE BEST" INDIVIDUALIST WORKING AS A TEAM MEMBER

Joe, a computer analyst, is motivated to be unique and outstanding, but is currently on a team project. As you read his achievement data, notice how important it is for Joe to differentiate his performance from others.

Joe's Achievement Data:

First Fight:

"At seven, I engaged in my first fight with a peer named Tom Daily. He was bigger and stronger and I lost badly. I then petitioned the school authority to mediate the unjust situation and was successful. I learned at that time that it is always better to negotiate settlements with more powerful adversaries and to solicit the help of the authorities to strengthen your position in disputes."

First Car:

"I had saved enough money to purchase my first car. It was a great prestige symbol to drive oneself to school, so I had to have a car. I found a 1950 Ford and it died about a week after I bought it. I had read a little about engines and was already pretty well experienced in electronics. I opened the hood and adjusted the only thing I knew how to: the ignition point gap. I tried to start the car and it ran. From that time on, I was convinced that I could fix anything on a car and still feel I know as much about automobiles and engines as anyone with amateur status and more than many people making a living at the activity."

Work in Computing Lab:

"I applied what I knew in electronics to design and construct a modern testing laboratory and eventually became the group leader. I taught myself FORTRAN, Basic, and operations on a GE Terminal connected to an IBM computer in a time-sharing mode. I learned more about computing than anyone in the Engineering Department and became an in-house consultant to that division. I created several meaningful computing systems and introduced Engineering to the use of computing in ratings calculations and design work. I laid the groundwork for computer simulation and laboratory control and data acquisition. I felt there was almost nothing I could not become or accomplish. I felt I was not appreciated by the corporation, but I felt that if I sought out and performed professional achievements, I would be treated fairly."

Data Systems:

"I created a major Information Management System and Data Acquisition System. By this time in my career, I had learned to organize, study, apply and repeat this process. I had learned how to interact with the users and create what they needed on the computer from what they said they wanted. I proposed a solution in several steps with benchmarks and time projections. I obtained user and local management consent and managed the installation of the hardware and creation of the software. I was there to instruct and debug and tune the systems.

"I felt I knew as much as or more than the users, the lab managers and the site managers knew about what they did and why they did it. I certainly knew more about how they did it. It was particularly satisfying to follow a sample through a complete analysis process and know that I made it possible to know where any sample was at any time, what the latest results of the latest test were, and that the environment I had created for the operators was safer, more accurate and more pleasant. I felt I had mastered another aspect of computing."

Comparison of Joe's Motivational Themes to His Current Job:

Joe is very motivated to differentiate his performance from others and to be recognized as performing in a unique and outstanding manner—in everything he does. He is also motivated to master a task or process and to have complete control over whatever he is doing.

His current assignment as a computer analyst is on a team that services a variety of users on a fairly routine application. This role simply does not give him what he needs in terms of opportunity for recognition and to differentiate his performance from others. So, because innate motivation is irrepressible, Joe finds other ways to express his "be unique and outstanding" motivation. He never fails to miss an opportunity to demonstrate that he knows more about the subject than his teammates or his supervisor.

Recommendations for Joe's Supervisor:

Joe would be best motivated to work in a role or assignment where any results are clearly the end product of his effort; he also needs recognition as an ongoing outcome from his work. If you can find legitimate ways to recognize him publicly for his efforts, he may not have to work so hard at getting the recognition himself. He needs a senior advisor role in a complicated technology. He will thrive in a position that provides recognition for his knowledge on a daily basis. If such a position is not available, you are doing no one a favor by keeping Joe in the role he is currently performing.

Recommendations for Joe:

You must recognize how powerful your motivation is to be unique and to be recognized as outstanding. Because your peers are also very talented, it is difficult for your supervisor to consistently single you out. Negotiate with your supervisor for a senior advisor role (on a difficult new technology) rather than a service role on a team of analysts. Also, establish activities in your personal life that would give you visibility and recognition. (Participate in a professional society; challenge your tremendous appetite to learn by mastering a new subject.) There is also some evidence that, because of your need to be recognized as being outstanding and unique, you may tend to overstate your role.

Comments:

Shortly after our discussion, Joe was terminated as part of a downsizing effort. Joe was devastated; being "fired" is a deep wound for anyone, but it is a nearly mortal blow for a person with his motivation. He has found a position as an expert consultant for a smaller computer company. He has a very independent role that is good for him and the company. It is a very flat organization and Joe really has no direct manager. His success with his clients provides daily recognition and feedback on his talents. He is a much happier man and now realizes that he was "working overtime" to squeeze some recognition out of his previous job.

MANAGE LIMITATIONS

The best way to identify any potential mismatch in your own situation is by comparing your Motivational Pattern with the Critical Requirements of Your Job—which is the topic of a forthcoming chapter. The following examples may alert you to some of the less obvious but common mismatches.

Common Mismatch Situations

✧   A person who is motivated to **build, develop and form** (put the "blocks" together and achieve a result that reflects all of the development steps—see a finished product—make something from nothing) is in a role that is primarily a maintenance role, which involves overseeing or administering but very little "building up" or "growing." This situation often occurs after a new project or product has been completed and the lead "developer" is positioned to continue as the lead person but now in a managerial capacity. The title may sound impressive for a while, but the maintenance role will soon be a real drag for this individual. "Builders" need to keep building!

✧   A person motivated to **become proficient and demonstrate competence** who has been in his job for some time—and finds there is virtually **nothing new to be learned and demonstrated.** Learning abilities are key for this motivation and after proving his ability in one arena, this individual begins looking around for other skills and subjects to tackle. Eventually, many people with this motivation seek totally new careers—most of the time without knowing exactly why they feel they must make a move. The best strategy for people with this motivation is to select a career field that is sufficiently comprehensive and changing so learning is an integral part of the profession. Many scientists and computer scientists with this motivation are happy campers!

✧   A person who is motivated to **excel and be the best** (wants to exceed the performance or expectations of others) needs to be able to measure her performance against some standard to confirm the excellence of her work. A mismatch situation for this person is any job/role that does not provide the kind of quantifiable results that allows the individual to measure (compare) her performance and thus confirm that she is indeed excelling. Best Fit Scenarios for this motivation include roles with quantifiable results (sales, profits, quotas, promotions, commissions). Of course, the ideal scenario for this motivation (if one is motivated to read and study) is in school itself, where the environment is clearly defined and opportunity for comparisons abound. The problem usually occurs when the individual enters the workforce and finds either no clear system for comparison—or that he is unable to attain the desired rating or ranking because the rules for the "contest" are less defined.

✧   People who are motivated to **gain a response from and influence the behavior of people** or other living things get their satisfaction from watching the "subject" respond as desired. These people are often seen as "movers" and "shakers." They like to make a difference. Because these individuals focus their energies on the behavior of others, they are often not the "expert" or the top performer. They may be passed over for leadership or other "people-oriented" roles and may end up in a behind-the-scenes role **with little or no opportunity for influencing** the behavior of others or gaining a response from their own performance. Best Fit Scenarios for people with this motivation are working directly with people—teaching, counseling, selling, managing, leading, confronting, serving, or caring for people or animals, in some cases.

✧ The person who is motivated to **comprehend and demonstrate by reducing to expression** focuses on understanding, defining and communicating insights into complex, difficult or puzzling matters. This person delights in exploring, probing and sorting out complexities. He will want to encircle or contain the whole of an idea or subject before his motivation is satisfied. If this individual is thrust into a situation where there are too many unrelated subjects, options or complexities to deal with, he is likely to get into trouble. People with this motivation need the opportunity to do their work thoroughly. Usually intellectual and motivated to work with intangibles, they can become "stuck" in their careers when they take longer to achieve a task than their colleagues. The typical "comprehender" needs an assignment with limited focus but also needs access to all parts of a problem or topic.

Managing Your Limitations

Progressing to increased responsibility in most professions does require some motivations that are not present in every Motivational Pattern. Listed below are some of the more common "limitations" that knowledge workers often face. Some suggestions for managing the limitations are also offered. **Don't forget that the best strategy is to find (or create) a role that is well matched to your strengths and where your limitations are not as relevant!**

Limited Motivation to Influence Others:

Influencing motivations are a very important aspect of both performance and career development for knowledge workers. People with influencing behaviors seek to influence others directly in order to secure a specific response or result. They want a definite action or conclusion to result from their involvement with others. They tend to be effective in breaking down the doubts or disinterest of potential customers. They are likely to be strong "closers" in sales interactions. They are usually effective in getting superiors to grant approval and support for proposals and actions. They will not hesitate to confront others on issues or performance. They will tend to hammer home the facts about a problem or situation in a way that will compel others to take appropriate action. Influencing behaviors cover a broad range from convincing, persuading, selling and confronting to explaining and describing to nurturing and getting others involved. Many knowledge workers, especially technical professionals, are motivated to explain and discuss, but may not be as motivated to convince, persuade and sell—and even less motivated to promote and "politick." In fact, the absence of this persuading/selling motivation often creates significant career problems for these individuals. Since they are not motivated to sell or to promote, they usually do not sell or promote themselves or their ideas and contributions. Often they end up, especially in larger organizations, "waiting to be discovered." They become downright angry and discouraged when colleagues seem to get more credit and more frequent promotions. Many become cynical as this phenomenon continues throughout their career and they repeatedly fail to have the impact that they want and need in order to be selected for increasingly responsible roles.

<u>Managing the Limitation</u>: Knowledge workers who are strong performers but do not possess motivation to convince, persuade and sell others often find a more compatible career home in a smaller organization, where both management and colleagues have an opportunity to know them and to see their contributions directly. Because employees also get to know more about their colleagues in a small organization, the interactions will be more like explaining and describing than selling and promoting. If you have this "limitation" and are working in a large organization, you may need to use other avenues for getting people to know you. If appropriate, you may want to write more reports and memos on your work or articles for professional journals. You may want to organize small group interactions where the mode is more talking/sharing experiences than formally presenting one's work. Another strategy is to "team up" with colleagues who are more motivated to influence.

Limited Motivation for Confronting Others on Their Performance:

You might be thinking...*This is a career problem for knowledge workers?* Yes, it is certainly a problem for many knowledge workers who are motivated to meet the needs of others or to gain approval from others. When people who are motivated by approval have to confront someone in a discussion of ideas or proposals, or on an interaction or customer service issue, they find it very stressful. Many will simply put off the confrontation as long as possible. Then, when it seems the issue can no longer be avoided, they will address it. By then, emotions are running high. Many times they confront aggressively (rather than assertively) and the results are usually not positive, making it a bad memory and causing the person to be even more reluctant to confront again.

Knowledge workers in supervisory or management roles are especially vulnerable if they are not motivated to confront because it is their responsibility to monitor the performance of others, and to address deficiencies. Unraveling personal problems among employees is another arena of supervisory responsibility that becomes a struggle for the supervisor who is not motivated to confront.

<u>Managing the Limitation</u>: While it is highly unlikely that you will ever enjoy confrontation if it is not part of your Motivational Pattern, there are some very effective processes and techniques for structuring interactions that have potential for emotional responses. Most utilize a "step" approach, and if followed carefully, will help you build skills and thus confidence for dealing with these kinds of situations. [79]

Many individuals who are not motivated to confront have learned to use other influencing skills to fill that void. They may be motivated to explain and describe, thus their strategy for dealing with confrontational issues could be providing ongoing discussion and information, which tends to dilute the emotional potential. Others are motivated to get people involved, which can have a similar "cooling" effect.

There is an important fact here: If you are not motivated to confront others on their performance, and do not possess other strong influencing motivations, stay away from supervisory and management roles that require this motivation for performing the critical aspects of the job.

Limited Motivation for Dealing With Abstract, Conceptual Subject Matter:

Based on the approximately 50,000 Motivational Patterns that have been prepared for knowledge workers in the past 40 years, it appears that only about 25% of this population is truly motivated to work with abstract and conceptual subject matter. [80] The remaining 75% of this population do not enjoy the process of moving from a premise to a tentative assumption to a statement of principle—they want to start with the principle. They are frustrated with research, philosophical speculation and testing hypotheses. Because they need more definition in order to sustain their interest and motivation, they want to work with more defined subject matter (e.g., knowledge or information, details, numbers, systems or processes). Fortunately, there are thousands of professional occupations and roles which are more applied and less abstract, so the opportunities overall are proportional to the nature of the supply. But, alas, some knowledge workers end up in jobs/roles that have less definition than they personally find motivating. In addition, their manager may not be motivated to provide needed definition and direction. These knowledge workers fail to maintain competitive performance because they can become somewhat "paralyzed" or hesitant to act when they do not have the level of definition needed for them to feel confident in their understanding of the situation and their plan for action.

<u>Managing the Limitation</u>: Mismatch in subject matter is probably the most difficult element to "manage" when there is a poor fit. The best strategy is to head for a role where there is a better match. But sometimes it does take a while to make the move and you may be expected to complete the task you are currently assigned.

Most of us tend to procrastinate when it is not sufficiently clear what action we should take.

One strategy to deal with this hesitation to act is to use "straw plans" as a way to "tease out" more definition and direction from your colleagues and your management. A straw plan is a tentative action plan that makes it easier for others to provide their perspective on a subject. Such a plan might include:

❖ Your description/understanding of the problem, situation or topic.

❖ Your ideas, suggestions of actions to be taken.

❖ Your estimation of resources needed.

The key to using this simple process effectively is to ask for input and response on each item as you present it. Then carefully listen to the responses and probe for more detail. Many knowledge workers are motivated to demonstrate their competence; they will find this kind of interaction very engaging. (Of course, you will need to be sure to give credit to ideas and insights that you gain or it may be more difficult to get the involvement next time!)

One of the reasons many knowledge workers may hesitate to initiate these kinds of discussions is that they, too, may have some motivation to demonstrate knowledge or to impress others and this feels like a sure way to look dumb! Doing the initial homework and practicing the discussion with colleagues can prepare you for the Big Time and the Big Issue when you really do need to have some more definition before you can act. But do remember that strategies like these will only provide temporary relief! If you are not motivated to deal with abstract and conceptual subject matter, identify the kind of subject matter that you are motivated to deal with and start your search for that kind of work. Again, our experience with thousands of clients says that there is a good "fit" job for you—and most probably, many more than one!

Limited Motivation to Work from a "Blank Sheet":

Many knowledge workers tend to be analytical problem-solvers who are highly motivated to solve problems that are "on the table." The troubleshooter's track record is often impressive if he has been given the latitude to solve the problems. These individuals often are "promoted" to staff-level strategic planning roles, frequently as part of a "rotation" program to prepare them for managerial responsibilities. Frequently neither the individual nor her manager understands how the motivations required for the visionary or strategic planning role differ from the troubleshooter, problem-solver role. While the troubleshooter works with an existing problem or situation, the strategic planner, almost like the artist, is facing a relatively blank sheet of paper. Unfortunately, evaluative and analytical motivations (which made the individual successful in problem-solving) are frequently not accompanied by the motivation to originate ideas, concepts and strategies. Both the quality and quantity of the planning effort suffer when a problem-solver faces the relatively "blank sheet" requiring the creation of plans of action that integrate all the angles and will enable the organization to reach future goals. For many a talented problem-solver, even a short period in a strategic planning role has meant career disaster. In the end, the organization rarely remembers the talented problem-solver; the image of the ineffective strategic planner becomes more powerful and more permanent.

<u>Managing the Limitation</u>: Probably the only temporary remedy that really works is for the troubleshooter to seek out the talents of a strategic thinker to assist in accomplishing the tasks at hand. While finding such a resource is not always easy, many individuals with more visionary motivations are underutilized and will welcome the invitation to participate. For the incumbent, it's really a matter of moving on to another role before his image in the organization is tarnished. We have met many of these mismatched individuals who say that it was the strategic planning assignment that derailed their careers. Probably the interaction with top-level management gives strategic planners a level of visibility that can be dangerous if not accompanied by performance!

Chapter 4. Making Job/Career Decisions

People without information cannot act responsibly.

Ken Blanchard

WHY DO SMART PEOPLE MAKE DUMB DECISIONS ABOUT JOBS AND CAREERS?

It is important for you to understand and respect the powerful nature of innate motivation, because your work and your life are impacted every day by its very existence. If you don't take charge of the direction of your work/life, and take the necessary steps to engage your innate passions in accomplishing a purpose that is meaningful to you, you take the risk of your destiny being directed or controlled by some outside force. You will be recruited to serve the purpose of some other agency.

A study released by the U.S. Bureau of Labor Statistics in April 2000 reported that the average person in the U.S. holds 9.2 jobs from age 18 to age 34. Nearly 87% of both men and women experienced at least one period of unemployment from age 18 to 34. [81] This obviously does not reflect a continuation of "lifetime" (cradle to grave) employment. It means that few of us are exempt from the dynamic changes in the work world, and we all need to be continually prepared to make decisions that keep us "aligned" with our innate motivation.

Peter Vaill [82] characterized the challenge of managing ourselves in today's work world, for which he coined the phrase *permanent whitewater*. He said: *Complex, interdependent and somewhat unstable systems require continual, imaginative initiatives and responses.* His words contain a wealth of wisdom and deserve careful reflection.

There IS simply no letup. Every day I talk to people who are trying to make decisions about their jobs, their careers and even their lives:

◆ A fast-track accountant is trying to decide whether to accept a rotational assignment in marketing—and if she accepts, how to best manage the "fit."

◆ A highly regarded lawyer has been encouraged to run for political office.

◆ A manufacturing process manager is trying to regain control over the "line" after a new micro-managing vice-president has come on board.

◆ A highly rated mechanical engineer is totally frustrated in his new position as a liaison with a governmental funding agency.

And, when I listen to my messages on the home-phone recorder, the quest for clarity and direction continues:

◆ A friend's son (National Merit Scholar) is trying to decide whether to choose an engineering major or a business major so he can decide which university to attend.

◆ My niece calls with the question: *Do you think I should go to graduate school?*

◆ My neighbor wants to talk about his next career. He calls it "Act II." Very wisely, he is planning for life after his corporate career.

Because we have all faced these or similar situations, we know that job/career decisions can be complex, primarily because others are also impacted by our decision. But these decisions become even more troublesome when we do not have sufficient clarity on the underlying facts:

◆ What we are "motivated" to do

    and

◆ The critical requirements for performing the role/career that is under consideration.

Most of us are not generally aware of the profound impact that these two sets of information have on the accuracy of the decisions we are making. Nor are we aware of specifically what it is that we are "motivated" to do or the critical requirements of the job! Without this basic information, we are unable to compare our "motivators" to the critical requirements for performing the role in question. If you have your Motivational Pattern in hand, you will be adequately prepared to describe what you are "motivated" to do. If you understand the process of identifying Motivational Patterns, you will also be much more prepared to gather the necessary information for defining the critical requirements for performing the role in question. With both sets of data in hand, you will be prepared to make an informed and accurate decision about your "fit" to the employment situation under discussion.

When managers make hiring and placement decisions, they usually depend on traditional information:

✧ For college hires—GPA, major field of study, college/university attended, participation in extracurricular activities, leadership roles and interpersonal skills.

✧ For experienced hires—more emphasis on performance in previous or present role, individual's career goals and an intuitive assessment of the "potential" of the candidate.

The individual, on the other hand, may be thinking:

✧ *Where will I be working? Is there much travel?*

✧ *What is the working environment like? (Dress down only on Fridays?)*

✧ *Do I like the work? Could I learn to like it? Can I learn to do it? Will I be bored after I once learn it?*

✧ *What about salary, benefits and promotions?*

In most cases, NEITHER the manager nor the employee have been prepared to give much attention to the really critical "job-fit" questions:

For the manager:

Is this person "motivated" to perform this job or role? Is there evidence that he or she has demonstrated the critical motivations in the past?

For the candidate:

Does this job/role provide the opportunity for me to do work that I am "motivated" to do? Will I be able to accomplish my purpose by working for this employer?

The answers to these questions provide the most accurate insights into whether this person (provided that he/she meets basic skill and knowledge requirements for this job) will be able to sustain competitive performance in the role AND find the work rewarding and fulfilling.

JOB-FIT = PERFORMANCE AND RETENTION

A hiring project with a multinational pharmaceutical firm illustrates this point. [83] This company had been experiencing an over 50% termination rate in its medical representative sales force. (These are the people who sell products directly to doctors and clinics.) When we asked about the qualifications for this position, we were told that recruits must have (1) a B. S. degree in some scientific field, (2) a high GPA and, (3) good interpersonal skills. The company felt they could train people with these basic qualifications to perform the work of the medical sales representative.

Because sales were dropping and replacement costs for the large number of terminations were zooming, the problem became a priority issue. As one would expect, some medical sales representatives were sustaining their performance, feeling quite satisfied with their work, and staying with the company. The Motivational Patterns of these individuals who had sustained their performance were developed and analyzed. Not surprisingly, those who had sustained high performance as medical sales reps had some distinct similarities in their Motivational Patterns:

✧ They were "natural relationship builders." Their achievements had strong evidence of initiating, building and sustaining personal relationships with others.

✧ They were proactive. They did not wait to be told what to do. They were not dependent on structure or requirements to perform.

✧ They were "informed influencers." They were not only skilled in influencing and selling; they also knew their products well. They explained and described their products, and thus influenced their customers by informing them about their products.

✧ They were effective organizers. They organized their time, their schedule, their materials and their interactions with the home office.

✧ They were enthusiastic about their subject matter. Their behavior demonstrated strong personal value for their products.

Given this new set of criteria for proven success as a medical sales representative, the company decided to set up a test. A group of new sales reps were hired. Half of these new hires were selected using the traditional criteria and half with the motivational criteria. All the sales reps were given a new product and a new territory. Their respective sales volume was recorded and compared over a period of about one year.

The sales representatives whose Motivational Patterns most strongly exhibited the above five criteria had sales of nearly double the others! By the end of the second year, those who were "motivationally" qualified were still going strong; several of the "mismatched" sales representatives had left the company, requiring costly time and effort to recruit, hire, train and relocate replacements.

Why Do "Selection Myths" Persist?

It seems so logical that managers who are making recruiting, selecting and promotional decisions should use the characteristics of superior performers as their "template" or "blueprint." Why then do the decision-makers fall back on the traditional criteria of degree (preferably from a prestigious university), grade point average, and "interpersonal" skills?

We believe there are at least three key reasons:

(1) Most managers are simply not fully aware of the profound nature of the Motivational Pattern and its value in predicting performance. As discussed by Arthur Miller in the foreword to this book and reported by the Gallup Organization, there is basically a gross misunderstanding about human nature on the part of both employers and employees. Organizations and their managers, with the best of intentions, continue to subscribe to the "becoming" philosophy that erroneously supports the concept that we can be anything we want to be. The Gallup story tells it very much like it is:

> *They tell their employees that everyone has the same potential. They encourage their employees to be open and dedicated to learning new ways to behave. They send their employees to training classes designed to teach all manner of new behaviors. From their perspective, one of the most admirable qualities an employee can possess is the willingness to transform herself through learning and self-discipline.*

The Gallup study found that truly effective managers (*the world's great managers*) did not share the "becoming" philosophy, but instead recognized that their job was to find a role that fits the talents of the person. Only *the world's greatest managers* seemed to have this *revolutionary insight.* [84]

(2) Sadly, many managers are not themselves sufficiently interested in behavior (as a subject matter) to devote time and interest necessary to explore the phenomena. Although the title "manager" implies managing people, many managers, especially at higher levels, are not actually "motivated" to actively manage the talents of others. Their lack of interest in the subject causes them to write it off as "soft stuff" or "black box" or worse.

(3) Historically, the evaluation of managerial performance has not been sufficiently rigorous or consistent to accurately tally the incredible costs created by inaccurate recruiting, selection, promotion and termination decisions. **In other words, managers have simply not been held accountable for the outcome of their hiring and promoting decisions.** This is changing rapidly and will cause managers to seek new ways for making more accurate human resources decisions. Organizations facing the tough competition are no longer able to ignore the costs of high turnover, currently calculated at $1^1/_2$ times an employee's annual salary. [85] They are beginning to take action. For example, Agilent Technologies in Silicon Valley reports that *over the next year or so, we will begin to assess undesired attrition in calculating managers' variable pay.* [86]

As the achievement stories in this book demonstrate, there is a wealth of data that could serve both employees and employers in making more accurate job and career decisions. It is all there, just for the asking. And, because it is *your* job and *your* career and *your* life, it is up to you to provide the evidence for why you will be the best "fit" for the job!

Chapter 5. Maximize Your Job-Fit

There are literally millions and millions of us who use only some of our giftedness in the job and then seek other outlets for our talents.

Arthur F. Miller, Jr.

ACCURATE INFORMATION IS KEY

Every job/career decision should be made with two sets of detailed information:

✧ Your Motivational Pattern.

✧ The Critical Requirements of the Job/Role.

Understanding your Motivational Pattern is the first step toward making good career decisions. Don't be fooled by its seemingly general nature. It effectively describes your successful working parameters. If you are not satisfied with the insights gained from your own analysis of your achievement data, seek some professional input. It is essential that you are able to make an accurate self-presentation of your Motivational Pattern.

If you realize that **everything outside your Motivational Pattern is vocationally wrong for you** and you examine any job/career possibility with this in mind, you have a tool for screening out poor career decisions and focusing on good ones. On the other hand, comparing your Motivational Pattern with a generalized idea of a potential job is a wholly inadequate way of using such a tool.

People usually make job/career decisions without sufficient information. They have a general idea of their own skills, a generalized summary from the personnel office, or the opinions of friends and associates who might know something about the job or career. Rarely do they make the effort necessary to acquire the detailed information necessary to make the appropriate choice.

To determine your fit to a job or role, it is important to compare your Motivational Pattern with the Critical Requirements of the job or role, described in similar terms. The following example (Example C) presents the Motivational Pattern of a Technical Specialist being considered for a Technical Sales/Consultant position. Read both the employee's pattern and the job requirements very carefully. Then examine the "Assessing Job-Fit" diagram (Figure B on the following page) to learn how motivations can be "matched" to job requirements.

Example C

Directions: *To learn the process for assessing your job fit, compare the Motivational Pattern of this Technical Specialist* to the critical requirements of a Technical Sales/Consultant role.*

*Note that the definition of **tech•ni•cal** *is 1. Of or relating to some particular art, science or trade.*
2. Having, dealing or pertaining to a knowledge or skill. Funk & Wagnall's Standard College Dictionary.

Technical Sales/Consultant

Employee's Motivational Pattern	**Requirements of the Job**
Subject Matter	**Subject Matter**
Computer Science/Math	Computer Science/Math
Data/Logic/Systems/Models	Data/Logic/Systems/Models
Abilities	**Abilities**
Evaluating (analyzing, judging merits, determining pros/cons)	Evaluating (analyzing, judging merits, determining pros/cons)
Creating (ideas, concepts)	Adapting (ideas, concepts)
Investigating by probing and inquiring	Influencing by selling, getting involvement
Overseeing by directing how it is to be done	Overseeing by facilitating, providing a way
Circumstances	**Circumstances**
Recognition	Behind-the-scenes
New areas to learn	New areas to learn
Difficulty, challenge	Low visibility work
Personal expertise	Difficulty, challenge
Operating Relationships	**Operating Relationships**
Key contributor	Influencer, facilitator
Motivational Payoff	**Outcome/Purpose**
Develop, demonstrate proficiency, expertise	Results obtained; sale closed; customer served

Figure B

ASSESSING JOB-FIT
Areas of Job-Fit and Job Mismatch for the Technical Sales/Consultant

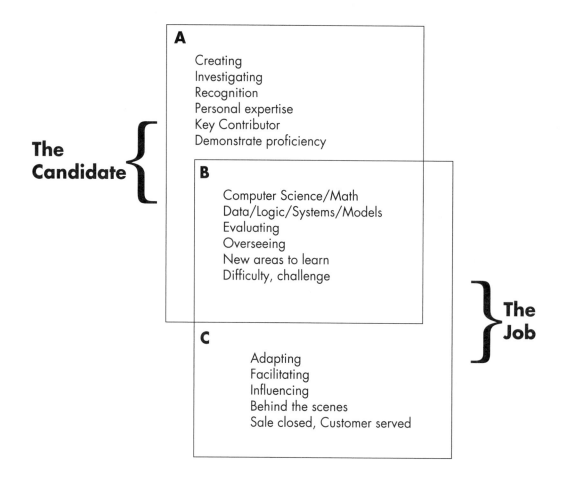

A = Motivational Pattern elements not required by the job.

B = Motivational Pattern elements required by the job and which the candidate is motivated to perform.

C = Job requirements that the candidate is not motivated to perform. (Job requirements that do not match the motivations.)

Is This a Good Job-Fit?

The Subject Matter required for the Job and the Employee's Subject Matter are well matched. Since "match" in the Subject Matter is one of the most critical aspects of job "fit," as well as one of the most difficult to change, this is an important point. Basically, it means there is a possible foundation for "fit" for this person to the job.

Some of the areas of mismatch are Circumstances and Motivational Payoff—which can sometimes be "shaped." (That is, something could be done to make this job a better fit.) For example, the employee is motivated by recognition of his expertise and the opportunity to demonstrate proficiency. Even if the client relationship calls for a "behind-the-scenes" support role, the supervisor could help the employee to meet these motivational needs by providing the employee frequent recognition and opportunity to discuss/present his expertise within the work unit. This also helps to fulfill the employee's need to be a key contributor.

The most likely cause of performance problems will be the mismatch of Motivated Abilities. The essential nature of the consultant's role is influencing and selling. The employee is motivated to analyze and create. So is this job a good "fit"? No, it is not. With assistance from an understanding supervisor, the employee could probably function effectively for a short time. But the consulting/selling nature of the position does not fully engage the employee's analytic and creative motivation. Long term, it does not meet the Dalton/Thompson research criteria for a position that "leverages one's strengths" and keeps the employee's career "moving."

Manage the Mismatches

Even "good fit" jobs will have some responsibilities for which you are not well matched. If you are asked to perform a "mismatched" assignment, you should initiate actions to manage the mismatch BEFORE you perform the task that does not "fit" you. Imagine a situation where the employee in the above example is tasked with the responsibility for presenting the group's products and services to a new and very important client. Probably the best way for the employee to address the issue is to:

- ✧ Team up with a colleague (who is motivated to sell) when calls are made on critical clients

  or

- ✧ Ask his supervisor to join the discussion, if the supervisor is appropriately motivated.

The worst but probably most common scenario occurs when the employee ignores the fact that he is NOT motivated to perform this task and tries to "pull it off." It is likely that the sales interaction will not go well. Eventually this will come to the attention of management. Then the employee's performance in sales interactions becomes a subject of discussion. Seemingly small and unimportant interactions can become major issues for the employee. Unfortunately, the employee may receive little constructive feedback but may not be allowed to handle that kind of client interaction again—which is another way that people can get "stuck" in their careers.

If for some reason it is not convenient to team up with a colleague or a supervisor to perform a mismatched task, you should discuss the situation with your supervisor. Tell her that influencing/selling is not a "motivated" ability and that you think some strategy and/or preparation is in order. Perhaps a rehearsal of the key selling points and the likely objections of the clients would be helpful, or a review of the clients' needs and how your product/service would meet those needs. Certainly a trial run of your presentation with colleagues playing the role of the clients would be useful.

Many employees are reluctant to be open with their supervisors about such "fit" issues. They may feel that the supervisor will see them as "deficient" and that they are adding grist for a negative performance appraisal. But, think about it. If you are not motivated to influence and sell, how long do you think it will take your supervisor to figure that out? The same dynamic applies to every other "fit" issue. Besides, most supervisors are impressed with employees who present strategies for avoiding and solving problems—and ultimately save the supervisor from criticism by his or her manager.

In these situations, you should let your supervisor know that you have recognized this "mismatch" in yourself and that you are taking steps to build your skills in question (reading books, taking courses, participating in Toastmasters, serving in your condominium association, etc.) but you know that it has not yet turned you into a silver-tongued salesperson and that you are primarily concerned with the overall outcome of these sales interactions.

Compare Your Pattern With Your Job

In order to effectively manage your performance, you should know how you "fit" your job. It is essential information for performance and career discussions with your supervisor. To accomplish this comparison, transfer the key elements from your Motivational Pattern (page 75) to the left hand column on page 151. Then describe your job in the right hand column of page 151. (Hint: The descriptions of critical requirements in the previous example might help you to describe more precisely the critical requirements of your job. You should also check your description of your critical job requirements with your supervisor, just to make sure you are both on the same track!) Using Figure C, follow the directions to assess the fit of your Motivational Pattern to your job.

Comparing You & Your Job

Your Motivational Pattern

Subject Matter: _____

_____

_____

_____

Motivated Abilities: _____

_____

_____

_____

Circumstances/Environment: _____

_____

_____

_____

Operating Relationship: _____

_____

_____

_____

Motivational Payoff: _____

_____

_____

Requirements of Your Job

Nature of Subject Matter/Content:

_____

_____

_____

Key Abilities: _____

_____

_____

_____

Circumstances/Working Environment:

_____

_____

_____

Working Relationship with Others:

_____

_____

_____

Purpose/Outcome: _____

_____

_____

Figure C

ASSESSING YOUR JOB-FIT

Directions: *By inserting the motivations in the appropriate section, you can quickly assess your "fit" to the job and determine areas that need to be managed.*

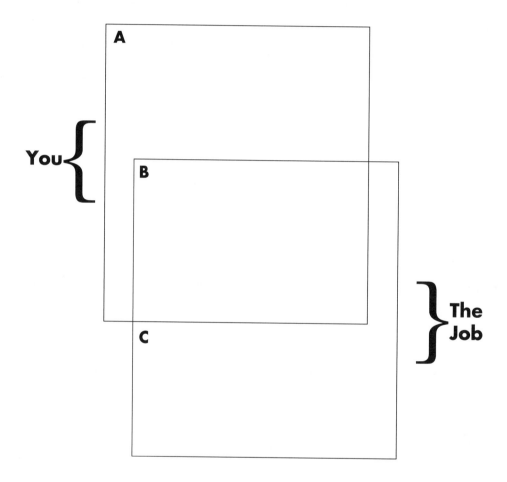

A = Motivational Pattern elements not required by your job.

B = Your Motivational Pattern elements required by your job and which you are motivated to perform.

C = Job requirements that you are not motivated to perform. (Job requirements that do not match your motivations.)

Use this visual to discuss your job-fit with your supervisor.

Does One of These Scenarios Describe Your Situation?

After you have completed the comparison of your Motivational Pattern to the Critical Requirements of your Job, assess the percentage of your fit by comparing your situation to the following statements:

A.　I spend at least 70% of my time doing work that I am motivated to do.

B.　I spend considerably less than 70% of my time doing work that I am motivated to do, but there is some opportunity to change my job/assignments.

C.　There is very little match of my Motivational Pattern to the Critical Requirements of my Job.

If none of these descriptions accurately reflect your situation, add your own descriptions of your "fit" situation below:

D.　_____

　　_____

What To Do About Your "Fit" Situation

Scenario A: Good fit

If you are spending at least 70% of your time working and learning in areas that are motivating to you, congratulations! You are in the one-third of employees who are actually doing work that is a good match to their motivations.

That doesn't mean you have nothing to do but watch your career unfold. There is still much to be done to manage your career. But you have overcome the toughest hurdle and can now focus on strategies for leveraging your talents.

Your Action Step:
Continue with the exercises in this book.

Scenario B: Moderate fit—possibility to alter job/role

If you are spending somewhat less than 70% of your time in work that utilizes your Motivational Pattern, but there is some opportunity to alter your job or assignments, there is probably sufficient potential to warrant your efforts. Most people find that serving in a better "fit" role within their profession will make their careers a better fit.

Your Action Step:
Schedule a discussion to talk to your supervisor about "fit" issues, using the outline

presented on page 155. Make it clear to your supervisor that this is neither a career discussion nor a performance discussion. It is your attempt to maximize your productivity by more precisely aligning your "motivated" capabilities with the needs of the business.

Scenario C: Poor fit

If there is very little match between your Motivational Pattern and the Critical Requirements of your Job, you should take this opportunity to explore other professions and occupations.

Your Action Step:
After you have read the next section entitled MANAGING YOUR CAREER, consider carefully the strategies described in the chapter on Creating Your Best-Fit Scenario.

NEGOTIATE FOR JOB-FIT

Being clear about your Motivational Pattern and the kind of situation that will best utilize your strengths prepares you for the real challenge of career management—negotiating for the kind of assignment that is the "best fit" for you. Fortunately, in tight labor markets, employers are usually more willing to accommodate both prospective and current employees in creating good "fit" work roles. [87] Even in times that were less competitive for talent, knowledge workers who negotiated for roles that met both their goals and the organization's needs found their management to be surprisingly receptive. Data collected from employees and their supervisors at Exxon Engineering in the early 90's, a period of slow growth and much downsizing, found that 75% of the employees who had presented a career development plan based on their Motivational Pattern had at least partial implementation within a one-year period. Most organizations reported only about a 25% implementation rate for employee-generated development plans during those years. [88]

Because your immediate supervisor has considerable influence on your assignments and career experiences, it is critical that you discuss and plan your career with her. Don't wait to be scheduled for an appointment. *Ask for an appointment to discuss how you can maximize your contributions.* Suggest a specific day; take whatever initiative it requires to get on his calendar. Use the outline presented on the following page to prepare for the discussion and as an agenda to structure your discussion. It is always a good plan to give your supervisor your agenda items (but not your answers) when you schedule the discussion. This gives your supervisor the opportunity to prepare and to recognize that this is not a meeting to request a promotion or a salary increase!

Suggested Outline for Job-Fit Discussion With Your Supervisor

(Use the "overlapping boxes" graphic on page 152 to visually illustrate your job-fit. For the first conversation, emphasize the "fit" as much as possible, and identify only one or two items in the other areas that you wish to discuss and address in this conversation.)

1. **What principal requirements of your present job make substantial use of your strengths?** (e.g., logical and analytical problem-solving, ability to design, ability to anticipate problems, ability to relate to customers, investigative abilities, ability to define structure and determine direction without guidance or instruction.)

2. **What requirements of your present job clearly fall outside your strengths?** (e.g., you are currently a team member, but are motivated to work alone; you are supposed to administer the program, but you are not motivated to work with details; the subject matter is intangible and abstract and you are motivated to work with tangible subject matters.)

3. **Is it possible to change or eliminate some of the responsibilities listed above in order to make better use of your strengths?** (Can your work role be redesigned to make better use of your talents? What would you change about your work to create the better "fit?")

4. **For those requirements that cannot be eliminated, what special controls/ procedures could be established to ensure acceptable performance?** (e.g., up-front discussion of expectations, closer checking and monitoring on progress, frequent updates, "teaming up" with a colleague who has complementary strengths or delegating to someone who is a better "fit" for the role?)

5. **What can you do in your present job to give yourself more opportunity to use and develop your Motivational Pattern, to build more capability in areas that you perform well and enjoy doing?** This is probably the most important part of the conversation. In order to make a persuasive case about how your motivations could be more beneficially utilized, you will need to have knowledge of specific current issues your supervisor and the organization are facing. It is much more compelling to make a proposal to address a specific business challenge than it is to ask for support to attend a workshop to develop a competency, even one that is on the organization's "critical skills" list. How can you learn more about specific business needs, especially those facing your supervisor? Ask your supervisor to discuss these problems and challenges with your entire group. A group get-together with a few pizzas makes an informal, participative setting that encourages Q and A. Lunch-time discussions with colleagues in other functional areas will provide a

broader perspective. Reading the company's annual report and strategic mission is a must. **The bottom line: If you know what challenges are facing your supervisor, you will be in a much better position to identify the right opportunities for you.**

LOOK THROUGH THE SUPERVISOR'S GLASSES

When discussing your performance and career issues with your supervisor, it is important to think about the nature of your supervisor's motivation and how his motivation influences his perceptions of your performance. To learn more about this phenomenon, I conducted a review of performance appraisals prepared by a selected group of supervisors over a ten-year period. The first step was to identify ten supervisors who had occupied supervisory roles in the organization for at least ten years. Then, a performance appraisal written by each supervisor for each of the previous ten years was randomly selected and retrieved from personnel records.

As I analyzed the ten appraisals written by each of the supervisors, I was amazed at the similarity of performance strengths and limitations that were addressed in the appraisals prepared by a given supervisor. At first glance, one would almost believe that each supervisor's documents represented ten years of performance appraisals on a single employee! It was evident that a dominant factor in preparation of these performance appraisals was the "glasses" through which the respective supervisors viewed their employees. ALL of the performance appraisals written by a given supervisor addressed similar performance strengths and limitations. For example, some supervisors focused on writing and speaking skills; others focused on the quality of the technical work. Still others found interpersonal and teamwork issues to be most important. I call this bias "looking through our motivational glasses." It is a bias that everyone possesses. And unlike my reading glasses, I cannot remove my "motivational glasses." Everything I see and do passes through the screen of my Motivational Pattern.

"Motivational Glasses" Exercise

The following example illustrates the point. Listed below are the key elements of Motivational Patterns from two individuals. Imagine that Person A is a researcher and reports to Person B, who is the supervisor. Read carefully the patterns of both individuals and think about the "motivational glasses" that Person B will be using to assess the performance of Person A. What limitations is Person B likely to see in Person A?

PERSON A	PERSON B
Abilities	*Abilities*
Learning by studying, reading	Learning by doing, trying
Investigating by in-depth researching	Investigating by interviewing, inquiring
Evaluating by analyzing, dissecting	Organizing by classifying, categorizing
Conceptualizing by hypothesizing	Influencing by involving, getting participation
Communicating by writing	Overseeing by monitoring, checking
Subject Matter	*Subject Matter*
Ideas, Theories, Philosophy, Phenomena	People—Individuals & Groups
Details, Particulars, Facts	Systems, Networks
	Money—Economics
	Results—Payback Potential
Circumstances	*Circumstances*
Lack of Pressure	Needs
Precise, Exact	Participative
Research	Group, Team
Visibility	Need for Immediate Response
Operating Relationship	*Operating Relationship*
Individualist	Manager
Motivational Thrust	*Motivational Thrust*
Comprehend and Demonstrate Understanding, Reduce to Expression	Gain Response—Influence Behavior

When Person B Is the Supervisor

Person B is a very people-oriented, interactive manager who is motivated to get people to do what is wanted and needed—and to do it now. Person A is an individualist, motivated to conceptualize and do in-depth scientific research. Person A wants to be able to completely understand and comprehend a subject before acting on the knowledge. Looking through the "motivational glasses" of one who wants response, Person B is likely to see Person A as:

✧ Taking too long to complete a task—not sufficiently productive.

✧ A "loner"—not a team player.

✧ One who frequently gets into "analysis paralysis."

✧ Having no ability to sell ideas.

✧ Having no political savvy.

When Person A Is the Supervisor

Now reverse the relationship: The scenario is Person A as the supervisor and Person B as the researcher. You might be thinking—*that would never happen. That is not the right "fit" for either of them.* You would be right about the "mismatch" for both but it does happen frequently. Many technical organizations firmly believe that in order to be an effective supervisor, one must be first an outstanding technical contributor. Person A has all the motivations that could make her an outstanding scientist who, in this scenario, has been promoted to a supervisory role. On the other hand, Person B is strongly motivated to work with people and has no science in his subject matter. It is quite likely that Person B was not a top technical performer and so, in many organizations, may be passed over for promotion to supervisory roles. Person B could be having some difficulty with a role as a researcher.

Looking through her analytical, science-oriented "motivational glasses," what limitations might Person A (the supervisor in this scenario) find in Person B who now occupies the researcher's role? Person B could be viewed by Person A as:

✧ A "sloppy" thinker, too impetuous, doesn't do his homework.

✧ Wastes too much time in discussion with other people—wastes their time as well as his own.

✧ Doesn't seem to be really interested in investigating the intricacies of science—gets involved in too many aspects of the subject that aren't directly related to the research.

✧ Can't seem to do anything alone—needs other people—not a very productive employee.

It is possible, of course, that Person B would be exhibiting many of these performance limitations in a role that does not "fit." However, because the supervisor does not recognize the value of Person B's talents, there is no attempt to create a better "fit" and leverage the talents that are present but not being utilized (i. e., people-related influencing motivations). In fact, Person A, the supervisor, may even feel threatened by these people-related motivations that she does not possess.

Of course, the best "fit" situation is the first scenario where Person A is the researcher and Person B is the supervisor. Their Motivational Patterns actually "fit" their respective roles and complement each other very well. But, even if the "fit" is there, incumbents are not always able to fully understand and thus appreciate the performance strengths in another person. Both parties may need some education on the concept of Motivational Patterns. For example, Person A really needs a supervisor who is going to keep the research integrated with broader objectives of the organization and not let it get off track into areas of primarily personal interest. Person A also needs a champion who will be able to "sell" the importance of Person A's research to management and keep them informed on the value added. On the other hand, Person B needs Person A's analytical and investigative talents to provide quality data and new concepts. By understanding the unique talents that each of them bring to the party, these two individuals will begin to see how they are really "made for each other." Their working relationship could be extremely productive and mutually beneficial if they both understand and thus appreciate the uniqueness that each party brings to the table.

Check Out Your Supervisor's "Motivational Glasses"

Your supervisor's assessment of your performance has long-term impact on your career development. You need to be alert to the uniqueness of your supervisor's motivations and be thinking about how a person with those particular motivational priorities would be likely to view your performance. How can you learn about your supervisor's Motivational Pattern? Of course, you can pay close attention to what he does—actions provide many clues. You can listen closely to the kinds of questions he asks and the priorities that he sets. Notice when he seems to be engaged and enthusiastic and when it is difficult to keep his attention. (A word of caution—these "investigative" approaches require interpretation and you may "bias" your perceptions with your own motivation!) You can also ask your supervisor directly what she expects from this particular assignment or what criteria will be used to evaluate your performance. Supervisors will often respond with a copy of the performance appraisal policy or the company's list of desired competencies. But persist and say you would also like to hear his personal opinion. One creative thinker asked the supervisor if she would talk to the group about her work experiences—tell them about some of the assignments that she had really enjoyed doing. (One can always do this in private conversation when the situation is appropriate, but a group setting makes you look less like an apple-polisher.)

Get On Board With Job "Fit" Concepts

It is always a great idea for employees and supervisors to learn together about the concept of motivated abilities and job "fit." Provide your supervisor and colleagues with an article or two to read on the subject (I would recommend "Mismatches—The Problem Isn't Bad Employees" by Arthur Miller, Jr. and Marlys Hanson, published in *Across the Board*, journal of The Conference Board, June 2000 or Peter Drucker's "Managing Your Career," *Harvard Business Review*, March-April 1999.) Offer to lead a discussion on the topic; point out obvious talents that members of your group have demonstrated. Talk about how these talents could be leveraged by assigning tasks that "fit" and how productivity is lost when the group does not recognize and utilize talents of the team members. Of course, the very best way to get understanding about each other's talents and how to best leverage these talents is to have Motivational Patterns prepared for all members of the group. Because Motivational Patterns contain only positive information (there are no deficiencies, only "mismatched" situations) the patterns can be shared with all team members. Strengths and limitations of the team as a unit can be identified and addressed. Individual strategic plans can be formulated to maximize the talents of the team members to reach team objectives. It's a terrific team-building process. You'll hear more about it in the chapter on team building.

SECTION B. MANAGING YOUR CAREER

Chapter 1. The "I Can Do Anything I Want to Do" Myth

Nothing estranges man more from the grand plan of his instincts than his learning capacity.
C. Jung

LEARNING: A DOUBLE-EDGED SWORD

Humankind's continuous impact on the conditions of our existence has resulted in a powerful, almost arrogant, confidence in:

✦ Our ability to learn

and

✦ Our capacity for transforming ourselves into what we want to be or believe we need to be.

In short, the more power man exerted over nature, the more his knowledge and skill went to his head, and the deeper his contempt became for merely natural and random phenomena, like the uniqueness of the individual. Jung [89] writes:

Man's consciousness orients itself chiefly by observing and investigating the world around him, and it is to its peculiarities that he must adapt his psychic and technical resources. This task is so exacting, and its fulfillment so advantageous, that he forgets himself in the process, losing sight of his instinctual nature and putting his own concept of himself in place of his real being.

There are powerful rewards (status, money, power, fame) for those who fulfill roles that are highly valued in a family, an organization, or in our society. We all want our talents and efforts to be valued and appreciated. Whether it is the son who can "take over the farm," the engineer who can also manage people, or the daughter who becomes a medical doctor like her father, the perceived advantages for fulfilling these roles can override the individual's own instinctual sense of what he or she is "motivated" to do.

We observe others, who seemingly possess similar abilities and intellect, performing in the chosen roles. We assume that we, too, can do anything we want to do, if we work hard enough. We usually make these decisions about "being able to" perform a particular role by assessing our abilities, especially our ability to learn. Like an iceberg, our abilities are what can be observed "above the water." But below the water lie our motives, the powerful dynamic that gives us the sustained appetite for using our "motivated" abilities to accomplish a given purpose. Because we are generally not aware of the existence of these motives, we fail to give them consideration. We fail to respect the powerful impact that they have on our behavior and performance. We lose sight of what we are "motivated" to do.

Knowledge workers are probably the most vulnerable to losing sight of their own passion and purpose because they, as individuals, usually have a varied set of learning motivations. Many are motivated to learn in several ways, sometimes covering the spectrum of learning by reading, studying and/or in-depth research as well as doing/ trying and participating in an activity. In other words, many knowledge workers learn quickly and easily. Many are better-than-average students, even top students, throughout their school years. To most, their experiences seemed to tell them that they are quite capable of learning almost anything they set their mind to learning.

But learning is only part of the equation; sustaining quality performance over time is the real test. As Peter Drucker reminds us: *What one does well—even very well and successfully—may not fit with one's value system.* [90] Many knowledge workers can indeed learn to perform a wide variety of activities, but if the activity does not tie into their passion and purpose, they will find it unrewarding and unfulfilling to continue the activity. Eventually, they will find it difficult to sustain competitive performance. In fact, many talented knowledge workers leave their organizations because their managers don't understand this aspect of work satisfaction. [91] Many managers assume that people who excel at their work are happy in their jobs. The fact is that strong skill or performance doesn't always reflect or lead to job satisfaction. The wise employees will recognize that they are not going to be able to sustain quality performance in roles that neither "fit" nor are motivating. These employees will seek other opportunities; they will need to act quickly if they want to move before the mismatch issue has diminished their image or their performance. With great discipline and perseverance, some individuals can (and do) make their situations work at some level. As previously discussed, the costs are significant for themselves and for others who depend on the quality and consistency of their performance.

> *Strong skill or performance doesn't always reflect or lead to job satisfaction.*

Knowledge workers need to know themselves as individuals who have a passion for doing certain things. Their efforts should be firmly focused on finding the right situations wherein they can express these passions. As Carl Jung said, *We can lose sight of our own passion and purpose through our own choices, as a tree or a stone cannot.* [92]

Knowledge workers can, and frequently do, lose their way because their abilities to learn take them into "unmotivated" areas. After much lost time and effort, they realize that learning a skill or acquiring knowledge does not assure sustained ability to perform or personal fulfillment.

LEARNING THAT "FITS"

You are probably thinking, *But how do I know what I should learn? There are endless demands and constantly increasing complexities that compete for my attention. Every assignment seems to require building some new competencies. And I am interested in so many things that it is difficult to choose a direction!*

David McClelland's definition of competencies (see the section on Understanding Innate Motivation) provides useful insight. **His research on competencies has resulted in the recognition that innate motivation is at the core of every competency.** [93]

That is, one must possess innate motives that are related to the competency in order to successfully acquire the attitudes, beliefs, skills and knowledge to sustain quality performance of the competency. In other words, what you are learning must be related to who you are or it won't bring sustained quality performance—much less fulfillment and enjoyment. You may be thinking, *Now that sounds very restrictive.* But the good news is that our Motivational Patterns are broad but also definitive. While providing us with plenty of options for growth, the process also surfaces "evidence" that is especially useful in helping us to determine WHAT it is we are motivated to learn.

For example, I remember Pat, who was a chemical engineer on her company's list for "performance improvement" counseling. Pat has a Ph.D. in Chemical Engineering from a prestigious school, but after only three years in her profession, her career was on the skids. In examining her work/life achievements, both she and I were surprised to find there was not a single reference to science, materials, devices, or even phenomena. Pat's achievements were all about excelling and being the best. (That's why she got her Ph.D. Her father was a chemist and encouraged that career field.) In describing her work/life achievements, she told about learning what she needed to learn to be the best in athletics, music, and academics—and then she would tutor her friends. She had even found fulfillment as an innovative Sunday school teacher. She was very motivated to learn by reading, studying and memorizing. More defined subject matter—knowledge and information as contrasted to concepts and theories— motivated her. Her college coursework gave her exact measures (grades) to confirm her excellence and excel she did! But when she entered the real world of solving ill-defined problems in a chemical research lab, she could find little "fit" to keep her motivated. (She was not motivated to investigate, which was the core of her job.) Even her fantastic learning motivations failed her as she struggled with the lack of definition and concrete standards by which to measure her performance.

> *What you learn must be related to who you are — or it won't bring performance and fulfillment.*

Taking her cues from her achievements that involved learning and tutoring, she decided to pursue a career in teaching and acquired a position at a junior college. A recent e-mail from her reported that she was enrolled in an on-line learning program and was acting as a consultant in a "pilot" for on-line courses at the college. She felt it was one of the best on-line programs in existence! It is probably an accurate assessment, since teaching is a good "fit" role for her, especially in a format where the progress made by her students could be clearly established. She is clearly engaged and challenged in her new role—and has made considerable progress by learning what "fits" her.

In another situation, I prepared a Motivational Pattern for Ken, a 30-year-old carpenter who had a back injury and could not return to his carpentry career. Understandably, he was quite concerned about what he was going to do, since he loved his work as well as the financial rewards. In examining his "motivated" subject matter, we found a recurring theme for mathematics, along with evidence of other "tangibles," like materials, structures, tools, etc. Since his injury, Ken had been thinking about construction estimating as a possible career direction, but he thought it was "wishful thinking." He was worried that he wouldn't be able to learn it, since he had finished high school with a GED and had no college experience. In looking at his achievement, there was evidence of learning in several areas, but the learning was by *doing and trying*, not by *reading and studying*. Thus, it was critical that he select a construction-estimating program that is very "hands on" as contrasted to academic in nature.

The "evidence" that was clearly apparent in his past achievements gave Ken the confidence that there was a solid basis for his choice of construction estimating as an alternative to carpentry. He also understood more about why high school was a problem—for him and thousands of other young men and women who are forced to endure teaching methodologies that do not "fit" how they learn.

Examine Your Motivation to Learn

Directions:
Review your Motivational Pattern and your achievement data for specific evidence for answers to each of the following questions:

How are you motivated to learn? Is anyone else involved when you are learning?

What are you motivated to learn? To what depth are you motivated to learn?

What are the learning outcomes that you seek?

One of the most important kinds of learning is in the maturing of your abilities developed through performing more complex and demanding achievement tasks. (For example, the sequence of my teaching achievements involves "playing school" with my brothers, tutoring friends in high school, teaching high school, training teachers, training employees, training managers, training other consultants.)

What "motivated" abilities or subject matters show evidence of "maturing" or sequential learning for you?

Chapter 2. Build on Your Strengths

The idea that we can choose to become what the world values is as misguided as the alchemist's ancient promise to transmute lead into gold.

Arthur F. Miller, Jr.

MOVE AHEAD OR FALL BEHIND

As new technologies and new ways of organizing work permeate the working world, many of us try to discover what new rules will apply in creating our future. What will be expected of us? What will we need to do or learn to maintain our value in the marketplace? In our profession?

Researchers Dalton and Thompson, whose work was introduced at the beginning of this book, conducted extensive studies on the careers of knowledge workers. Their research was conducted initially in the 1970's [94] and repeated in the 1990's. The authors reported that their findings stood the test of time and, in 1994, the characteristics that differentiated "stuck" from "moving" employees remained the same: [95] The responses from hundreds of interviews with employees and managers had five recurring themes. The knowledge workers who continued to "move" in their careers:

✧   Knew how to leverage their strengths.

✧   Continued to build skills and knowledge that were valued by their organization(s).

✧   Performed well in areas valued by their organization(s).

✧   Performed well and had good experience at each stage of their career.

✧   Knew how to build relationships.

Based on the Dalton and Thompson research, employees who continued to "move" in their careers did a better job of meeting the organization's expectations for growth in their performance over the period of their employment. Dalton and Thompson identified the most common development phases that organizations seemed to expect from their employees. They called these phases of development "Career Stages." They described four stages of career development that are presented in Figure D:

Figure D

CAREER STAGES

	Central Task	Working Relationship	Challenge
Stage I	Performing tasks under supervision	Helper	To accomplish task within time and budget
Stage II	Establishing a distinctive competence	Individual Contributor	To develop an recognized expertise without becoming "narrow"
Stage III	Guiding Developing Influencing	Mentor Champion Integrator	To develop greater breadth of skills - to work through others
Stage IV	Shaping direction (organization or technical)	Director Sponsor Strategist	To exercise appropriate power in initiating actions, influencing decisions

CAREER STAGES MODEL (96)

Central Features of the Four Stages

Figure D identifies specific characteristics of each stage, including:

- ✧ The central task to be performed.

- ✧ The nature of the relationship to others in performing the work.

- ✧ Critical challenges that must be met to perform well in that stage AND to move to the next stage.

As you review the Career Stages Model and read the descriptions for each stage, identify the stage in which you are primarily performing. (Sometimes your responsibilities will involve more than one stage.)

The Career Stages Model is very useful in helping knowledge workers to understand that every organization has certain expectations for their employees' development. **Organizations expect that the nature of the employee's contribution should progress over time, through these stages, if the employee is to sustain and enhance his value.**

It is important to note that organizations differ significantly in the distribution of employees in each stage as well as the length of time the employee is expected to remain in each stage. Some organizations have more opportunity for Stage I and II personnel (e.g., fast food chains) whereas others have proportionately more Stage III and Stage IV roles (consulting firms). Research organizations typically have a longer Stage I (three to seven years) and more opportunity for growth in Stage II and Stage III technical leadership. Smaller, start-up organizations may have a very limited Stage I period; Stage II may be short as even new employees are expected to contribute to team leadership, mentoring and customer interface.

Because of the uniqueness of expectations for development in each organization, the most effective use of the Career Stages Model is as a reference point for stimulating discussion with management and colleagues to get their perspectives on "how it works around here." One way to do this is to present the Career Stages as the researchers have described them, and then to ask your manager and your colleagues if that model reflects their experience in this organization. Does the model accurately describe the development this organization expects from its employees? What else does this organization want? Are there aspects of the model that do not apply to this organization? Is this how career development really works at Company XXXX? What are the best strategies for getting the needed experiences and responsibilities in each stage?

The Career Stages research helps us understand some of the major career challenges of knowledge workers. Obviously, some knowledge workers have Motivational Patterns that will quickly align with the expectations of their organization; it will be relatively easy for these knowledge workers to "leverage their strengths." For example, knowledge workers who are motivated to influence and to oversee the work of others will be more likely to move quickly to Stage III and Stage IV leadership and management responsibilities. But employees who are motivated to work as individual contributors, and who may have more motivation to analyze or create than to influence, can find the transition to these Stage III and Stage IV roles difficult as well as unfulfilling.

Herein lies a major organizational systems issue: **The organization's expectations for the development of its employees can create major career problems for individuals whose Motivational Patterns are not aligned with that organization.** The researchers were quick to state that they were reporting the way the systems *were*, not necessarily the way the systems *should be*. [97] The compensation and promotional systems based on the organization's expectations reward the performance and development that meets those expectations. But it is very difficult to accurately measure different contributions with the same yardstick. What happens to the individual researcher who plods away for years developing a unique expertise that leads to a breakthrough cure? How about the outstanding teacher who has to become a school principal to build her income and acquire adequate financial resources for her retirement? Or the counselor who is very motivated to counsel individuals who must now take on a role of securing new clients, which is totally not her "bag." One can readily see that organizational career systems create thousands of "mismatch" cases that are extremely costly to both employee and employer as individuals attempt to "become" what the organization expects and rewards. The classic example is, of course, when strongly individualistic contributors try to make a shift to overseeing others. The organization, as the old saying goes, "loses a good engineer and gains a bad manager."

Organizations create mismatches as employees try to meet expectations.

Listed below are a few of the more common career "mismatches" created by organizational expectations and career development systems. Check the list to see if any of these challenges might apply to you. Remember, too, that each of these situations can be reversed:

Your Strengths	Your Organization's Expectation
To perform your specialty expertise	To become a generalist
To create innovative new products	To apply "off-the-shelf" products
To do in-depth research and analysis	To develop the business
To troubleshoot and solve problems	To do strategic planning
To work as an individual contributor	To become a mentor or supervisor
To sell products	To manage the sales function
To teach and/or counsel	To administer, oversee
To be a team leader	To be an executive manager
To lead an organization	To integrate several organizations

"Dual" Career Ladders

The researchers did report that some organizations are moving toward development systems that provide greater opportunities for *non-managers* to play Stage III and Stage IV roles. These organizations have implemented policies and practices that provide alternate routes to these more responsible and valued stages. Called "dual" or "parallel" career ladders, these systems are often criticized by technical employees as being a parallel "stool" rather than a ladder! But the researchers found significant examples of organizations that are providing more career growth for their technologists. Some of the reasons for this trend include the following:

✧ *The combination of knowledge and entrepreneurial initiative is becoming more important to many organizations and to their ability to compete. Capital is still an important factor in competing, but ideas and innovation are more important than they have ever been.*

✧ *It has become easier for people with good ideas for new products or services to leave a company and start up their own firm—or to work as independent contractors. Venture capital for someone with a good new technical product has become easier to obtain.*

✧ *The popular culture and the media have created a milieu in which more people are likely to be willing to attempt starting up their own small companies.* [98]

This all adds up to new opportunities for those employees who are capable of making strong technical contributions. If these people do not find the opportunity to influence and to be rewarded for what they have to offer within their current organizations, they are more likely to move on. Every organization, feeling the competition for top technical talent, *will be working to create conditions where able professionals will not have to occupy formal management positions to gain influence over decisions where their knowledge is important.* [99] New technologies, telecommuting and the rise of "free agent" workers have opened the door to entirely new systems of organizing work. The expectations for employees' performance over the span of their careers will change rapidly. This puts even more pressure on individuals to keep abreast of the changing expectations.

Select an Organization That Matches Your Motivation

Knowledge workers must be prepared to deal with the reality of their organization's expectations for development. They must understand that, if they expect their compensation to increase each year, the value of their contributions must also increase. Knowledge workers need to understand development from the perspective of their employers and actively seek to *leverage their motivation* to meet the organization's needs and their goals. Thus, a critical responsibility for effectively managing your career is to investigate potential employers to be sure that your Motivational Pattern will be aligned with their expectations for development. Ask for examples of individuals who are doing what you want to do. Can these people be identified on an organization chart? How long have they been with the organization? How are their functions valued in this organization? How have their responsibilities progressed? How about their salaries? Who is seen as being influential and powerful in this organization? You should also ask for examples of individuals who seem to keep "moving" in this organization and get some detail on their career activities. Likewise, ask for examples of individuals who seem to be "stuck" and for discussion on why they have not progressed.

> *You need to establish that your employer can accommodate your motivations, because you cannot successfully change your motivations to accommodate the employer!*

You need to establish that your employer can accommodate your motivations, because you cannot successfully change your motivations to accommodate the employer!

If you are motivated to create innovative software, do not join a company where the main thrust is to develop applications for off-the-shelf programs. If you are motivated to develop and perform a specific technical expertise, look for an employer whose overall mission is closely aligned with your specialty; your growing expertise will more likely to be valued over time. (I always think of the career struggles that electronics engineers have in oil refining companies.) If you are not highly motivated to work with technical depth and are working on your MBA, stay away from research-focused organizations. If you are in Human Resources, look for an organization with a reputation for strong support, not just lip service, for that function. Examine the proportion of HR staff to the number of employees. Look at their programs and systems. Are they up-to-date or does the function seem like a starving stepchild? It does take a bit of investigation to determine the organization's expectations for the development of its employees, but as we say, the view IS worth the climb!

Develop Critical Skills That "Fit" You

Management can contribute significantly to the employee development process by identifying both the future direction of the organization and the specific skills/knowledge deemed necessary to meet these strategic goals. **Employees can use this information to develop more targeted learning strategies, designed to build skills that leverage their motivation to meet the needs of the organization.** Some organizations provide information on what they call "Business Drivers." It is another way of saying "this is what we need to do best in order to succeed." For example, one of the world's largest pharmaceutical companies defined "think big, think global" and "move fast, move local" as two of their Business Drivers. Other drivers that revealed the company's strategic intent addressed R & D productivity, product access, customer outreach and product commercialization. Because each of these drivers require specific skills to execute, such information can be critical in formulating a career and development strategy that matches your talents.

However, in lieu of providing specific information on organizational direction and related skills, many organizations are choosing to develop lists of **competencies** deemed to be needed by the organization. You will recall that competencies, as described by McClelland, include knowledge, skills, attitudes and beliefs but have innate motivations at their core. This means that characteristics that can be taught and learned (e.g., knowledge and skills) are integrated with characteristics that cannot be changed (e.g., innate motivation). Individuals who are aware of the role of innate motivations know that it is very difficult, if not impossible, to acquire and sustain competencies that are not built on their innate motivations.

The Gallup Organization offers a word of caution about the practice of using competencies:

> *Even though designed with clarity in mind, competencies can wind up confusing everybody. Managers soon find themselves sending people off to training classes to learn such "competencies" as strategic thinking or attention to detail or innovation. But these aren't competencies. These are talents. They cannot be taught.*[100]

But organizational information on future direction and critical skills can be very useful for employees in identifying the kind of work-related experiences in which they can leverage and develop their talents. Most employees do recognize that meeting the organization's expectations for development is a critical part of managing their career development. However, this topic can become problematic in a career discussion if the employee has not "done his homework" and prepared some suggestions for how he/she plans to develop those critical skills. (Again, don't depend on your supervisor to provide specific suggestions. Make her job easier by taking the initiative to offer some mutually beneficial suggestions.) **The best strategy is to determine the competencies that are priorities in your organization AND aligned with your motivation.** You will then be better prepared to suggest what you would like to do to meet your organization's needs AND continue your development.

Chapter 3. Getting the Entrepreneurial Bug?

Entrepreneur: one who undertakes to start and conduct an enterprise or business, usually assuming full control and risk.

Funk & Wagnall's Standard College Dictionary

THE PRIORITY CAREER CHOICE OF GENERATION X

America's 23 million small businesses employ more than 50% of the private workforce and generate more than half of the nation's gross domestic product. Small businesses are the principal source of new jobs in the U. S. economy. No wonder entrepreneurship is such a hot topic! However, according to statistics collected by the Small Business Administration, 50% of all businesses in the United States fail within the first four years. The success rate for entrepreneurial activity is not great! [101]

Because of the increased numbers who join the entrepreneurial ranks each year, the business of entrepreneurial training and education has blossomed. Colleges offer degree programs in both undergraduate and graduate study. Two-year colleges offer associate degrees and certificate programs. Seminars, books, tapes, and assessment instruments offer guidance and tools for the experienced as well as the novice.

Journals and periodicals report case studies of those who make it big. Some entrepreneurs are successful by taking huge risks in niche markets; others pursue well-planned ventures into mature competition. And there are all kinds of entrepreneurs. Some are past masters in their field, and some are "charmers." Some are truly investigators; others build their businesses from their networks. How does one decide if indeed one has the *potential* to be an entrepreneur?

A popularized form of assessing one's entrepreneurial bent is a questionnaire with a rating scale. In most of these exercises, respondents are provided a list of characteristics deemed critical to entrepreneurial success and instructed to rate themselves on a scale of:

1.   This is unlike me.

2.   This is somewhat like me.

3.   This is very much like me.

Typical items include the following: [102]

Entrepreneurial Checklist

- ✧   I have a burning desire to work for myself, to be on my own. I basically dislike working for others.
- ✧   I am self-starting, self-disciplined, and persistent.
- ✧   I am able to set long-term goals and stick to them, even when faced with difficult obstacles.
- ✧   I am creative and always looking for novel approaches and ideas.
- ✧   I am realistically confident that I can succeed at what I put my mind to.
- ✧   I am willing to take the real risks—financial and personal—that are inevitable in being an entrepreneur.
- ✧   I make genuinely sound decisions, and I am willing to make hard decisions.
- ✧   I am willing and able to market my services, in fact I actually enjoy selling when I am proud of the product.
- ✧   I am well organized and pay attention to details.
- ✧   I am flexible, adaptable and comfortable with significant ambiguity and change.

While these questions do provoke one to think about characteristics that seemingly could be related to success as an entrepreneur, there are some significant problems with this type of assessment:

1.   If I am sufficiently interested in becoming an entrepreneur to participate in the exercise, I am likely to bias my responses and find many of these items to be "very much like me." This is a well-established bias in self-assessment, otherwise known as wishful thinking!

2. How can I be sure that these are really the critical characteristics for a successful entrepreneur? What is the research base for these assumptions?

More Than a Risk Taker!

A more reliable and accurate way of assessing your entrepreneurial motivations is to examine your past behavior. Is there evidence of entrepreneurial characteristics in your work/life achievements? This approach assumes, of course, that you know something about the behaviors of successful entrepreneurs.

In their book *Competence At Work*, the Spencers report a study for the United States Agency for International Development. [103] It was a cross-cultural study designed to identify competencies that predict business formation and success within and across cultures. A criterion sample of 216 successful and less successful entrepreneurs was identified. Each entrepreneur was interviewed for two to three hours to obtain a detailed account of how the entrepreneur started and operated the business. They were also asked to identify four other key situations they experienced while running the business.

Several statistical analyses were used to identify the competencies that best distinguished the "superior" from the "average" entrepreneurs. Using a stepwise multiple regression of competencies against the successful entrepreneur criterion rating, the researchers found only three competencies to be statistically significant: "Superior" entrepreneurs had all demonstrated competencies in:

1. Initiating and developing business relationships.

2. Seeing the potential of ideas and acting to develop that potential.

3. Monitoring the activities and work of others.

There were other competencies that all the "superior" entrepreneurs did not share, but each of them did possess and repeatedly demonstrate these three competencies. The "average" entrepreneurs had other competencies; some even had one or two of these competencies. However, the set of three appeared to be the differentiating factor. How can this information be used to identify entrepreneurial behavior?

How to Identify Entrepreneurial Motivations—an Exercise

Assume that you are a venture capitalist who is making a choice about where to invest your money. Examine the achievement data from two prospective entrepreneurs and select the candidate that demonstrates the Spencers' three criteria for superior entrepreneurs. Assume that both candidates have presented comparable business plans; they have appropriate education for their fields; and they have presented themselves effectively in the individual interview.

Entrepreneurial Prospect #1: Leslie's Achievement Data

✧ "As president of a college social organization, I transformed a troubled chapter into an efficiently running organization. I thought a lot about what went wrong the previous year. There were a lot of inefficiencies and an enormous amount of time was required to achieve marginal results. I decided upon certain themes and ran the chapter with those themes in mind. I wanted the chapter to achieve these goals with maximum efficiency because every student's time was valuable. I wanted all the time spent conducting our business to be worthwhile for those participating. Payoff: The successful results of our various programs.

✧ "Started Investment Group for stock purchase. I identified my goal for the initial purchase as learning about the stock market through involvement. I thought of friends who need to be aware of investment options as their income rises. I contacted potential members by phone, explaining my idea. I followed up phone calls with a written memo containing a schedule for forming the group and proposed operating procedures. Payoff: The group experienced steady growth in investments.

✧ "Established Aggressive Savings Goal to achieve ultimate goal of buying property. I expanded the details of my budget and analyzed my performance against this budget every month. Committed to cutting out expenditures that were of little benefit and I became more aware of how I spent every penny. I encouraged my partner to participate and form an arrangement for joint ownership. Payoff: Achieving my goal by being in a position to purchase property."

Entrepreneurial Prospect #2: Ananda's Achievement Data

✧ "Made money providing lunches for roofers. Lived in a neighborhood where many roofs were being repaired. Decided there was enough going on to make it worthwhile to get involved. Watched roofing operations and tried to figure out what they needed that I could do. Overheard discussion about workers not having any place to have lunch. Talked my mother into letting me provide free lunch one day to the workers . . . then took orders and made/sold lunch after that. Got Mom and Grandmother to make the lunches which I delivered and went to other sites looking for more business. Payoff: Figured out a way to make some real money that summer . . . even though I was only 12.

✧ "Worked for a highway contracting firm and was offered a partnership. My parents were divorced during my junior year in college. As my mother and grandmother were left with my five younger brothers and sisters to raise, I felt they needed some help. A classmate offered me a job with a family construction firm, as a project engineer on a highway project. I was responsible for the crew doing the line and grade work for a 2.5 mile stretch of state highway and drainage work. We completed the project in less than one year, and I was offered a partnership. I turned it down in order to have an opportunity to travel. Payoff: It was a tough job and my neck was on the line a lot, but I hung in there. It was a great place to gain experience and to make the money we needed.

✧ "Started my own real estate development company from scratch. I always wanted to run my own business, so I finally decided to try it. I formed a new company, completed a business plan, purchased a subdivided parcel of land and quickly started developing the site. After hiring a small crew, we designed and built high quality custom homes, and successfully sold out the project at a profit in a very tough market. It was especially difficult because one of my children was hospitalized and I was faced with huge medical bills. Payoff: I felt especially good about proving to myself that I could run my own business, despite an extremely difficult environment. My customers were pleased."

Did you choose Leslie or Ananda?

Ananda has demonstrated all three of the Spencers' Entrepreneurial Criteria. There is evidence of:

1. Building business relationships (mom, grandmother, customers, offered a partnership).

2. Seeing the potential of an idea and acting on it (lunches for construction crew, making money in construction, starting own business).

3. Monitoring the work of others (being responsible for the crew, hired the crew to build custom houses).

While Leslie has interesting accomplishments, he has not supplied recurring evidence to support the existence of the three entrepreneurial criteria as established in the above-referenced research.

ARE YOU MOTIVATED TO BE AN ENTREPRENEUR?

You may be thinking, *Well, I just want to be a consultant, not really a full-blown entrepreneur.* But your entrepreneurial bent (or lack thereof!) has a tremendous impact on whether you will REMAIN in business.

Directions: Before you quit your day job, take the time to reflect on your life/work achievements. Is there evidence in YOUR achievements of the three criteria that the researchers found to be foundational to successful entrepreneurs? Review your data and identify the specific words that provide that evidence. List these words after the each of the three criteria.

My Evidence for Being a "Motivated" Entrepreneur

(1) Initiating and developing business relationships:

(2) Seeing the potential of ideas and acting to develop that potential:

(3) Monitoring the activities and work of others:

Then, if you are satisfied that you probably do meet the basic criteria, take the time to read carefully Elaine Biech's book on *The Business of Consulting*.[104] It offers thoughtful insights into the pros and cons, plus a whole lot of very practical suggestions on how to start and sustain a consulting practice.

Can You Be Trained to Be an Entrepreneur?

If we look at the amount of money spent on training around the world, it is obvious that our cultures place a great deal of faith in training processes and support this belief quite generously. While there is evidence to support training to build specific skills and knowledge, there is little evidence to support the successful and lasting change of innate motivation that impacts how these skills and knowledge will be used.

David McClelland, [105] renowned for his work in motivation research, was not satisfied with his understanding of *what psychological factors might be responsible for the fact the training* (in this case, training to develop entrepreneurial behaviors) *was effective for some participants and not for others.* He concluded that, **in some cases, the training had led to an increased desire to have impact or to be recognized as a success for some men, which does not translate into taking the entrepreneurial, moderate-risk steps necessary to improve business.**

In other words, participants responded differently to the training. That's hardly a surprise! It should cause us to think about the fact that if someone has innate entrepreneurial motivations, he or she will probably listen to and participate intently in such training, then hurry out to put it to work. But for the participants who are not so motivated, listening and participating will be a chore. They will probably be thinking of ways they can use the skills and knowledge to pursue their own passion and purpose.

So my answer to the question *Can you be trained to be an entrepreneur?* is: Yes, you can be trained to be an entrepreneur if you have some evidence in your Motivational Pattern for the basic behaviors. However, if there is little or no evidence of your having demonstrated these entrepreneurial behaviors in your life/work accomplishments to date, and you really want to have your own business, you should start looking for a partner to complement your motivations.

Building Entrepreneurial Teams

We know that only a very few people are "motivated" to do everything, but many times we behave as though it were true for everyone. We act as though we truly can "do anything we want to do." Start-up businesses, where cash is short and tasks are endless, are especially prone to "making-do" with whomever is on board. Some people do seem to "be able to do anything." They often do this at high personal cost, including their physical and mental health. Sustaining their performance in a role that doesn't "fit" is another story. The high failure rate of small businesses tells us that this strategy doesn't work for long.

In examining small businesses that do work, the staff at People Management International LLC identified four basic Motivational Patterns that seem to be critical to the long-term health and profitability of start-up businesses. [106]

Simply stated, the essential Motivational Patterns needed to make a business work include the:

❖ **Inventor/Developer**: Often the idea person who is interested in creating and investigating, usually motivated to work on concepts and products.

❖ **Entrepreneur:** More interested in profitability and potential. Usually a strategist and intuitive decision-maker with strong influencing motivation, builds business relationships, monitors the work of others.

❖ **Promoter:** Motivated to communicate and promote. Interested in people and ideas; serves as a catalyst or "spark plug" in creating action.

❖ **Manager:** Motivated to oversee the work of others, to organize and to bring structure. Sets goals, responds to problems, wants to bring things to completion, improve and make things better.

Rarely does one find all of these motivations in one person. Most of us just do not have this breadth and scope in what we really enjoy doing and do well. The obvious strategy is to determine the nature of your entrepreneurial strengths and then find others to complement your strengths. And when you start your search, don't forget the "past behavior" part! You will want to do a thorough analysis of any prospective partner's Motivational Pattern. It is one of the best ways to really get to know a person. You will want to share your pattern with them, too. It's much easier to identify potential problems BEFORE you have taken out a loan on the equity in your home!

Chapter 4. Mid-life Crisis, Job Mismatch or "Plateaued"?

To stay mentally alert and engaged during a 50-year working life, one must know how and when to change the work one does.

Peter Drucker

WHEN LIFE IS A BORE

Trevor is about 45 years old, a 20-year employee of a Fortune 10 organization. He has a B.S. in Accounting and two Master's Degrees, one in Accounting and an MBA. He came to me after a presentation on mid-life crises and "plateauing" and asked if he could talk privately. When we were alone, he said *I just sat there sort of astounded when you were going through the description of such a crisis, when one can't seem to find excitement or enjoyment in anything. Even though I am constantly busy with something, I feel totally bored. I go home in the evening and crash. I don't even want to go out to dinner with the family or to the health club to play basketball with my son. Life has become routine and totally unexciting. I have no goals. I feel no sense of future. I am going nowhere. I move without energy. I am merely enduring.*

Trevor said his performance as an accountant had been average or above most of his career, but lately his performance had slipped. In today's competitive environment, he recognized the vulnerability that this implied, but he said even the fear of being laid off did not get him going again.

When we talked about his work, he said that he felt his job was a pretty good "fit." He enjoyed the accounting system that he supported and the clients, but there was not much learning in his work anymore. He had done about everything at least once and most of it several times.

When we examined Trevor's descriptions of his life/work achievements, there was a strong theme for learning. He wanted to develop knowledge or skill to a point of competence and then demonstrate his proficiency in performing a task or responsibility. Then he wanted to move on to new learning and new demonstration. His current job had turned into a maintenance role, which is obviously not a good "fit" for a person who is motivated by learning.

It is fulfillment of our motivational purpose that puts meaning and excitement in our lives.

I asked Trevor why he had not talked to his supervisor about his situation. He said he had been told that he would probably not get promoted to another level, and that salary increases would be small at best. So what incentive was there to ask for something new to do?

Trevor, like many people, did not understand how profoundly our Motivational Pattern impacts our daily existence. He did not understand that it is fulfillment of our motivational purpose that puts meaning and excitement in our lives. He did not recognize that running out of "motivational gas" at work was impacting his attitude toward life in general. He thought that the previous promotions and salary increases were the motivating forces. However, upon examining his stories of life/work achievements, he noted that learning and demonstrating new competencies were at the core of every accomplishment that he had cited.

Trevor decided to take responsibility for his situation. Waiting for his supervisor to talk to him about the reasons for his drop in productivity seemed to be a high-risk strategy. He decided to set some learning goals for himself, both for his work and for his life. He suggested to his supervisor that he learn a new computer application that his group was going to implement, and then he could teach it to others in his group. This would be a perfect "fit" for his learner/demonstrator motivation. His supervisor was surprised and delighted that he asked for this added responsibility. It also saved her from having to confront Trevor's slipping performance.

Trevor also decided to take a night school program in accounting systems for the health care industry. He was very interested in public health and thought he would move into health care as a "retirement" career.

When I met with Trevor about three months later, he looked like a different man; he said he felt like one. He was still shaking his head in disbelief that he had allowed his disappointment with lack of promotion and salary increases to drown his motivational instincts to learn and perform, and that his disappointment had such negative impact without his recognition of the cause.

Trevor's experience is not at all unique. In fact, it is so common that we generally term this period of the blahs a mid-life crisis. In working with the many individuals who report these mid-life crises symptoms, it appears that individuals can sustain mismatch situations only so long. Then they really do run out of "motivational gas." For many, this happens in their early 40's. While I have not done rigorous data collection to document my impressions, I cannot recall interacting with a single individual with mid-life crisis symptoms that was highly involved in a "good fit" work situation. I have also worked with many individuals who have resolved their mid-life crises with a change in their work situation and without changing spouses or having liposuction.

Different Kinds of "Plateaus"

Trevor's situation is often characterized by the word "plateaued." Webster's New Collegiate Dictionary defines *plateauing* as "reaching a period or phase of stability, forming a plateau; leveling off." In a career sense, we most often think of being *plateaued* when we are no longer being promoted or are seen as not having the potential of advancing further in the organization. Dr. Judith Bardwick in her book entitled *The Plateau Trap* [107] helps us to more completely understand the subject by describing three different kinds of plateaus:

Position Plateau—the End of Promotions Caused by an Organization's Hierarchy or Structure

There is an end point to every career, even for the President of the United States! Being Position Plateaued is inevitable. However, with flatter organizations and reduced numbers of "rungs" in both management and technical ladders, employees are likely to become Position Plateaued at a younger age than their predecessors. Of course, many employees anticipate this problem and make a career move if it is an issue for them. Position Plateauing is usually a significant problem only when promotion is a very strong motivator for the individual. For example, individuals who seek personal advancement as payoff for their achievement activities are often devastated if they are Position Plateaued.

Contribution Plateau—When People Know Their Job Too Well and Have Little Opportunity to Learn and Contribute Something New

This happens when people "master" their job and there's just nothing new anymore. They have done the work so long that the challenge is gone. A Contribution Plateau is not related to the amount or type of work nor to one's level in the organization. It can happen any time or any place and generates as much stress as a Position Plateau for the person who is motivated to learn or meet new challenges. The good news about the Contribution Plateau is that it needs never to occur! It is preventable and if it has occurred, it can be remedied.

Life Plateau—When People Find Little Fulfillment in Any Area of Life and Nothing is Fun or Exciting Anymore

The Life Plateau is more profound, more total and thus more serious. It can be brought about by a Position and/or Contribution Plateau. Individuals suffering from this kind of plateauing can be very busy or they may not be busy at all. But their lives have become routine, repetitive, hum-drum, "gray," dreary, predictable and downright boring. There is no forward momentum, no sense of future—the person will say that he/she feels like there is movement, but toward nothing. Individuals often resign themselves to this state and simply seek to endure.

Trevor, the accountant, was probably experiencing all three kinds of plateaus. He was Position Plateaued; he had allowed himself to be Contribution Plateaued; all this resulted in his being Life-Plateaued—which is much like a mid-life crisis. By understanding his Motivational Pattern, he was able to develop strategies to directly address the outcome or payoff that he sought from his achievement activities. For Trevor, the outcome he seeks is learning—developing new proficiencies and having the opportunity to demonstrate those proficiencies. Once he had identified the specific problem, he was on his way to finding his own ways to do just that. Mid-life crisis resolved!

Chapter 5. Create Your Best-Fit Scenario

Work should be the full expression of the worker's faculties, the thing in which he finds spiritual, mental and bodily satisfaction.

Dorothy Sayers

IF IT'S TO BE, IT'S UP TO ME!

The door has been opened wide for us! No period in human civilization has provided such possibilities for change. Never before in the period of human history has each individual had such a possibility of directly influencing his or her course and destiny.

In fact, it is more than a possibility; it is a responsibility! Many have gone so far as to call this period the *Age of Individual Responsibility.*

But many knowledge workers approach this responsibility tentatively or with difficulty. Some of us have become content (and yes, even lazy) and have placed the responsibilities for our careers in the hands of others. We may truly expect to be taken care of by our organizations.

We may still be seeking answers, to find out w*hat we should be when we grow up.* We may have little practical experience with building our own vision and strategies. Most importantly, only a small percentage of individuals is actually *motivated* to work from a blank sheet!

Robert Fritz, a well-published authority on the power of our *basic orientation* as the single most influential component affecting the outcome of all our actions, asks the question in a more precise way: *What result do you want to create?* [108]

Isn't this where most of us check out when we simply cannot describe the results we want to achieve in a sufficiently articulate form to serve as the vision for our career/life?

But wait! Haven't you just carefully examined the life/work achievements that you most valued, and developed a summary statement of what motivates you? Have you not described:

✧   **The end result you are seeking?**

✧   **How you want to relate to others?**

✧   **The subject matter(s) with which you wish to work?**

✧   **The abilities you want to use again and again?**

✧   **The circumstances that are most motivating to you?**

Those statements are not a product of your imagination, but an extraction from your enjoyable life experiences! What has brought you satisfaction and fulfillment in the past will provide you similar benefits in the future. If you can accept this as a vision of the best fit for you, you can use it as the foundation for your actions to develop both your strategies and your work situation.

Because your Motivational Pattern, when understood properly, really defines what you want out of your work and your life, you can transform it into a "Best-Fit Scenario" for your lifework.

Do not make the mistake of extracting one or another quality and saying it is typical of you. Only as integrated with all the other parts can one part properly be understood. For example, individuals often tell me that they are motivated to "work with people." There are many ways to work with people—and only by examining all the parts of the Motivational Pattern does one learn the ways in which this person wants to work with people. Does she want to teach or instruct people? Sell or persuade them? Perhaps it is to oversee or manage them—or even to confront them? What purpose is the individual seeking by working with people? Does she want to excel, to impress, to control, or to gain response? What kind of circumstances does she need to be motivated in her work with people? She may need a defined problem to address; others need an open and unstructured situation. Be sure that you address all five parts of your Motivational Pattern when you speak about your motivations!

The way to create your "Best-Fit Scenario" is to synthesize the elements of your Motivational Pattern into a single statement. The format for creating this statement is presented below:

Outline for My Best-Fit Scenario

A job working with— summarize your subject matter; *e.g., people, ideas, numbers, structural things.*

Where the conditions of the work— summarize your circumstances; e.g., *project oriented, require operating under stress, and allow some freedom of movement.*

And where I can operate— summarize your way of operating or relating with others when you work; e.g., *a member of a team, or in a defined role, or in a leadership capacity.*

Using my motivated abilities to— summarize your motivated abilities; *e.g., investigate for the facts, analyze their significance, improvise a solution, organize others involved, oversee the implementation.*

And which leads to— insert your one motivational payoff or outcome; *e.g., a finished product, chance for advancement, greater responsibility, recognition for my contribution.*

To give you an idea about what you are trying to create, read the following examples carefully:

Examples of Best-Fit Career Scenarios

Sales

A job in sales working with people, merchandise and money. The conditions of work are not too structured and allow me to tackle and solve problems that come up, and require me to keep a cool head in the face of a lot of pressure. I can operate pretty much on my own; using my abilities to evaluate people, make friends with them, sell them on myself and my product, keep my merchandise neat and orderly and carefully account for my sales and cost of sales. All of which leads to opportunity for participation in the ownership or profits of the business.

Product Development

A job working with people and instrumentation; where the conditions of work require deadlines and constant attention to details, and there's a need for technical support. I can operate as a member of a team; using my motivational abilities to analyze and solve problems, implement solutions, draw on people and technical resources. All of which leads to an end product that enhances the quality of life and earns me some recognition for my contribution.

Employee Relations

A job working with people and ideas; where there is a need to develop new programs, a requirement of responding to the concerns of the community, and every situation is a new one. I can operate on my own, but have others in the group to learn from; using my abilities to listen and maintain confidentiality, meet people and tell them about different kinds of careers, improve communications between employees and their management, and develop training programs. All of which leads to people who are happier and more effective in their work.

Product Management

A job working with people and a product; the conditions of work are constantly high-paced and goal-oriented. I can operate as the leader and coordinator to implement these goals; using my motivated abilities to analyze the facts and decide on the best course of action, monitor progress, and keep communication flowing. All of which leads to the successful marketing of a product I think is worthwhile.

Machinery Maintenance

A job working with machinery and its maintenance—where the conditions of work make clear what is expected of me, and each job can be completed before going on to the next. I can operate with others as part of a team, using my abilities to learn how new machinery works, set up a maintenance schedule, repair broken parts, improvising with what is available, and explain to operators how to properly use machinery. All of which leads to opportunity to work with greater variety and complexity of machinery.

My Best-Fit Scenario

Directions:

Now, using the space provided, transform your Motivational Pattern from page 75 into your Best-Fit Scenario. Your Best-Fit Scenario should describe the most productive and fulfilling job/career situation for you. Use it to communicate your career interests to your management. Identify organizational needs/roles that are a good fit for your vision. Remember, one or more of your life/work achievements may offer some great clues about the kinds of situations that are the "best-fit" for you! (Your Best-Fit Scenario can also be used to define your Job Objective on your resume.)

A Job Working With . . . (Insert subject matter.)

Where the Conditions of the Work . . . (Insert circumstances.)

Where I Can Operate . . . (Insert operating relationship.)

Using My Motivated Abilities To . . . (Insert motivated abilities.)

Which Leads To . . . (Insert motivational payoff.)

FINDING A NEW CAREER

If you are in a situation that calls for an evaluation of your job/career direction, you may find the SIMA® JOB MATCH useful. This computerized program compares the elements of your Motivational Pattern to over 400 professions and occupations. Each profession/occupation in the computerized match has been characterized by the motivational elements critical to the performance of the respective job/role.

The SIMA® JOB MATCH provides an objective perspective of the professions and occupations that would be a good "fit" for your Motivational Pattern. It is most useful for individuals who are making initial career choices or who are looking for a better "fit" career. Individuals who are planning for a second or third career may also find the information helpful. The SIMA® JOB MATCH will suggest areas for further investigation through Critical Requirements Interviewing, which is discussed below. If you are interested in learning more about the SIMA® JOB MATCH, please contact us at mhanson539@aol.com or www.motivationalpattern.com.

CRITICAL REQUIREMENTS INTERVIEWING

When you have completed your Best-Fit Scenario and have a generalized notion of a "good-fit" job or career, you will want to get more specific information about the job/ role. This is also an effective strategy anytime you are asked to consider a new assignment or are being "redeployed." Job descriptions rarely provide the kind of detail needed to make an informed decision. The following technique can be used at any level of your job/career research, but it is essential when you are seriously considering another position.

In conducting this interview, you will probably want to start with an incumbent in the desired (or a similar) position. (Be sure to tell the incumbent that it is not his/her job you want!) You will get your best information at this level. If the position appears to be a match, you may want to have a similar interview with the supervisor to broaden your perspective.

If you are doing this kind of interviewing in your organization, should you inform your supervisor about your activities? This is a much-debated question and depends on the policies, practices and culture in your organization. But remember that you do want to build a mutually supportive relationship with your supervisor. Thus, being open about your career interests and related activities is generally the best policy. To be sure, check it out with some of your politically astute colleagues who seem to know how to keep their careers moving without alienating the boss.

Questions for the Critical Requirements Interview:

The basic approach to the Critical Requirements Interview is similar to describing your achievements. You are trying to get past generalities and get down to the essential requirements (details, details, details!).

As information is provided, ask "door-opening" kinds of questions that will allow you to get at detail. For example:

What is involved in handling the customers? How do you go about setting up your day's run?

Could you give me some more details on what's involved in providing market services?

What are the detailed steps in making such a survey? How do you do that?

What do you mean by coordinate?

What's involved in that?

This kind of "digging" can be interspersed with more general questions that may put the person at ease. Consider any or all of the following as good questions:

What are your duties during your usual day?

Are these typical of most days?

What is your working environment like?

Are there advantages you can see in your occupation?

What about the disadvantages?

What do you foresee as long-range challenges and problems?

What are the toughest problems you must deal with?

What sort of person do you think would enjoy your occupation?

What type of person would not be satisfied?

What skill should a person possess in order to be good at this profession?

In what ways do you work with people?

How does your occupation affect other aspects of your life?

What background is needed?

What are some of the biggest problems this company faces?

How would the average employee describe working in this company?

Ask any other question which is relevant to your motivation. If the person seems open, you may want to share your "best fit" scenario and ask how the position under discussion compares to your scenario.

Avoid questions that can be answered with "yes" or "no" answers. (e.g., Do you like your job?) Also be aware that the interviewee is giving you a picture of this position as seen through his or her "motivational glasses." That is why it is always important to get more than one perspective about a position.

If you're getting good answers to your questions, you should begin to have a clear idea of whether the performance of the job's critical responsibilities will require motivators that you possess. For example, is this a sales or consulting position? Are you motivated to influence, explain and sell? Or is this an analytical, problem-solving job and perhaps you do not possess the required "motivated" analytical skills. You may not have a perfect match for all the responsibilities, but it is key that there is a match of your motivators to the critical responsibilities of the position. Be honest about your comparison!

SECTION C.
RECOGNIZING THE TALENTS OF OTHERS

Chapter 1. Your Role as a Manager or a Leader

The best way to help an employee cultivate his talents is to find him a role that plays to those talents.

Gallup Organization

THE MEAT IN THE SANDWICH

In these days of unpredictable change, everyone is looking to you, the manager, for direction and guidance. Top executives expect you to translate their vision into profits. Your peers expect you to "hold up your end of the tent;" they want your unit to contribute equitably to the organization's efforts. Your employees want to know whether they have security in this organization and how their careers will progress. They need to know what the organization expects from them. They want feedback and coaching on their performance.

And you have to accomplish all of this by effectively utilizing the most important resources you have—the people you manage!

The basic challenge that is the core of all these managerial responsibilities is the challenge of managing people's talents. It's getting the right person in the right job at the right time to produce the right results! (Sounds like my story of the work on the family farm!) What many managers and their organizations fail to recognize is that it's a lot more than just right-person/right-job/right-time. It is a matter of continuing to develop that person's talents to meet the individual employee's goals as well as the business needs. Job security and loyalty have gone out with the buggy whip; the new employer-employee contract promises interesting work and the opportunity to build marketable skills in exchange for commitment to excellence.

Remember, the key to employee performance and retention is job-fit that provides intrinsic motivation—the work itself is motivating to the employee. Managers should understand each employee's passion and purpose in sufficient detail to be able to make accurate decisions regarding his assignments and development. The manager's goal should be to help each individual utilize his unique talents to the fullest in meeting business needs.

In less competitive days, organizations were less demanding of their managers and their employees. Marginally productive employees (both managerial and non-managerial) were often retained for their career lifetimes, but not in today's profit-oriented world. There is no room for time-consuming low producers and problem employees. There is more pressure on you, Mr./Ms. Manager, to make accurate selection and assignment decisions. You are expected to get the job done right the first time.

The fitness of your organization to compete is dependent on the "fit" of the workforce to the mission of the organization. When people do things because they want to, not because they are told to, they perform at their best. Reliance on power and control over time diminishes the capacity of individuals and organizations to excel. To be a competitive manager, you must build a sound track record of making accurate decisions about the use of people's talents. That is what the job of management is all about.

So how do great managers do it? How do they select a person, set expectations, motivate and develop each and every one of their employees? How do they release the potential energy of all their people?

One of the ways to learn more about what effective managers do is to think about the managers for whom you have worked. Think of the manager that you felt was the most effective and describe what that manager did that made you believe she was so effective. Can you list 4-5 items? (You may have to consider the behaviors of more than one manager.)

Effective Behaviors of My Managers

- ✧ _____
- ✧ _____
- ✧ _____

You may want to ask some of your friends and colleagues to respond to this question, so that you get perspectives from individuals who have different Motivational Patterns. (Obviously, what each of us wants and needs from a manager depends on his own motivational needs.) It is also interesting to note that salary increases and promotions are rarely mentioned, and when mentioned, it is usually in the context of a manager "fighting for me." Listed below are some of the more frequent responses:

Most Effective Behaviors of Managers

- ✧ Took a personal interest in me—understood what my strengths were and helped me to find assignments that were good for both the company and me.

- ❖ Increased my sense of competence by talking to me about my work and demonstrating trust in me. Asked my opinions and trusted me with confidential information.

- ❖ Served as a sounding board—just listened and helped me to clarify my thoughts. Helped me to assess risks.

- ❖ Helped me to learn the organization's "ropes"—gave me inside information and instruction in dealing with organizational realities such as politics, power struggles, and personalities.

- ❖ Taught me about the organization's values, cultures and tradition.

- ❖ Protected me from an unfair attack and organizational pressures. Provided support by intervening in conflicts that could have ruined my career.

- ❖ Influenced other decision-makers to give me responsibility.

- ❖ Increased my visibility in the company by advertising my good qualities and accomplishments.

- ❖ Got me into selective training programs, responsible positions on committees, etc.

- ❖ Used her position to get me access to resources, funding, in-house contacts I needed.

- ❖ Truly understood and appreciated my strengths—did not try to mold me into his form.

- ❖ Encouraged me to set higher standards—not to be satisfied with the ordinary. Really pushed me to develop MY potential.

- ❖ Served as a role model in a variety of situations.

- ❖ Knew when to intervene and when to let me do it myself.

EMPLOYEES JOIN COMPANIES, BUT LEAVE SUPERVISORS

One of the interesting outcomes that consistently appears in results of employee surveys is that supervisors have a tremendous impact on both the performance and satisfaction of employees. For example, the employees of Supervisor A (located with his/her team on one side of the hallway) may report (on average) that the company is a great place to work, their talents are being well-utilized and developed, and that there is plenty of career opportunity in this organization. On the other hand, the employees of Supervisor B (located in the same facility with a very similar function) may provide information that is directly contrary to the results from Supervisor A's employees. Anyone who has reported to more than one supervisor in the course of his/her career doesn't need a "meta-analysis" to be convinced of the fact that the employee's performance and satisfaction are most directly influenced by the employee's immediate supervisor. However, the Gallup Organization has provided just such an analysis. Based on interviews with one million employees and 80,000 managers, the six issues found to be most directly related to employee retention and business outcomes are the following:

1.   *Do I know what is expected of me at work?*

2.   *Do I have the materials and equipment I need to do my work?*

3.   *Do I have the opportunity to do what I do best every day?*

4.   *In the last seven days, have I received recognition or praise for good work?*

5.   *Does my supervisor, or someone at work, seem to care about me as a person?*

6.   *Is there someone who encourages my development?* [109]

If you reflect carefully on that list of relevant issues, you will recognize that the process of understanding and utilizing an employee's Motivational Pattern is the mechanism through which the supervisor can address these issues.

Are You the Right Person for the Job?

Managers and Leaders have a serious responsibility to *liberate the potential in everyone and to develop the capacity to guide others to places you (and they) have never been before.* To maximize productivity AND employee satisfaction, they must learn what others really WANT to do, as differentiated from what they CAN do. They must be able to recognize what others find personally enjoyable and rewarding and to avoid the trap of *If it works for me, it should work for you.* They must be able to recognize that while Employee A wants specific directions and requirements spelled out, Employee B wants unstructured and undefined work, and both employees will turn in better performances if they have the appropriate scenario. Employee C needs a daily pat-on-the-back; Employee D could care less about recognition. And these are just the more common differences! (Please remember that while this may sound very complex and difficult to those who are not "gifted" for managerial roles, a truly "motivated" manager or leader will intuitively be attuned to the unique needs of his employees.)

Managers and Leaders need to arouse intrinsic motivation and to make it possible for others to do good work. They know that no one does her best when feeling incompetent or out-of-their-element. Managers and Leaders must search for opportunities for people to exceed their previous levels of performance. They must go out of their way to help others engage their passions to accomplish their purpose!

What if by virtue of examining your own talents, you discover that identifying and making decisions about other people's talents are NOT among your "motivated" abilities? Spending your career (and your life) in management could be an exercise in frustration, involving you in a lifetime of work that you truly do not find rewarding. Because you are not as interested or "motivated" to perform the work of management, your performance as a manager may not be as competitive and you may fall short of your career goals. Because you do not find your role rewarding and satisfying, it will be difficult to lead and inspire others. It is very hard to "pour from an empty pitcher," as the old saying goes.

Chapter 2. Build Teams Based on Motivation

The purpose of a team is to make the strengths of each person effective, and his or her weaknesses irrelevant.

Peter Drucker

GET THE RIGHT PEOPLE TO DO THE RIGHT JOBS

Teams are groups of people who need one another to get something done. Teams do not develop themselves; they require systematic hard work. To build a successful team, you don't start out with people—you start out with a job. You ask:

✦ What are we trying to do?

✦ What are the key activities?

Then, and only then, you ask:

✦ What does each of the key people have by way of strength? How do the activities and the skills match?

And, just as important, everyone needs to know what each one of the other people is going to do. You identify individual strengths, and then you match the strengths with key activities, and position the players to take action. A common mistake is to believe that because individuals are all on the same team, they will all think alike and act alike. One manages individuals on a team. A team melds the performance and the strengths of individuals into a joint effort.

The challenge is to create working roles for people that fit them better and thus enable them to give full rein to their gifts and abilities. It's an empowering concept that allows the individual to leverage his strengths for the benefit of the team and the organization.

Team building, if used to match team activities to performance strengths, can do much to legitimatize the motivational differences between team members. Teams that are built with understanding and appreciation of the unique contributions of individuals offer both employee and employer the benefits of enhanced performance. We all recognize that the silver-tongued orator will bring something different to the "party" than will the analytical investigator or the creative designer. Effective team building based on the "matching" of activities to strengths is really the application of common sense.

In fact, there's a new "buzz-term" that depicts that kind of work environment that teams should really reflect. The term is "hot group." A hot group is a group that is totally passionate about a task. Hot groups have always existed; they just have a new name. (The term "skunk works" describes a somewhat similar situation.) With a marked demand for innovation, new products and technology, these kinds of groups are more important than ever. They can be found in all industries, but they are the nucleus of activity for technology companies. Examples of hot groups that you may recognize include Bill Gates and his friends at Harvard and the folks who put together the Macintosh.

What sets the hot group apart from conventional work groups is its attitude toward its work:

> *These groups consider what they do as fun. It's so much fun they often lose track of time and work around the clock accomplishing the task at hand. Hot groups are loosely structured, freewheeling and democratic. They are not interested in your rank in the organization. The only thing they're interested in is your willingness to contribute.* [110]

"THE MISSING INGREDIENTS"—A CASE STUDY IN BUILDING A TEAM

One of the best ways to observe the dynamics of teams is to examine the actions and strengths of an operating team. The following case study examines the management team at a small company I shall call "Zudco Devices." Zudco has about 300 employees and has been engaged in the manufacture and distribution of specialized medical devices for about five years. Initially, the organization was very profitable and enjoyed high morale and employee retention. About a year ago, profits began to drop, even in a favorable market. Employee turnover was high and interpersonal conflicts frequent.

The Zudco Management Team

To help you remember this cast of characters, we have assigned names that are somewhat descriptive of their motivational strengths. A thumbnail sketch of each is provided:

(1) CHIEF EXECUTIVE OFFICER Victor Cavalier had been a leader in student government in high school and college. The lack of participation from students left Victor disenchanted with his role as president. He approached his leadership role at Zudco by getting all employees involved in a "Leadership Challenge Seminar." However, the new "I'm a Leader" buttons lost their gleam in the late night hours, while everyone was working to meet the endless changes demanded by clients.

(2) CHIEF OPERATING OFFICER Moxy Molder had always been an organizer. She always had ideas on how she and her friends could make some cash. But overseeing the projects weren't nearly as much fun as getting them started. This seemed to be true in her role at Zudco, where Moxy was off starting something new and leaving no one responsible for routine maintenance and quality control.

(3) CHIEF FINANCIAL OFFICER Chintzy Earnmore found his niche early in life. He monitored his siblings as they performed their household chores and distributed their allowances accordingly! As a young accountant, he distinguished himself with vigilance in negotiating contracts. But employees often found his decisions to be "penny-wise" and "pound-foolish."

(4) LABORATORY MANAGER Rory Bustabrisket was a bit of a genius as a child, creating new chemicals and applications with his chemistry set. He was still at his best when he was in the lab. He was at his worst in meetings with employees who wanted direction and feedback on their work.

(5) PROCESS ENGINEER Fred Fixer created his first production line when he worked in his uncle's footstool factory. Later, he made pizza production lines more efficient and was a lifesaver on Zudco's manufacturing line. But his talents for solving systems problems often went untapped because he rarely spent the time needed to explain and "sell" his ideas and his capabilities.

To help you think about the individual and collective strengths on this team, Figure E below summarizes the key contributions of each member of the management team:

FIGURE E

WHAT ARE THE MISSING INGREDIENTS IN THIS MANAGEMENT TEAM?

	Fred Fixer	Chintzy Earnmore	Moxie Molder	Rory Bustabrisket	Victor Cavalier	?
INVESTIGATE				X		
ANALYZE	X	X	X	X	X	
DESIGN, DEVELOP	X		X	X	X	
OVERSEE PROCESS	X					
INFLUENCE		X	X	X	X	
- - - -						
- - - -						

The Missing Ingredients:

Directions:

As you study the Zudco Matrix, ask yourself:

What are the other critical responsibilities for the Zudco Management Team? In the two columns at the bottom of the chart, add two key MISSING INGREDIENTS for this management team.

When the Motivational Patterns of these five management team members were reviewed, it was clear that none of the five members of this team were "motivated" to:

✧ Oversee or actively manage the work of others.

✧ Coach, encourage, and develop individuals.

The Management Team at Zudco presents a classic organizational problem, especially in smaller companies where the inventor/developer often teams up with colleagues who are motivated to deal with the financial, sales and manufacturing functions. They may involve other partners with capabilities to offer vision and strategy, but many times do not address the need for effective "people management" until there is a problem, or lots of problems.

For example, the following are some of the issues identified by Zudco's employees as *detracting from the effectiveness and profitability of the company:*

✧ No consistency in how employees are treated.

✧ No priority/accountability for management responsibilities.

✧ Everyone needs to hear customer's feedback.

✧ Management communication should be to all employees.

✧ Tension/power struggle at the top.

✧ No consistency in managing and rewarding performance.

✧ No consistent authority-responsibility at lower levels.

✧ Limited communication between functional areas.

✧ Insufficient orientation/training for new employees.

✧ Slow response time to issues identified by employees.

✧ Need more discussion of competitive markets and new technology.

 ✧   Too much reworking.

 ✧   Selling before product is ready.

 ✧   Limited effort to retain/develop employees.

Basically, the employees said, "These managers are not managing this company."

What Should This Management Team Do?

Obviously, the best long-term solution would be to add another member to this team. The team needs an individual who has a "pattern" of demonstrated motivation as a manager or strong team leader and who is strongly motivated to work with individuals. After reviewing their own Motivational Patterns and learning more about the impact of their collective patterns on the operations at Zudco, the Management Team was much better prepared to select a real "manager" as contrasted to one who would only occupy the role.

In the interim, the Management Team decided to build on the strengths of others in the organization who were not currently on the Management Team. Each Management Team member had one or two individuals in his or her functional area who had demonstrated some team leadership or managerial talents; these individuals were promoted to Team Leader roles to address the many "people managing" issues surfaced by the employee surveys.

Eventually, the new manager linked these Team Leaders into a cohesive management system. She found ways to engage some of the Management Team's talents in new ways. For example, Victor was an effective leader when the task was to inspire and motivate rather than to oversee and manage. Moxy was great at getting new things going, as demonstrated with a new performance management system. (But don't count on her to maintain it!) Fred Fixer would offer his practical and useful insights if the Management Team asked for his input and then actually listened to what he had to say.

Through the insights and understanding provided by the Motivational Patterns, the Management Team at Zudco was able to:

 ✧   Redistribute duties to better match strengths.

 ✧   Build action plans with each person to improve his or her performance.

 ✧   Encourage the use of "teaming" to cover voids.

 ✧   Solicit new members to find ways to use their strengths.

The process of identifying their Motivational Patterns, and then assessing their collective motivations against their responsibilities, gave this Management Team a new respect for their colleagues. It turned a finger-pointing power struggle into an informed discussion and an action plan. It works every time. Knowledge is a very powerful antidote.

Chapter 3. Prepare Your Children for Their Lifework

It is the rare mother who can see the seed, encourage its emergence, and yet not mess with its individual direction.

James Hillman

THE FOUNDATION OF SELF-ESTEEM

Relating his comments to the analogy of "flying," Thom Black [111] says:

> *The wind that keeps children in the air is their parents' positive responses to the use of the child's natural abilities. The more positive acknowledgment given, the more freedom children feel to use their wings, and the more they are used, the stronger they become.*

Earlier in this book, I wrote about my experiences in growing up on a farm and how the good "fit" of the child's abilities to the work on the farm seemed to increase the "value" of the child. Because there is so much work and so many kinds of work on a farm, there is opportunity for almost everyone to get some positive response for their work. (There are, however, exceptions, like my brother who was basically a researcher. His investigative and observational abilities were not highly useful—and thus not highly valued—in an agricultural setting. He was the proverbial "duck out of water.")

Finding the right kind of opportunities for children to engage their motivations is probably the most important work the parent has to do. But in today's suburban world, the opportunities for positive responses as a natural outcome of doing real work are greatly diminished. More children end up being the "duck out of water" just because the nature of the "water" can be limited. Yes, there are the standard household chores and yard maintenance, but it takes special effort on the part of the parents to make these tasks as high value and esteem-building as, for example, driving a truck in combining season when you are eight years old. Parents have to be much more attuned to orchestrating situations that "fit" the uniqueness of their children. Getting children into the right situations and helping them to avoid the wrong ones requires a great deal of attention, insight and creativity on the part of the parent.

Finding the right way to recognize the achievements of a child is also critical to building confidence in his natural abilities. Thom Black [112] makes a strong point of differentiating between AFFIRMATION and REWARDS. He defines affirmation as a *statement of love that creates a climate of warmth and appreciation.* (Examples include *I love you; You're my special boy; You are one terrific kid.*) Affirmations are essential and foundational, even vital. However, they are not words of REWARD, which is a statement of fact that describes the quality and value of a child's work or play. (Examples include *Your drawing is very colorful; I especially like the reds; You climbed that tree very skillfully; That was very considerate of you to share your cookie.*)

Rewards may be verbal or physical. The verbal ones may be addressed directly to the child or spoken to someone else within earshot of the child. In either case, they relate to an activity your child has been involved in; they are statements that recognize the quality of her work or play. Every reward statement is connected to something the child did while using his natural abilities. Reward statements should be given whenever a child does good work. Statements about the quality and value of what your son is attempting or your daughter is building provide the energy and enthusiasm necessary for them to (continuing Thom's flying analogy) "soar."

Remember that the most important rewards your child receives will come from YOUR mouth. Pay careful attention to your child's daily activities so that the rewards you give are real, reflecting something he has actually done. In other words, be sincere. Kids know the difference.

Thom Black makes another very important point: If you don't provide your child with rewards, someone else will. And the rewards could come from the wrong people or at the wrong time or in the wrong place. Rewards are very powerful; the overriding need for encouragement can cause a child to form damaging relationships and do unhealthy things. Sometimes this occurs even when you are offering better ones at home. It is less likely to happen, however, if you are rewarding your child at home. Children who are properly rewarded are better equipped to withstand ill winds that threaten to push them off course.

Looking Back

When I read Thom's words, I think about our experiences raising our own daughter and son. Both my husband and I launched our careers through academic achievement; both of us are highly motivated to read/study, to meet goals/requirements and to work with ideas/concepts. When our children came along, we fully expected that they would have a "double shot" of natural motivation for academic achievements. We were also fully equipped with what Thom Black calls the "good kid list." We had some very well established expectations about what our kids should be and do.

So we were unprepared, to say the least, to deal with the reality that our children were both unique individuals with their own talents and interests. Both of them are very different from either of us and from each other. Our daughter demonstrated her interest in the visual arts very early. In fact, I recently found one of her first drawings stuck between the pages in my cookbook. She wasn't quite two years old when she sketched a bird sitting on a branch outside the kitchen window. She drew murals on her bedroom walls and painted trees that covered the doors. She made costumes endlessly and organized plays with the neighbor kids. Once she created a monologue depicting a grandmother in a rocking chair that put her real grandmother is absolute stitches. While we noticed her creations and provided the necessary audience, I think we could have been much more specific in identifying and REWARDING the nature of her talent that made these creations possible. I think we said more about her cuteness and energy than we did about her ability to create scenarios and to depict emotion.

Recognizing a child's natural abilities builds self-esteem.

She did well in school, but the consistent message on her report cards was "does not work to her ability." She was often caught daydreaming and never seemed to really care about whether she had good grades or not. In high school, her interest in art and drama continued and we provided private art lessons. But we mainly talked to her about doing something with her art that would make money. Since neither my husband nor I have artistic talents, we provided little comment or showed much interest in the specifics of her art. We probably offered few "rewards" for the use of her abilities to accomplish something that interested her. We said a lot more about trying to get some decent grades so she could get into a "good school."

After two years of community college, she went on to art school without our support. Her determination finally convinced us that she was going to be a fine artist, whether we liked it or not. We helped her financially to complete B.A. and M.A. programs at one of the nation's best art schools and to do an internship with a well-known artist. We were still concerned with the challenge of supporting herself as a fine artist, especially since she had also married an artist. We kept trying to help her explore other ways to express her talents: computer graphics, computer animation, advertising and marketing efforts for my consulting company, as well as co-training in my career workshops. Since she needed the money, she did the work but it was always a struggle. After 10 years of trying to balance her painting and these other efforts, she recently decided that she is going to paint full-time. It's the right decision; she should have taken that step years ago.

Unlike either of us, our son is highly motivated by physical activity and the outdoors. He always distinguished himself in competitive physical activities, usually in roles where he could impress someone with his individual talent. For example, in soccer he was the best kicker and goalie. As a five year old, he won a "Big Wheels" contest; his driving as a teenager was a continuation of that motivation! His real love was fishing. Even when he was a toddler, he would beg to go watch the fish in the pond, and then he would devise schemes to catch them. Schoolwork was always a drag for him. We sent him to a church-sponsored elementary school that was, in retrospect, totally wrong for him. When he started high school, he transferred to the large public high school in our community. I think he was really lost in the classes that were huge compared to his elementary school. He made friends but not always the right kind of friends. He also found "rewards" for his abilities in fast driving and partying. It was a wasted four years that caused both him and us a great deal of pain.

Of course, we talked to him about his future until we were hoarse. He did express an interest in being a forest ranger, and with our encouragement, he enrolled in a two-year college. The first semester he was on the honor role, but the enthusiasm soon waned. After a couple of years, he decided he could make more money working as a carpenter, like his best friend. After a year of long commutes and long, hard hours on the job, he ended up with a tough bout of mononucleosis. By this time, my husband and I were getting a little wiser, and so was he. One day he said, "I need to play the cards I've been dealt." We thought about what might work for him and probably because of our farm backgrounds, we felt some kind of a farm would probably be a good fit. After looking at many options, we ended up with a walnut orchard and he runs the operation. He is also very mechanically inclined, so he is very capable of operating and maintaining the equipment. He has taken a great deal of interest in making the orchard more productive, planting additional trees and experimenting with fertilizers and irrigation techniques. And best of all, he has built a successful guiding service, offering a variety of fishing adventures in California's inland waterways.

Recognizing and rewarding natural abilities creates a bond of respect between parent and child.

I think when he was younger, we could have done a lot more to reward him for the talents that he exhibited. We spent too much energy pushing him toward what we had in mind. He ended up building stronger relationships with friends that did "reward" him for his "impressive" behaviors, which were to his detriment. We lost our influence with him in many important arenas.

Consistently rewarding (as defined by Thom Black) and recognizing your child for his natural abilities creates a powerful bond of respect between parent and child. No one else will ever take your place if you fill this responsibility carefully. I think of my father who always looked at my report card. He expected to see all A's, so a B was a big discussion. His attention to the results I had achieved was an important signal for the value he placed on my ability to learn by reading and studying. I remembered that respect on other occasions when I had to make choices about my behavior. I didn't want to do anything to diminish his respect for my performance in any scenario.

SELECTING LIFEWORK

Few things that we do as parents have any longer lasting impact than that of helping our children to transcend into adulthood and select their lifework. Discovering a child's passion is the beginning of finding the adult inside. In his book *Kicking Your Kid Out of the Nest*, Thom Black offers some practical strategies for learning about and reinforcing your child's natural abilities. Not surprisingly, the best approach is to listen for *stories of passion. You never know when these stories will come out . . . but they happen every day. You just have to listen for them—listen for expressions of enthusiasm, desire and interest. Listen for words that describe the thrill of doing something well. Ask exactly what happened. Ask what they enjoyed the most. Write down what you observed. Look for a pattern. Watch and listen for things that repeat themselves.* [113]

How young adults uses their free time is a key factor in getting insight into their motivators. (What activities does he select? Does she work with tangibles objects like equipment or materials? What seems to be his favorite activity? Who are her best friends? What does he seek in a friend? Does he prefer to be alone?) However, beware of evaluating your child in situations where she has been told what to do. These settings often reveal what she doesn't do well, but seldom reveal what she does well.

As children become teenagers, parents can help them prepare for their lifework by helping them find jobs that use their natural abilities. Parents need to be aware that many teen jobs are not what they used to be. Twenty years ago, teen jobs like being a file clerk provided the incumbent with an opportunity for kinship with adults, caring mentors and new self-confidence. Adults at the office included young men and women in their work routines and in the office breaks. They made them feel involved. In today's fast food industry, where most teens find work, teens associate almost exclusively with other teens and have very limited contact with other adults, especially managers. With teen employment at a 25-year high, and the service sector bidding up wages for young workers, there is a growing concern about teen jobs.

New research suggests the kids might not be learning what their parents think they are on the job. A five-year study by the Alfred P. Sloan Foundation of more than 7,000 teens found a mismatch between adults' expectations and teens' actual job experiences. Adults typically assume that teens will learn skills and gain valuable contact with adults to equip them for the future. But many teens report they are hired because of qualities they already have—such as good communication skills or punctuality. They don't see their jobs as related to their futures.

Such jobs do little to equip kids to set meaningful career goals, which presents a big problem for today's adolescents. Though they are the most ambitious generation of teens in history, they aren't getting enough guidance in aligning their ambitions with reality, leading them to make poor college choices and, often, to grow alienated. [114]

Experts in youth employment recommend guiding teens towards jobs that match their interests. Working in a vet's office might be a great experience for the animal-lover, or a nursing home for a people-helper. A role as an office assistant in a real estate office would be a useful experience if sales were an interest. The money they earn is not as important as the opportunity to explore the employment world in their area of interest.

Children who have the opportunity to engage their innate motivations in activities that they (and others) perceive as valuable and useful get a real head start on building self-esteem. Researchers in the "twins studies" did find that self-esteem was a major arena in which parents do have an opportunity to significantly impact the development of their children, whether biological or adopted. [115]

PART III
KNOWING WHAT YOU NEED

Section A.
Act II – One Last Chance to Be Who You Are

Section B.
Creating What Will Be

SECTION A.
ACT II – ONE LAST CHANCE TO BE WHO YOU ARE

Chapter 1. How to Maintain a Purposeful Life

We cannot fully give up the throne nor the drive that took us to it.

James Hillman

For most of us, a major portion of our lives is focused on pursuing our careers and raising our families. Retirement from our corporate careers or finishing the business of raising children brings us to another important phase of our lives. Because people are retiring earlier and living longer, this period in our lives is lasting longer than it did for our parents. Earlier emphasis on physical fitness and health care makes it possible for more active participation in leisure, hobby and "second career" activities. Growth in real estate and stock market investments have also made a financially secure retirement a reality for many of the millions of "baby boomers" now reaching retirement age.

In this phase of their lives, people generally have more resources and fewer responsibilities. It is a time that is less driven by both financial needs and social expectations. We no longer have the pressure from ourselves, our family and our culture to be become a manager, to be promoted, or to make partner-in-the-firm status. Many people are basically free to do what they want to do. More and more "retirees" have both the resources and the health to support most of their choices.

Because both the potential quality and length of this period has expanded substantially, it deserves (and requires) more planning and preparation…and a new name. **Preparing for Act II** seemed to capture the appropriate sentiments for this specialized planning process. If you are interested in learning more about it, please contact us at mhanson539@aol.com.

Act II is a time that can be used to accomplish all those things that you have dreamed about doing in your life. It is a time to build new relationships, participate in new adventures, and engage in activities that truly bring meaning to your life. It is also a time for maintaining a purposeful connection to the world. It's a time for giving back some of what you learned. The following quote from a typical Act II individual tells the story:

> *"In Act I, I pursued my career and raised my family. Now, in this stage of my life, I have come into my own. This is my time for creativity, continued learning and exploration. I have plenty of energy, and plenty of resources. It is my time to enjoy new relationships, appreciate family and friends and to explore the spiritual side*

of life. It is also my time, if I choose, for giving back to society—for sharing the wisdom of my experience."

Many of us are not sure that we know what it is we want to do in our Act II. We may have spent our lives primarily focused on the needs of others, on our careers, or our family. We may have given little thought to Act II scenarios, other than dreaming about the day when we no longer had to face the traffic twice a day or work late into the night on yet another proposal.

When the day finally comes that we truly can do what we want to do, we may not be able to orchestrate the kind of Act II that is as fulfilling as we had anticipated. We may find our concept of an ideal Act II in conflict with our partner's scenario. Seeing no way to accommodate both scenarios, we end up doing nothing. We may try a few months of travel or golf or our favorite charity, but we soon begin to feel like our life has lost a sense of meaning.

Whether we were self-employed or worked as an employee, or spent our lives raising our families, in Act I our lives had a distinct purpose. We could define ourselves by our title or role. The challenge of meeting the needs and fulfilling our responsibilities provided a structure for our efforts and gave a sense of meaning to our outcomes. In most cases, our Act I roles also provided opportunities for socialization and to build relationships. Most roles also required new learning to keep up our performance helping our children with their homework!

In Act II, many of these conditions are no longer present. How does one replace and augment these important aspects of life? In many years of working with Motivational Patterns, I have learned that a truly essential ingredient to a purposeful, meaningful life is having the opportunity to use and develop your motivations to accomplish purposes that are meaningful to YOU. This important fact does not change when you transition from Act I to Act II. In fact, it becomes even more critical for you to understand the kind of situations that provide you satisfaction and enjoyment. In Act II, you have much more responsibility for generating the necessary scenarios. The structured roles of Act I will no longer be in place to automatically provide meaning and purpose in your life.

RETIREMENT PLANNING BASED ON MOTIVATIONAL PATTERNS

Why is it difficult for so many people to find interesting things to do once they retire? One reason is that they are often overwhelmed by the many alternatives that are available. They are not confident that they will select something that indeed will work for them. Added to this hesitation in choosing an activity can be a shyness that often accompanies a dip in self-esteem when one no longer has a defined role or job. The shyness may turn into a "Who would want me?" attitude, while the mirror continues to record declining physical abilities and appearance.

But the most powerful reason why retirees have trouble finding meaning and purpose in Act II is that they have failed to adequately prepare for this new phase of their life.

For guidance on creating what you want to do in your Act II, you can look to your life/work achievements. By identifying the underlying themes of what you have enjoyed and found satisfying in your life to date, you can gain tremendous insight into the nature of experiences that will give you purpose, meaning, fulfillment and enjoyment in the future.

The themes from your life/work achievements provide superbly accurate criteria for assessing the myriad of activities available to you. Use them to create the scenario that you will find satisfying and enjoyable. Because you will be motivated by those activities that "fit" you, you will be naturally engaged in the activity and will continue to participate and to develop your skill. Act II "retirees" often are disillusioned by initial attempts to become more involved because they choose the wrong activity. When they do not find their participation to be enjoyable or satisfying, they disengage. Often they do not realize the true reason for the discouraging outcome.

Performing activities that are "motivating" reinforces our sense of self-worth.

For example, many retirees are counseled to get involved in "volunteer" activities, visiting nursing homes, helping the homeless, etc. While this is a tremendously rewarding activity for anyone with innate motivations for helping and caring for, nurturing, or simply interacting with people, I know many individuals who do not have any elements in their Motivational Patterns that would make these kinds of volunteer activities satisfying and enjoyable. They may make the effort to please a spouse or to ease their conscience, but if meeting needs is not a part of their motivation, they are unlikely to find that such activities give their life meaning or purpose. The advice to retirees to "get involved in a plateful of interesting activities" needs to be qualified. Get involved in a plateful of activities that are motivating for you!

Doing things that are "motivating" reinforces our sense of self-worth. This is a powerful dynamic that profoundly impacts our entire life, and generating self-worth is critically important in Act II. In this phase of our life, we are less likely to be involved in structured roles that define our value for us. Many retirees "keep busy" but still have difficulty in sustaining the meaning and purpose in their lives. In Act II, we must be proactive in creating roles that use and develop the motivators that are the essence of our being, our Motivational Pattern. There is a payoff for the effort. Researchers at the Southern Illinois University surveyed all the persons who visited the Senior Center at the Illinois State Fair. The results showed that, for both men and women over age 54, those who work full-time or are active in volunteering or hobbies find their lives "more interesting and satisfying" than do those who are retired, work part-time or do little volunteer or hobby work. [117]

To illustrate the point, let me introduce you to some Act II candidates.

I met Harry and Helen in a PREPARING FOR ACT II workshop. Married 35 years with two grown sons, they appeared somewhat uncomfortable sitting together by a workshop table. Helen coughed nervously.

Harry is a Ph.D. Engineering Manager for a large oil company; Helen is a homemaker who has tried a number of part-time career strategies but didn't express much satisfaction with any of them. Harry could retire this year with a very comfortable pension or he could continue his employment. Their first grandchild is about to arrive and Helen's Act II plan at the beginning of the workshop was to move to New Jersey to be able to see her grandson every day. Harry didn't really have a retirement plan; he said something about having to get some hobbies going. He was not supportive of the plan to move to New Jersey because it meant retiring now. They openly indicated that this had been a matter of major disagreement.

Many people simply fail to respect their innate motivations.

At first blush, this appeared to be an "opposites attract" pair. Harry's "motivated" interests revolve around technology and processes. Helen is more motivated to work with individuals and engage in artistic expression. What they learned from comparing their Motivational Patterns is that they are both motivated to learn and to teach. They both get great satisfaction from learning something new, demonstrating their knowledge and proficiency and then repeating the process.

At the end of the workshop, each participant was asked to explain to the group his or her key learning from the experience. Harry said: *It changed my thinking about retirement. I was concerned about how to fill up the hours in the day, especially when I don't even have a hobby. Now I am thinking about defining a new direction and purpose for how we spend the rest of our lives together.* Helen said: *I was amazed that we found we had so much in common. We both like to learn and to teach. Why hadn't we figured that out before?*

Why don't people figure this out themselves? Actually, some people do! However, many more people struggle with lack of knowledge and even more important, the lack of respect for the profundity of their Motivational Pattern. Harry had given up earlier career aspirations of being a professor in order to provide a "better living" for his family. Helen tried substitute teaching to accommodate her parental responsibilities but had found the discipline problems overwhelming. She had found a volunteer job working with developmentally disabled children to be very satisfying. Armed with new evidence that teaching was indeed a good "fit" for her, she set goals for completing the required certification. (She acknowledged that her son and daughter-in-law had not shown much enthusiasm for her moving plans.) Harry already had the necessary credentials. He planned to test his skills by teaching a community college course. They were actually holding hands as they walked through the parking lot to their car.

Dick and Carol were in the same workshop. Both in their second marriages, they initially seemed very aligned in their career/life/retirement goals. He is a very successful lawyer in his own practice with seven-figure revenues. She was a top-producing certified financial planner who had chosen to be a full-time mother about three years ago. They are both goal-oriented and very disciplined to achieve their goals, whether it was being top in their class or first in athletic competitions. Both are physically attractive, physically fit, talented and successful people. So why were they in the workshop? Since Carol had elected to move from her career to motherhood, she had experienced some feelings that were new to her. She found herself feeling depressed for days and weeks at a time. She wanted to be with her daughter, she loved her elegant home and seemed to thoroughly enjoy her reputation as the "gourmet" entertainer. She couldn't put her finger on what was missing.

A successful Act II requires preparation, just like other phases of life.

Dick was frustrated with trying to understand her change in attitude. And she was becoming a bit irritated with Dick. Even though his law business was a smashing success, he seemed to be continually getting side tracked on new schemes, like selling comic books or starting satellite businesses.

When they looked at their Motivational Patterns, they found some insights. Carol, not surprisingly for a top salesperson, is highly motivated by being able to differentiate her performance from others, and by measurable results that confirm her excellence. She also needs personal attention, recognition and interaction as part of her daily existence. She simply could not sustain herself in the absence of these elements from her daily life.

Dick's activities are motivated by acquiring expertise and material objects. He is truly motivated to acquire what is desired and to exercise control over what is owned. In addition to being motivated to build up wealth, he wants to broaden the nature of his responsibilities and projects and to expand and perfect his knowledge base. He has a tremendous appetite to satiate. It's not a new dynamic to him. It is what has made him first in every class he has been in.

So on closer examination, there seemed to be a growing problem with their alignment in career/life goals. After some discussion, Carol decided to take a part-time position as a financial planner. Dick decided to try acquiring knowledge about child-care businesses—and to get more involved with the daily care of his daughter.

How do we keep our plans for the future as vital as our memories of the past? And how about our life partners? What are their plans? Can we work these plans together? How can we make the most of the rest of our lives together? A successful Act II requires understanding and preparation, just like the other phases of our lives have required.

SECTION B:
CREATING WHAT WILL BE

Chapter 1. The SIMA® Ten-Step Guide

To be what we are and to become what we are capable of becoming is the only end of life.
Robert Louis Stevenson

Discovering the existence and nature of your Motivational Pattern is just the first step in the exciting adventure of knowing what you want and need. Based on our experience in helping individuals to achieve a meaningful and productive understanding of their patterns, the following Ten-Step Guide has been developed. Read each step carefully and think about how you would use your unique motivations to address that step and execute those ideas.

STEP ONE: AMPLIFY YOUR BASE OF SELF-KNOWLEDGE

Your Motivational Pattern is a comprehensive and integrated set of motivations. It is not likely that you will be able to fully understand all of its complexities in one pass. In fact, we encourage individuals to take some time each day to think about what went well and what was enjoyable. Link the experiences with the elements of your Motivational Pattern. Nail down any doubts or obscurities by analyzing the real evidence that you experience each day.

To gain additional understanding of the power and pervasive nature of your motivations, generate another set of your achievement experiences and use them to test each major conclusion about yourself. Verify each element by reciting evidence from these achievements.

Another very effective way to understand and appreciate your uniqueness is to study the uniqueness of others. Take the time to ask others what they enjoyed about that last project or what they believe they contributed to the project. Notice how some people respond to recognition and how others could care less if either their contributions or presence are recognized. Watch your supervisor in staff meetings; does he become uncomfortable at any particular times? If you are working on a team, ask your colleagues what tasks they would prefer to do. Before long, you will notice that people give very different responses to your questions. They report very different contributions and they seek different outcomes.

This process of learning about the motivations of others is particularly useful in family relationships. Spouses and other family members may initially wonder what is going on and question your motives, but they will soon be overwhelmed by your genuine interest in what they enjoy doing and feel they do well. Socially, learning about the motivations of others is a winning strategy. Most people enjoy being asked about their achievements. Ask the person next to you on the plane what she did this week that she really enjoyed doing. At first, she may not know how to answer. Keep trying. You will find some people will not be able to recall anything they did during the week that they enjoyed doing and felt they did well, so extend the period to a month or a year. If there is still no response, encourage them to read this book—and get a life!

STEP TWO: CHECK IT OUT WITH YOUR FRIENDS AND CO-WORKERS

Reality test your self-understanding as well as where your giftedness may be a pain to others. Give your Motivational Pattern to people with whom you work. Ask them to comment on whether they see these motivations in action. (Remember, if you are in a mismatch situation, they may not see all of the real "you.") Elicit examples that support their observations. Ask for examples that may help to identify areas of "limitations" that need to be more carefully managed. For example, individuals who are motivated to "be the best" are often very reluctant to share their patterns because they feel others will view them negatively. In reality, most of their close contacts already have recognized some aspect of the motivation and may have misread the intentions. The disclosure often brings better understanding and less resistance to achieving one's Motivational Payoff.

This process of sharing your Motivational Pattern (both orally and in writing) gives you practice in deciding what you want to say to others about yourself. Most of us do not speak candidly or descriptively about our strengths. We assume that others will figure out who we are, but then we are disappointed when they are wrong or when they don't make the effort. Don't wait to be "discovered." Tell people what it is you enjoy doing and do well. Don't make the mistake of assuming that your work will speak for itself! Be prepared to speak accurately and concisely about your passion and purpose.

STEP THREE: EXAMINE WHO AND WHAT YOU SEEK TO AVOID

Become aware of the selective nature of your will in even the most ordinary of circumstances. Compile a "What Bores Me Most" checklist and then tie each conclusion into your Motivational Pattern. See if you can invent a way to use your motivated abilities to make the activity more meaningful for you. For example, I am bored with social chatter. I am only truly engaged when I am working on overcoming an obstacle (which includes overcoming my "ignorance" or lack of knowledge about a subject or person) or helping others to overcome their obstacles. This motivation was a severe handicap at a cocktail party, until I discovered that people love to talk about their work/lives, especially if someone is really listening and asking questions that take them further into their favorite subject.

When you have some experience with your pattern, you will find yourself gravitating toward those individuals and circumstances that allow you to think, speak, and act according to your own Motivational Pattern. You will also avoid individuals and circumstances that frustrate the free exercise of your motivations. Experiences and people that constrain or devalue your motivation will only serve to drain your energy and impede your progress.

STEP FOUR: RECOGNIZE HOW YOU GET INTO EMOTIONAL TURMOIL

By paying attention to when you get upset, what makes you angry and when you get depressed, you can recognize the connections between your Motivational Pattern and your emotions. Start by describing—in writing—one or more recent examples of each situation where you had a distinct emotional reaction (anxiety, impatience, anger, depression, frustration, embarrassment, tears). Identify and explain the reason for each reaction in terms of your Motivational Pattern. For example, I can become downright demoralized when I come up against an obstacle that I cannot overcome, like discrimination in the workplace.

STEP FIVE: SHAKE HANDS WITH THE COMPULSIVE YOU

Remember, if you don't learn the cause of your excesses, you are condemned to repeat them. Trot out all the things that your friends and co-workers have said about you and your Motivational Pattern which were less than positive. Check out how obsessive you were under these circumstances. Describe those times when you got into trouble (lost a friend, got into a shouting match, fired, publicly criticized, trouble with the police, DWI, fight, separation, divorce, long-lasting argument). Again, identify and explain the source of these behaviors by linking the reasons for your behavior to your Motivational Pattern.

STEP SIX: NOW, ABOUT THE DARKER SIDE...

While Motivational Patterns are "amoral" and do not address character issues like loyalty, honesty or morality, they do serve to alert us to what could be called the "dark side." Because innate motivations are so powerful, we can be guilty of "going over the line " in exercising our passions to achieve our purpose. For example, if we are motivated to impress others, we may be given to exaggeration (even untruths) in order to more fully accomplish our purpose. If we are highly motivated by recognition, we may be guilty of being less than truthful about the role we actually played or the contribution we made. If we are motivated to win and prevail, we may be more tempted to take unfair advantage of others—or, heaven forbid, indulge in some downright cheating if the "win" is sufficiently important!

You need to fully acquaint yourself with any tendencies you may have to "cross the line" to achieve your intended purpose. How far are you willing to go to get what is motivationally significant to you? Like you did in Steps Five and Six, describe situations where your behavior was less than honest—a bit "dark," as we say. Maybe you told a lie (big time, small deal, half lie) or didn't keep your promise. Perhaps you were unjust and didn't fulfill your obligation, or maybe you used your power improperly. Again, tie in the reasons for that inappropriate behavior to your Motivational Pattern.

STEP SEVEN: RECALL A BAD JOB-FIT

A very accurate "thermometer" for measuring your job-fit is how you feel about going to work in the morning. Note the days that you can hardly wait to get to work, when you wake up excited about the coming day's events. Also note the days that you have a hard time getting started. Keep a record that connects your procrastination or poor performance to mismatch situations. Note which of your "to do" items remain on your list week after week. Identify items (both positive and negative) that seem to recur in your performance evaluations, regardless of who does the assessment. Dig into the details when you are looking at job-fit. Identify the critical requirements for performing the job and then figure out where you fit and where you don't. Describe the duties and decisions that you didn't like and what you did about them. Describe the effect you had on others. Estimate what you cost your organization in that job, not only what you didn't produce but what loss of productivity you cost others.

STEP EIGHT: CLEARING YOUR DECKS

Identify those activities in your life (at work and at home) that drag you down and have to go. Rate the activities on a scale to indicate their importance. For example, some people spend excessive amounts of time and energy just thinking about (and dreading) some of their responsibilities. It could be monthly accounting, the annual tax return preparation, the care of the lawns, or even routine housecleaning that is dragging you down. Do you really need to be dragged down by these events or could you "manage" these situations differently? Is there someone else who may find these activities more enjoyable and rewarding? Could you team up with someone who could supplement your contribution and keep you involved for your part? Maybe you just need to bite the bullet and hire someone else to do it!

"Managing" friends (and relatives) who take up your time without contributing to your well being can be more difficult. I have found that simply by telling people that I am heavily committed to a particular project (which I usually am), they will call or interrupt less frequently. Arranging for specific time to meet or have lunch (like once a month) can also work to maintain a relationship but minimize the time and/or negative impact involved.

STEP NINE: FOCUS ON THE RESULTS THAT YOU TRULY WANT IN YOUR LIFE

When an organization fails in the utilization of an employee, they have many more options to exercise. When you mess up the management of your own motivational assets, you are in a much different position. **You only have one lifetime in which to get the results that you want.**

By understanding your Motivational Pattern and the profound impact that it has on your sense of fulfillment, you are in a much better position to differentiate between that which you truly want and that which your culture or environment has taught you to want. **The more you realize that what you truly want matters, the more selective you become about what you want.** You recognize the importance of your deepest wants, and the less important ones take a secondary place.

How do you know whether your aspiration or goal is something that you truly want? The test is to check your vision or desired result against your Motivational Pattern. If this desire is fulfilled, will you feel fulfilled? What evidence is there from your past achievements? What elements of your pattern actually "fit" this outcome? How does the activity or result "fit" with what you need to be motivated and satisfied? People who know and respect their motivations know instinctively what works and doesn't work for them. Others are more vulnerable to external forces.

One way to more accurately define what it is that you want is to actually visualize the results you would like to have in each of the important areas of your life—and then check your vision out against the elements in your Motivational Pattern. Robert Fritz, noted authority on visionary strategies,* offers some guidance for how to create what you want. He suggests:

✧ Focus on the results that you want, not the process. (If you want something that you think will lead to something else, you are focusing on the process.)

✧ See whatever it is that you want in the present—not in the future.

---

*If you are having difficulty translating your Motivational Pattern into what it is that you truly want in your life, I would recommend reading Robert Fritz's book, *The Path of Least Resistance* (published by DMA, Inc., 27 Congress Street, Salem, MA, 01970) and doing all of the exercises he suggests. He offers more techniques for translating what truly matters to you to what you want out of your life.

✧   Focus on what you want, not on avoiding what you don't want.

✧   Don't evaluate what's possible.

To prepare for this exercise, re-read your work/life achievements and review your Motivational Pattern. Respect what appears in your work/life achievements. Think carefully about how those achievements gave you what you wanted.

Define What You Want

Directions:

Picture each aspect of your life exactly the way you would want it to be. See yourself in the scenario and environment that you seek. Think about what it is that you truly want. Depending on your own motivation, you may want to work on these over a week's time, focusing on one aspect of your life each day. (I find that people get the best results from this exercise when they find a relaxed position and close their eyes to envision what they want—and then make notes about their thoughts on one area before they move on to the next.)

YOUR CAREER/WORK: What do you see yourself doing? What is your "best-fit" scenario?

YOUR RELATIONSHIPS: What do you need from your relationships? What are you bringing to these relationships?

YOUR HEALTH: What do you want to have in your physical, mental, emotional and spiritual health?

YOUR HOME: What should your immediate living environment be? Is it the way you want it to be?

YOUR MONEY: What kind of a relationship do you want with money? What role does money play for you?

YOUR LIFE'S PURPOSE: What do you want to have accomplished by the time your life ends on this planet?

OTHER AREAS OF MY LIFE:

After you have defined some specific results for each area, develop both short term (to do in the next six weeks) and longer range (in the next year) goals and action steps for each area. Select the top three action steps and write these in large, colorful print. Post them in places where you will see them several times every day—maybe on the mirror in your bathroom. You will feel terrific when you take down your completed action item and replace it with the next one!

STEP TEN: DECIDE TO BECOME ALL THAT YOU ARE

Inspiration occurs to an individual when he is out of his ordinary senses, but he must recover his ordinary understanding if he is to comprehend what has appeared to him and how to turn it to use. [118]

Unpacking your Motivational Pattern takes a lifetime of effort. It may be perceived all at once but true understanding comes slowly. But the power of Motivational Patterns works in such a way that what you will do follows from what you have previously done and leads to <u>what you must ultimately do</u>. Your passions and purpose are truly enduring, and if you respect and encourage their expression, they will serve to fulfill your promise and to guide you to your place in the world. But it is important to translate the initial inspiration into practical action. The following is a quick way to make sure that you get started on the right track:

In a way that is meaningful to you, identify three key "motivated" abilities that clearly demonstrate your most "motivating" strengths. Then identify three action items that will take these motivated abilities to new heights!

Example: One of my "motivated" abilities is teaching or training. I have performed successfully as both a teacher and trainer for many years, primarily in classroom or workshop settings. I plan to join the National Speaker's Association to build my platform speaking and presenting skills so I am able to present more effectively in larger and less participative audiences.

My Motivated Ability	What I Have Done	What I Will Do
1. _____	_____	_____
2. _____	_____	_____
3. _____	_____	_____

REWARDS FOR THE "GOOD FIT" LIFE

It takes great courage to invest one's life with meaning. Many of us are simply not willing to make the effort. But the view is worth the climb. If the life you live provides you the opportunity to use your passions to achieve a purpose meaningful to you, you are already getting what you want.

You are spending your life doing what you want to be doing. What a privilege!

And there is much more! Your family and your colleagues routinely see you "in your best" suit, exhibiting your best talents. You have benefit of their appreciation for the contributions that you make using your best talents. Their compliments and the results you achieve are constant fuel for your growing sense of self-worth.

At a time when almost everyone else is trying to find his or her direction in a turbulent "whitewater" world, you feel confident that you have chosen the right direction. Yes, there will be corrections from time to time, but you know the basic requirements that provide you with the necessary alignment. You are focused on your horizon.

You feel more confident of your place in the world and your station in life. You are less vulnerable to envy, jealousy and other negative emotions. The bigger house in the gated community doesn't seem as important as what you are going to do tomorrow. Nor does the neighbor's new sports utility vehicle, or that dress that only recently was high priority. As a matter of fact, many situations that used to be stressful seem to have lost their punch.

You find that your relationships are more engaging; even learning about the motivations of others is quite captivating. Those who are close to you notice that you are more respectful of their needs. You are more willing to help them get what they want out of life as well.

You are more motivated to expand your capabilities and responsibilities. You look forward to taking an evening class, doing some reading, searching the Net to keep current in your areas of interest.

Instead of having to drag yourself out of bed and to work each morning, you wake early because you are excitedly anticipating the day's activities. The days and weeks seem to be full of excitement and fulfillment. There is no sense of drudgery, routine or monotony.

You may do more charitable work and become more involved in your community and other civic activities, if these are activities that fulfill YOUR passions and purpose. Or

It takes great courage to invest one's life with meaning.

you may find your job, your career, your family, your golf game, or your antique glass collection more rewarding for you than these activities. It all depends on what is in YOUR Motivational Pattern. And there is nothing wrong with you if you march to a different drummer; in fact, the whole concept of Motivational Patterns is about marching to your own drummer. It's the only way you can be a fulfilled person with a meaningful life and thereby contribute to the welfare of humankind.

You find that it is easier to stick to your diet, because you are not going through those "valleys and peaks." You haven't had a cold or flu this year. You have kept to your exercise schedule. Somehow, you don't feel the need for that drink after work. You would never start smoking again!

Who do you know that is living their life this way? Who in your circle of family and friends is reaping the rewards of using their passions to accomplish a purpose meaningful to them?

When I ask myself this question, my father comes first to mind. He always said he had everything he wanted there on the farm. I never quite understood what that statement meant then, because I could hardly wait to see what was beyond the prairie's edge. But Dad's purpose in life was to meet the challenge of surviving without help from others. He prided himself on the fact that he had never worked for anyone else (for compensation) in his entire life. He was never very impressed with the degrees my husband and I accumulated. He said we would end up spending our lives "working for somebody else." When he passed away, he owned so few personal items (besides his land, cattle and machinery) that we could find very few items to keep as remembrances. I found two decks of playing cards, which he had used so many times playing solitaire that the distinguishing "spots" were barely visible. Every once in awhile, I take the cards out and hold them, remembering how little time and money he spent on the accouterments of life. He was truly dedicated to living the life he wanted to live.

You may not be inspired by my father's story. Depending on your Motivational Pattern, it may seem like utter failure to spend one's life in relative solitude on a prairie ranch. You may be more inspired by the story about my friend Stephan, a multi-millionaire who started a world-renowned human resources consulting company, or Carla, another friend who raised and home-schooled four children and now has ten grandchildren, some of whom she is also home-schooling. But I trust that by now, you are clear about WHY one scenario might depict what you want whereas the other has little or no appeal. The secret, of course, lies in knowing what engages YOUR passion and achieves YOUR purpose.

Doing work that you love to do helps to sustain the value of your performance.

For many individuals, work/life decisions often come back to monetary issues. Will I be able to make a good living? Will I be able to support my family? Will I be able to enjoy a comfortable home and travel?

In making your work/life decisions, keep in mind that doing work that you love to do is an important strategy for sustaining value for your performance over a lifetime. And, after talking with hundreds of individuals about their careers and their lives, I am totally convinced that the best way for you to feel prosperous is by engaging your passions to accomplish a purpose that is meaningful—to you.

REFERENCES

1. Drucker, Peter, "Managing Oneself," HARVARD BUSINESS REVIEW, March-April, 1999.

2. Buckingham, Marcus and Donald Clifton, NOW, DISCOVER YOUR STRENGTHS, The Free Press, January, 2001.

3. "Liar, Liar, Pants on Fire," TRAINING & DEVELOPMENT, November, 1999.

4. RECRUITING AND RETAINING EMPLOYEES, a Consortium Benchmarking Study by ASTD & SHRM, June, 2000.

5. ibid.

6. Hillman, James, THE SOUL'S CODE, Random House, 1996.

7. Buckingham, Marcus and Curt Coffman, FIRST BREAK ALL THE RULES, Simon & Schuster, 1999.

8. ibid.

9. Sapolsky, Robert, WHY ZEBRAS DON'T GET ULCERS, W. H. Freeman, 1998.

10. Miller, Arthur F. Jr., WHY YOU CAN'T BE ANYTHING YOU WANT TO BE BUT YOU WILL LOVE BEING WHO YOU WERE DESIGNED TO BE, Zondervan Publishing House, 1999.

11. Buckingham, Marcus and Curt Coffman, FIRST BREAK ALL THE RULES, Simon & Schuster, 1999.

12. Drucker, Peter, "Managing Oneself," HARVARD BUSINESS REVIEW, March-April, 1999.

13. Kagan, Jerome, GALEN'S PROPHECY, Basic Books, 1994.

14. Vaill, Peter, LEARNING AS A WAY OF BEING, Jossey-Bass, 1996.

15. Dalton, Gene and Paul Thompson, NOVATIONS, Gene W. Dalton & Paul H. Thompson, 1993.

16. Czikszentmihalyi, Mihaly, FINDING FLOW, Basic Books, 1997.

17. Miller, Arthur F. Jr., WHY YOU CAN'T BE ANYTHING YOU WANT TO BE BUT YOU WILL LOVE BEING WHO YOU WERE DESIGNED TO BE, Zondervan Publishing House, 1999.

18. Buckingham, Marcus and Curt Coffman, FIRST BREAK ALL THE RULES, Simon & Schuster, 1999.

19. Brewer, Jack, Marlys Hanson, Rich Van Horn and Keith Moseley, "A New Dimension in Employee Development: A System for Career Planning & Guidance," PERSONNEL JOURNAL, April, 1975.

20. Moir, Elizabeth B. and Keith E. Moseley, "Career/Life Planning for Employees at Lawrence Livermore National Laboratory," UCRL 86206, October, 1981.

21. Hanson, Marlys, CAREER/LIFE PLANNING PROGRAM AT LAWRENCE LIVERMORE LABORATORY, THE PILOT PROGRAM AND AN EVALUATION, Master's Thesis, California State University, Hayward, CA, 1976.

22.   Hanson, Marlys and H. Fred Shultz, "Matching Employees to Their Work: A Mutually Beneficial Career Management System in Exxon Engineering," Ninth Biennial IEEE-USA Careers Conference, Minneapolis, MN, 1996.

23.   Justice, Blair, WHO GETS SICK, Jeremy B. Tarcher, Inc., 1998.

24.   Wright, Lawrence, TWINS AND WHAT THEY TELL US ABOUT WHO WE ARE, John Wiley and Sons, 1997.

25.   Khalsa, Dharma Singh, M. D., BRAIN LONGEVITY, Time Warner Books, 1997.

26.   Matteson, Michael T. and John Ivancevich, CONTROLLING WORK STRESS, Jossey-Bass Inc., Publishers, 1987.

27.   May, Rollo, THE DISCOVERY OF BEING, W. W. Norton and Company, 1983.

28.   Kohn, Alfie, PUNISHED BY REWARDS, Houghton-Mifflin, 1999.

29.   Justice, Blair, WHO GETS SICK, Jeremy B. Tarcher, Inc., 1998.

30.   ibid.

31.   ibid.

32.   ibid.

33.   Chesney, Margaret, Ph. D. et al, "Work Environment, Type A Behavior and Coronary Heart Disease Risk," JOURNAL OF OCCUPATIONAL MEDICINE, Vol. 33, No. 3, August, 1981.

34.   "Long Term Residents," Cover Story, SARATOGA NEWS, Saratoga, CA, November 24, 1999.

35.   Fox, Mathew, THE REINVENTION OF WORK, HarperCollins, 1995.

36.   Khalsa, Dharma Singh, M. D., BRAIN LONGEVITY, Time Warner Books, 1997.

37.   Roizen, Michael, M. D., REAL AGE—ARE YOU AS YOUNG AS YOU CAN BE, Cliff Street Books, 1999.

38.   Goodall, Jane and Dale Peterson, AFRICA IN MY BLOOD, Houghton-Mifflin, 2000.

39.   Williams, Juan, THURGOOD MARSHALL, AMERICAN REVOLUTIONARY, Times Books/Random House, 1998.

40.   San Francisco Chronicle, Obituaries, Victor Borge, December 24, 2000.

41.   System of Identifying Motivated Abilities ®, PMI Shares, Avon, CT., 1963.

42.   Hillman, James, THE SOUL'S CODE, Random House, 1996.

43.   Internal Report, People Management International LLC, 1999.

44.   Revis, G. F. TEACHER TRAINING, Vol. 2., No. 4., May, 1948.

45. Wright, Lawrence, TWINS AND WHAT THEY TELL US ABOUT WHO WE ARE, John Wiley and Sons, 1997.

46. SIMA® RESEARCH AND HANDBOOK, PMI Shares, Inc., 1992.

47. Searle, John, INTENTIONALITY, Cambridge University Press, 1995.

48. Norton, David, PERSONAL DESTINIES, Princeton University Press, 1976.

49. Maslow, Abraham, TOWARD A PSYCHOLOGY OF BEING, Van Nostrand, 1988.

50. Jung, Carl G., THE ARCHETYPES AND THE COLLECTIVE UNCONSCIOUS, Princeton University Press, 1959.

51. Wright, Lawrence, TWINS AND WHAT THEY TELL US ABOUT WHO WE ARE, John Wiley and Sons, 1997.

52. ibid.

53. ibid.

54. Wright, William, BORN THAT WAY, Routledge, 1999.

55. Hamer, Dean and Peter Copeland, LIVING WITH OUR GENES, Doubleday, 1998.

56. ibid.

57. Scarr, John, CHILD DEVELOPMENT, "The Minnesota Adoption Studies: Genetic Differences and Malleability," University of Minnesota, 1983.

58. McClelland, David, HUMAN MOTIVATION, Cambridge University Press, 1987.

59. Herzberg, Frederick, "One More Time: How Do You Motivate Employees?" HARVARD BUSINESS REVIEW, January-February, 1968.

60. Kohn, Alfie, PUNISHED BY REWARDS, Houghton-Mifflin, 1999.

61. ibid.

62. McClelland, David, HUMAN MOTIVATION, Cambridge University Press, 1987.

63. Internal Report, People Management International LLC, Avon, CT, 1999.

64. Internal Report, People Management International LLC, Avon, CT, 1999.

65. Herzberg, Frederick, "One More Time: How Do You Motivate Employees?" HARVARD BUSINESS REVIEW, January-February, 1968.

66. Bartolome, Fernando and Paul Lee Evans, "Must Success Cost So Much?" HARVARD BUSINESS REVIEW, March-April, 1980.

67. Norton, David, PERSONAL DESTINIES, Princeton University Press, 1976.

68. SIMA® RESEARCH AND HANDBOOK, PMI Shares, Avon, CT, 1992.

69. Spencer, Lyle and Spencer, Signe, COMPETENCY AT WORK, John Wiley and Sons, 1993.

70. Nietzsche, Friedrich Wilhelm, et al, A NIETZSCHE READER, Penguin Classics, 1978.

71. Miller, Arthur F., Jr., "This is Your Wake-Up Call" - foreword to this book.

72. Buckingham, Marcus and Curt Coffman, FIRST BREAK ALL THE RULES, Simon & Schuster, 1999.

73. "What They Don't Teach You at Harvard Business School," WORKING WOMAN, February, 1993.

74. Betof, Edward, and Frederic Harwood, JUST PROMOTED, How to Survive and Thrive in Your First Two Months as a Manager, McGraw Hill, 1991.

75. CEO'S BITE THE DUST, CNN Financial Network, August 2, 2000.

76. LaVelle, Alisa, "Managers Often on the Fast Track to Burnout," The San Francisco Sunday Examiner and Chronicle, August 27, 2000.

77. SIMA® Taxonomy, PMI Shares, Avon, CT, 1963.

78. Internal Report, People Management International LLC, Avon, CT, 1999.

79. Miller, Sherod et al, CONNECTING WITH SELF AND OTHERS, Interpersonal Communications Programs, Inc., Littleton, CO, 1988.

80. Internal Report, People Management International LLC, Avon, CT, 1999.

81. "Number of Jobs Held: Results from a Longitudinal Survey," US Bureau of Labor Statistics, www.stats.bls.gov/newsreels.htm, April, 2000.

82. Vaill, Peter, LEARNING AS A WAY OF BEING, Jossey-Bass, 1996.

83. Proprietary client data, Marlys Hanson & Associates, Livermore, CA ,1989.

84. Buckingham, Marcus and Curt Coffman, FIRST BREAK ALL THE RULES, Simon & Schuster, 1999.

85. RECRUITING AND RETAINING EMPLOYEES, a Consortium Benchmarking Study by ASTD & SHRM, June, 2000.

86. Lublin, Joann, "Holding the Stars," San Francisco Chronicle, October 4, 2000.

87. Butler, Timothy and James Waldroop, "The Art of Retaining Your Best People," HARVARD BUSINESS REVIEW, September-October, 1999.

88. Hanson, Marlys and H. Fred Shultz, "Matching Employees to Their Work: A Mutually Beneficial Career Management System in Exxon Engineering," Ninth Biennial IEEE-USA Careers Conference, Minneapolis, MN, 1996.

89. Jung, Carl G., THE UNDISCOVERED SELF, Little, Brown and Company, 1957.

90. Drucker, Peter, "Managing Oneself," HARVARD BUSINESS REVIEW, March-April, 1999.

91. Butler, Timothy and James Waldroop, "The Art of Retaining Your Best People," HARVARD BUSINESS REVIEW, September-October, 1999.

92. Jung, Carl G., THE ARCHETYPES AND THE COLLECTIVE UNCONSCIOUS, Princeton University Press, 1959.

93. McClelland, David, HUMAN MOTIVATION, Cambridge University Press, 1987.

94. Dalton, Gene and Paul Thompson, "Are R & D Organizations Obsolete?" HARVARD BUSINESS REVIEW, November-December, 1976.

95. Dalton, Gene, presentation at the Ninth Biannual IEEE-USA Careers Conference, Minneapolis, MN, 1996.

96. Dalton, Gene and Paul Thompson, NOVATIONS, Gene W. Dalton & Paul H. Thompson, 1993.

97. ibid.

98. ibid.

99. ibid.

100. Buckingham, Marcus and Curt Coffman, FIRST BREAK ALL THE RULES, Simon & Schuster, 1999.

101. Wells, Janet, "Sour Economy, Sweet Opportunity," San Francisco Chronicle, January 14, 2001.

102. Irish, Dick, "Do You Really Want to Be an Entrepreneur?" THE COSTCO CONNECTION, November, 1997

103. Spencer, Lyle and Signe Spencer, COMPETENCY AT WORK, John Wiley and Sons, 1993.

104. Biech, Elaine, THE BUSINESS OF CONSULTING, Jossey-Bass, 1999.

105. McClelland, David, HUMAN MOTIVATION, Cambridge University Press, 1987.

106. Internal Report, People Management International LLC, Avon, CT, 1999.

107. Bardwick, Judith, THE PLATEAU TRAP, AMACOM, 1986.

108. Fritz, Robert, THE PATH OF LEAST RESISTANCE, DMA, Inc., 1984.

109. Buckingham, Marcus and Curt Coffman, FIRST BREAK ALL THE RULES, Simon & Schuster, 1999.

110. Lipman-Blumen, Harold Leviatt, "Hot Groups: Seeding Them, Feeding Them and Using Them to Ignite Your Organization," Career Search, San Francisco Chronicle, August 24, 2000.

111. Black, Thomas, BORN TO FLY, Zondervan Publishing House, 1994.

112. Black, Thomas, KICKING YOUR KID OUT OF THE NEST, Zondervan Publishing House, 1996

113. ibid.

114. Shellenbarger, Sue, "Work and Family," The San Francisco Examiner and Chronicle, July 11, 1999.

115. Wright, Lawrence, TWINS AND WHAT THEY TELL US ABOUT WHO WE ARE, John Wiley and Sons, 1997.

116. Browne, Joe, Dave Cornett and Marlys Hanson, "Preparing for Act II," Partners in Life Planning, Houston, TX, Charlotte, NC and Livermore, CA, 1998.

117. Duncan, David and Rita Whitney, "Retirement, Work and Volunteering: Effects on Mental Well Being," Presentation at the annual meeting of the American Public Health Association, Washington, D. C., 1985.

118. Hillman, James, THE SOUL'S CODE, Random House, 1996.

APPENDIX

Motivational Pattern Practice Case

The following is a practice case to give you some experience in identifying the "evidence" for the different motivational elements. You will use this same process to identify your own Motivational Pattern.

There are five parts to the Motivational Pattern: Motivated Abilities, Subject Matter, Circumstances, Operating Relationship and Motivational Payoff. Each part is presented below along with an example of achievement data from Mark.

I. Motivated Abilities

These are the abilities that recur in achievements so they emerge as themes. The individual never seems to tire of using these abilities. There may be other things that he/she "can do" but these are the abilities that they are motivated to use.

Motivated Abilities are organized in the following categories:

Learning	Creating/Developing	Influencing
Evaluating	Organizing	Doing
Planning	Overseeing	Performing

Directions: Read Mark's achievements noting the words that are **bolded** to identify the **Motivated Abilities**. Use the checklists on pages 58–61 to identify the recurring **Motivated Abilities**. See the Motivational Pattern Summary on pages 237–238 for "answers."

Excerpts from Achievements of Mark

Before age 10:

"**Fixing up** a crow's wing—**taking care** of the bird for about a month and letting him fly away when he was well."

Remaining grade school years:

"**Formed** my own "Indian tribe" and **became** the chief, **built** an Indian hut out of twigs and it even stayed up for a while. My tribe **grew**—a girl and three fellows—then a problem started—a doubt of my authority—had an Indian war—didn't make out too good on that one—but remained chief of my little tribe—was a very successful tribe and lasted nearly three years—just **organizing** it was satisfying—and making **it stay together**."

Teen Years:

"**Working** with my animals—had one good cow—old Hazel—she developed mastitis—poor Hazel was a pretty good producer but not the best—father wanted to sell her—I **objected**—she was one of my cows so I **called** the vet and he came out—**worked** with this cow three days straight—it stopped and never came back—became one of our best producers—father was ready to give up—**stopped him** from selling another cow—**loved** my cows and **raised** all my calves—it was nothing but **plain work making them grow**—making them healthy, tame."

Twenties:

"**Became** officer in Navy; received exceptional and outstanding fitness reports. **Took over** a pretty much run-down education and information office and **built it up** to the point where everybody knew about it—**got rid** of a couple of employees—had them **transferred out**—**built up** a library—**wrote** instructions as to what I **expected** people to do before they went up for their first fleet wide examinations—**learned** my first lesson—you don't work with officers, you work with chiefs."

II. Subject Matter

This is what the individual is motivated to work with or through. It may range from something concrete (like mechanical devices) to that which is abstract (like concepts or ideas).

Subject Matters are organized in the following categories:

Data	Mechanisms	People
Intangibles	Sensory	
Tangibles	Technical	

Directions: Read Mark's achievements noting the words that are bolded to identify the **Subject Matter**. Use the checklists on pages 63–65 to identify the recurring **Subject Matter**. See the Motivational Pattern Summary on pages 237–238 for "answers."

Excerpts from Achievements of Mark

Before age 10:

"Fixing up a **crow's wing**—taking care of the **bird** for about a month and letting **him** fly away when he was well."

Remaining grade school years

"Formed my own "Indian **tribe**" and became the **chief**, built an Indian **hut** out of **twigs** and it even stayed up for a while. My **tribe** grew—a **girl** and three **fellows**—then a **problem** started—a doubt of my **authority**—had an Indian **war** - didn't make out too good on that one—but remained **chief** of my little **tribe**—was a very successful **tribe** and lasted nearly three years—just organizing it was satisfying—and making it stay together."

Teen Years:

"Working with my **animals**—had one good **cow**—old **Hazel**—she developed **mastitis**—poor **Hazel** was a pretty good **producer** but not the best—father wanted to sell her—I objected—she was one of my **cows** so I called the vet and he came out— worked with this **cow** three days straight—it stopped and never came back—became one of our best **producers**—father was ready to give up—stopped him from selling another **cow**—loved my **cows** and raised all my **calves**—it was nothing but plain work making them grow—making them healthy, tame."

Twenties:

"Became **officer** in Navy; received exceptional and outstanding **fitness reports**. Took over a pretty much **run-down** education and information **office** and built it up to the point where everybody knew about it—got rid of a couple of **employees**—had them transferred out—built up a **library**—wrote **instructions** as to what I expected **people** to do before they went up for their first fleet-wide **examinations**—learned my first **lesson**—you don't work with **officers**, you work with **chiefs**."

III. Circumstances

There are certain themes that trigger the motivation or certain environments critical to your motivated behavior.

Circumstances are organized in the following categories:

- What triggers your motivation . . . How did you get involved in the activity? *(Look for mention of needs, problems, competition, and causes.)*

- How well structured was the activity involved? *(Was there mention of instructions, requirements, and/or specifications?)*

- What were the working conditions or environment? *(Was there pressure, stress, risk, requirements, satisfactions?)*

- What was the end use or result of the activity? *(Was there interest in meeting goals, making money, quality and efficiency?)*

- Do you seek recognition in your achievements? *(Do you talk about audiences, awards, visibility, notoriety?)*

Directions: Read Mark's achievements noting the words that are bolded to identify the **Circumstances.** Use the checklists on pages 67–68 to identify the recurring **Circumstances.** See the Motivational Pattern Summary on pages 237–238 for answers.

Excerpts from Achievements of Mark

Before age 10:

"Fixing up a crow's wing—taking care of the bird **for about a month** and letting him **fly away when he was well.**"

Remaining grade school years:

"Formed my own "Indian tribe" and became the **chief,** built an Indian hut out of twigs and it even stayed up for a while. My tribe grew—a girl and three fellows—then **a problem** started—a **doubt** of my authority—had an **Indian war**—didn't make out too good on that one—but **remained chief** of my little tribe—was a very successful tribe and lasted nearly three years—just organizing it was satisfying—and making **it stay together.**"

Teen Years:

"Working with my animals—had one good cow—old Hazel.—she developed **mastitis**—poor Hazel was a pretty good producer but not the best—father wanted to sell her—**I objected** - she was one of my cows so I called the vet and he came out—**worked with this cow three days straight**—it stopped and never came back—became one of our **best producers**—father was ready to give up—**stopped** him from selling another cow—loved my cows and raised all my calves—it was nothing but plain work **making them grow—making them healthy, tame.**"

Twenties:

"Became officer in Navy; **received exceptional and outstanding fitness reports.** Took over a pretty much **run-down** education and information office and built it up to the point where **everybody knew about it**—got rid of a couple of employees—had them transferred out—built up a library—wrote instructions as to what I expected people to do before they went up for their first fleet-wide examinations—learned my **first lesson**—you don't work with officers, **you work with chiefs.**"

IV. Operating Relationship

There is a particular way you like to relate to others in work situations. This factor will indicate how best to manage you and whether you are motivated to manage others.

Operating Relationships are organized in the following categories:

- Individual Contributor: does not depend on others to take action.

- Influencer: influences others to take action, but doesn't seek continuing overall responsibility for managing others.

- Manager/Leader: works through others in accomplishing an end, and seeks overall responsibility.

Directions: Read Mark's achievements noting the words that are bolded to identify the **Operating Relationship.** Use the checklists on pages 69–70 to identify the recurring **Operating Relationship.** See the Motivational Pattern Summary on pages 237–238 for answers.

Excerpts from Achievements of Mark

Before age 10:

"Fixing up a crow's wing—**taking care of the bird for about a month** and letting him fly away when he was well."

Remaining grade school years:

"**Formed my own "Indian tribe"** and **became the chief**, built an Indian hut out of twigs and it even stayed up for a while. **My tribe** grew—a girl and three fellows—then a problem started—a doubt of my authority—had had an Indian war—didn't make out too good on that one—but **remained chief of my little tribe**—was a very successful tribe and lasted nearly three years—just organizing it was satisfying—and **making it stay together.**"

Teen Years:

"Working with my animals—had one good cow—old Hazel—she developed mastitis—poor Hazel was a pretty good producer but not the best—father wanted to sell he—**I objected**—she was one of my cows so **I called the vet** and he came out—worked with this cow three days straight—it stopped and never came back—became one of our best producers—father was ready to give up—**stopped him** from selling another cow—**loved my cows** and **raised all my calves**—it was nothing but plain work **making them grow—making them healthy, tame.**"

Twenties:

"Became officer in Navy; received exceptional and outstanding fitness reports. **Took over** a pretty much run-down education and information office and **built it** up to the point where everybody knew about it—**got rid of a** couple of employees—**had them transferred out**—built up a library—**wrote instructions as to what I expected people to do** before they went up for their first fleet-wide examinations—learned my first lesson—you don't work with officers, you work with chiefs."

V. Motivational Payoff

There is a singular result you are motivated to accomplish, which, when attained, is always satisfying. Achieving this result produces satisfaction and joy.

Motivational Payoffs are organized in the following categories:

- Focus on personal performance, comparison with others (*I was the tallest, the first, the best, the champion.*)

- Focus on dominance or power (*I was in charge; I overcame the feat.*)

- Focus on object or effect on the object (*I made it work, I made it happen.*)

- Focus on defined effort, purpose, goal (*I finished the project, I met the needs.*)

- Focus on the process involved (*I built the chair, I was able to do it.*)

Directions: Read Mark's achievements noting the words that are bolded to identify the **Motivational Payoff.** Use the checklists on pages 72–73 to identify the recurring **Motivational Payoff.** See the Motivational Pattern Summary on pages 237–238 for answers.

Excerpts from Achievements of Mark

Before age 10:

"Fixing up a crow's wing—taking care of the bird for about a month and letting him **fly away when he was well.**"

Remaining grade school years:

"Formed my own "Indian tribe" and became the chief, built an Indian hut out of twigs and it even stayed up for a while. My tribe grew—a girl and three fellows—then a problem started—a doubt of my authority—had an Indian war—didn't make out too good on that one—but remained chief of my little tribe—was a very successful tribe and lasted nearly three years—just organizing it was satisfying—**and making it stay together.**"

Teen Years:

"Working with my animals—had one good cow—old Hazel—she developed mastitis—poor Hazel was a pretty good producer but not the best—father wanted to

sell her—I objected—she was one of my cows so I called the vet ar
worked with this cow three days straight—it **stopped and never cam**
one of our best producers—father was ready to give up—stopped
another cow—loved my cows and raised all my calves—it was noth
work making them grow—making them healthy, tame."

Twenties:

"Became officer in Navy; received exceptional and outstanding fitness reports. Took over a pretty much run-down education and information office and **built it up to the point where everybody knew about it—got rid of a couple** of employees—**had them transferred out**—built up a library—wrote instructions as to what I expected people to do before they went up for their first fleet-wide examinations—learned my first lesson—**you don't work with officers, you work with chiefs."**

Mark's Motivational Pattern Summary

I. Motivated Abilities

Learning by	*Doing, trying*
Evaluating by	*Assessing worth, value*
Planning by	*Defining tasks to be done*
Creating/Developing by	*Growing, building up*
Organizing by	*Providing structure*
Overseeing by	*Directing detailed work of others*
Influencing by	*Convincing, persuading, encouraging, nurturing*
Doing by	*Maintaining*
Performing by	

II. Subject Matter:

Data	
Intangibles	*Values*
Tangibles	*Animals*
Mechanisms	*Methods, procedures*
Sensory	
Technical	
People	*Groups*

III. Circumstances:

What triggered your motivation? How did you get involved in the activity?

Respond to a need or problem

What degree of structure/definition do you need?

Brings order, structure

What working conditions or environment motivate you?

Difficulties, obstacles

What end use or results do you seek?

Greater effectiveness

Do you seek recognition?

Visibility

IV. Operating Relationship:

How do you work best with people?   *Overall Responsibility for Others –Director*

V. Motivational Payoff:

The primary result you want to achieve:

Focus on the object: Make work and make effective.

PASSION AND PURPOSE
Group and Individual Training Services

If you are interested in using the concepts presented in this book to maximize individual and organizational effectiveness, you may want to access the following training resources:

JOB-FIT AND YOUR CAREER: one or two-day sessions designed to help employees match and build their capabilities to meet individual goals and organizational needs.

COACHING AND MENTORING FOR SUPERVISORS AND MANAGERS: custom-designed sessions to build management skills for recognizing, utilizing and developing employee talent.

TRAIN-THE-TRAINER WORKSHOPS: Team training with an experienced trainer plus step-by-step trainer's guide to prepare you to deliver either or both of the above workshops.

TRAINING TO BE A SIMA® COACH: Individual and/or group instruction designed to provide you a systematic understanding of motivation; to build your skills for recognizing and developing individual, team and executive potential.

For these training resources or to order copies of *PASSION AND PURPOSE*

Contact

Marlys Hanson & Associates, Inc.
E-mail: mhanson539@aol.com

QUICK ORDER FORM

MY ORDER:

Please send me _____ **copies of PASSION and PURPOSE.**   **Books:** _____
    Price per copy (1 to 20 copies) $19.95 each
        Discounts for Volume Purchases

Shipping by Air: (Priority or First Class Mail)   **Shipping:** _____
U.S.: $4.00 for the first book and $2.00 for each additional book.
International: $9.00 for the first book; $5.00 for each additional book (estimated).

Sales Tax: Please add 7.5% for books shipped to California addresses.   **Sales Tax:** _____

                                                  TOTAL: _____

Name: _____

Address: _____

City: _____ **State/Country/ZIP:** _____

Telephone: _____ **Email Address:** _____

Payment: Check Enclosed: _____   Credit Card: ____MasterCard ____VISA

Card Number: _____

Name on Card: _____ Expiration Date: _____

I understand that I may return any item for a full refund—no questions asked.

Please send me FREE information on: ___ seminars/presentations ___ consulting.